Unchained Eagle

4th ALLIED P.O.W. WING

4

RETURN WITH HONOR

*The Story of the First B-52 Crewmember
to be Captured in Vietnam*

Robert G. Certain, Navigator, Charcoal 1

Library of Congress Cataloging-in-Publication Data
Certain, Robert G., 1947-
Unchained Eagle by Robert G. Certain.
Includes bibliographical references and index.
ISBN 978-0-9826180-0-4

1. Certain, Robert., 1947-2. Episcopal Church--Clergy--Biography.
3. Prisoners of war--Vietnam-- Biography. 4. Vietnamese Conflict,
1961-1975--Prisoners and prisons, North Vietnamese. 5. Prisoners
of war--United States--Biography. 6. Vietnamese Conflict, 1961-1975--
Personal narratives, American. I. Title.
BX5995.C39A3 2003
283'.092–dc21
[B] 2002192781

Unchained Eagle

By Robert G. Certain

What Readers Have Said...

"… a great story. I hope it will be read by many." President Gerald R. Ford

"Worthwhile." Supreme Court Justice Sandra Day O'Connor

"… a reality check for anyone who imagines that pastoring a large congregation with substantial resources is a walk in the park." Charles Hoffacker, The Living Church

"… a gripping story. I thoroughly commend it." Donald Armentrout, *Sewanee Theological Review*

"… a compelling story of a man who struggled with his experience and in the process found his faith." William Dopp, *The Church Times*

"Robert Certain's personal story keeps the reader interested from beginning to end. Whether you are interested in Vietnam history, or spiritual autobiography, you will find something here that intrigues and inspires you. I highly recommend it." A reviewer. Amazon.com

"It made me laugh, cry, and think." A reader

"I can hardly put it down." A reader

"I salute you for your forthrightness, honesty, candor and trust." Lawn Griffiths, *East Valley Tribune*

"I can only say that I firmly believe that anyone who reads it, no matter what their station in life, will be better for having read it." Ken Bower, Veteran

"The title was very fitting. This author has certainly led an interesting life. He is quite the man to overcome all of those obstacles along the way. He illustrates that The Lord does move in mysterious ways." John Ellis, Veteran

"A well done account of the author's feelings and thoughts from being shot down in a B-52 to becoming and being an Episcopal priest. He gives detail but he makes it so readable that I found it a real page turner. A very interesting look at how the author deals with his Post Traumatic Stress from his ordeal." James A. Heathcote

"This revealing biography will take you through the fog and friction of war, the deprivation of a prison camp, his calling of God to the priesthood; balancing married life, children, ministry and Air Force responsibilities that will transform you in unexpected ways." Sherry Colbert

"From the time that I started reading the first page of *Unchained Eagle* until I finished reading the last page, I was completely absorbed in the account of Father Certain's life as a military officer and church leader. He has provided special insights into the trauma that the war experience caused for many military personnel. I highly recommend *Unchained Eagle* as a must-read autobiographical work." Harry Bowman

Panning for Gold in the Muck of War
Introduction to the Second Edition

When combat troops come home from war, we have been profoundly changed. Some of that profound change is not so good; but some of it can actually lend us a greater understanding of who we are, what society is about and what international relations are about. Our wartime experience can bring a wealth of understanding—and that is part of the reason that I wrote *Unchained Eagle*, the chronicle of my journey from the prisons of Hanoi to full freedom nearly three decades later.

My initial and most long-lasting response to Vietnam and Hanoi was spiritual and psychological growth. I believe those years gave me greater insight and empathy as I became a Christian priest, ministering to people experiencing loss, circumstantial confinement (illness, disability, broken relationships), and loss of power. During the years in seminary I learned skills in theological reflection, counseling, and prayer that would serve me and my parishioners well in following decades.

Even as a well-trained caregiver, I was treated on two occasions for clinical depression. The first time was in the late 1980s, soon after my sister-in-law was diagnosed with Huntington's Disease (see chapter 13), and I had the sense that all parts of my life had been uprooted and were spinning out of control. The second occurred at the end of a major capital campaign in the church I served in the spring of 2000 (chapter 1). During treatment for each of these experiences I was diagnosed with post-traumatic stress disorder (PTSD), a diagnosis I rejected.

My reasons for rejecting the diagnosis were multiple and complex. First, my professional life was successful and gratifying. Second, I considered my depression to be a natural result of especially stressful circumstances. I also rejected the idea that I could have PTSD because I was not a "real" combat veteran.

I had flown 100 combat missions over Southeast Asia in a B-52, and all but one of them was uneventful insofar as any direct enemy contact was concerned. Even the 100th mission, on which I was shot down and became a prisoner of war, did not count much in my mind when compared to the multiple battles of our ground forces. I downplayed my POW experience because it lasted only 100 fairly benign days, not the years of torture and deprivation known by the men who had been held much longer. Finally, the stigma of mental illness was a burden I did not want to carry. It was bad enough to have to consult a psychiatrist for depression and to take psychotropic drugs to get through it; but that regimen would be relatively short. Insofar as I knew at the time, PTSD was incurable and maybe even untreatable. Consequently, as soon as I felt better about myself and the world around me, I threw off the chemical crutch and withdrew from any rigorous therapy. As you will read, those decisions did not serve me very well nor did they help the people I loved the most, my family, to understand my demons.

A few years ago, my wife and I went on a tour of Alaska, including the famous gold fields. While there, we tried our hand at panning for gold. I discovered that it takes a good technique and a lot of patience to wash away copious amounts of mud to find the little flakes and nuggets of the precious metal hidden within. At the end of the day, it was not the technique, the water, or the mud that we valued – it was the gold. Finding the "gold" in combat experience can be accomplished with similar diligence.

Combat stress has been called a lot of different things: shell shock, battle fatigue, post-traumatic stress disorder. For a decade or two after Vietnam, most people's understanding of Post Traumatic Stress had to do with things like hyper-vigilance, nightmares, anger management, and startle reflex. Over time we have also recognized social and psychological withdrawal, a refusal to talk about and to process the experience of war, anniversary depression, and emotional upheavals as part of the long-term effects of combat.

I came out of Hanoi, went into seminary and then straight into parish ministry. I had always equated what was going on inside my soul from early December until Easter day with the liturgical season – until I heard about anniversary stories. I realized then that the season formed the brackets, the "bookends", of my incarceration in the prisons of North Vietnam. I was shot down one week to the day before Christmas, and I was released two weeks before Holy Week. So what was going on inside of me was related to this timeframe and brought certain emotions, behaviors, and ways of looking at life into the liturgical context of the church. This insight led me to practice some self-care (extra time off, shorter work days, more prayer and meditation) to get through the difficult days.

About ten years after I came home from Vietnam, I was taking a class on communication skills and pastoral response. One of the lectures had to do with being very aware of people's anniversary events – the deaths of spouses, children, parents, friends, family – because long after the rest of us have quit sending flowers, cakes, and casseroles and have gone on about our lives, that person, whether they remember the specific date or not, will have some emotional upheaval on the anniversary of the death. Suddenly, I had a deep realization of my own anniversary story.

I had always experienced the season beginning with Advent (around the first of December) through Easter day as a time of tremendous stress. Each year, I was focused on making everything work right: extra education, fellowship, and liturgies as well as cultural parties and dinners. The amount of tension I felt, however, was more than these events could have caused.

Another manifestation, apparently unrelated to my wartime experience, was impaired decision making. Neither I nor anyone around me understood why I made some decisions under stress. Only when I was introduced to "Eye Movement Desensitization and Redirection" (EMDR) therapy in 2001, did the "ghost of Christmas past" finally leave me. The idea of EMDR is that the trauma is lodged in one hemisphere of the brain, and alternate "solutions" are in the other, and the two are not communicating. As explained on the institute web site, "When a traumatic or very negative event occurs, information processing may be incomplete, perhaps because strong negative feelings or dissociation interfere with information processing. This prevents the forging of connections with more adaptive information that is held in other memory networks." By alternate side sensory stimulation (vision, hearing, and feeling) during therapeutic retelling of the traumatic event, the client is enabled to make significant changes in response to events that mimic the originals.

In most manifestations of post-combat stress, the veteran is not stuck in the past, reliving the memory of combat. Rather, when the themes of warfare repeat in an entirely different set of circumstances, the resulting decisions will likewise be thematically similar to the decisions made in the initial event. Because I completed writing the war story in 2000, when I engaged in EMDR, I knew two things: first, the 100 days from Advent to Easter was more than a liturgical experience; second, as I reviewed the written story, the most vivid, detailed writing was about that final mission. That last mission, which ended after eight hours and twenty minutes, takes about 8,800 words to tell. Five years in a parish takes about 6,500 words.

The themes of that mission were keys to this final transformation of an old liability into a new asset. First of all, there was disappointment that I had to fly, because my crew was supposed to go home that day. Another theme was the danger of the target. It was Hanoi, the second most heavily SAM defended city in the world. On taxi out, we had an earth tremor. Before we took off, we shifted our takeoff position two times. After we took off, we had a mechanical problem that had to be fixed. Four hours into the flight, we had a rendezvous issue with the tanker and had to overcome a critical challenge. We had a flight planning error that we had to solve in the air and on the fly. Then, as we got into the target area, we entered a jet stream with a 90 knot tailwind. My job as navigator was to get there on time to the second, and that is exactly where we were—on time to the second. Unfortunately, we were shot down ten seconds short of the target. If we had been a few seconds early or a few seconds late, the missiles might have missed. My decision at the time, after a quick assessment of the situation, was to eject—take my chances with the parachute and with the enemy on the ground rather than with 160,000 pounds of jet fuel in the airplane.

Since that night, there have been several times in my life when we entered major events, major projects in church life, where all of these themes were repeated. We had to decide on difficult schedules and overcome multiple obstacles. Each time, as we approached probable success, my anxiety level would peak and I would have resumes mailed to everybody—I would be ready to leave, to eject. The most difficult project for me was the conduct of capital funds campaigns, which were always done during the Advent-Easter cycle. When September 11, 2001 occurred, I found all of the emotions boiling up from the past, but at the wrong time of year. I finally followed the good advice of my Navy doctors and engaged in EMDR therapy. I came home from Vietnam in 1973, and I found the key to unlocking the chains of prison twenty-eight years later.

The point of telling the story of my experience is to give insight to other veterans and their families as they tackle the effects of their own combat long after they have left the field of battle and the military. Most of us come home, leave the service, return to our families and careers and make good livings and good contributions to society. Even so, the intense experience of warfare leaves us with some important work to do if we are to fully utilize the positive aspects of those days in our life back in the world.

Bringing the troops "all the way home" is not just the responsibility of the Department of Defense; nor even a shared responsibility with the Department of Veterans Affairs. All of us – employers and family members, churches and synagogues, physicians and veterans themselves – have a vested interest in converting combat liabilities into assets for societal leadership. We all have a responsibility to pan for the gold.

Those of us who have been there have a role to play in the full and complete return of those who come after us. By sharing my experience, strength, and hope in the pages of this book, my hope is that other veterans may be able to gain insight into their own stories and find new ways of finding the value in the silt of their troubling times. Families, friends, service organizations, and faith communities are likely to be the people who facilitate the vast majority of this work – as it should be. Putting the story on paper was also a very big part of how I was able to finally exorcise the "ghost of Christmas past" by identifying the specific events within which the troubling themes of trauma were hidden.

For those of us who need a little expert help, the VA, Vet Centers, and private medical care should be available. For my own part, I used both the Vet Center (a free service) and an EMDR clinician I found on their web site: http://www.emdr.com. That experience was amazing. Thirty days (and about four sessions) into the process, my wife said, "I don't know what you're doing in therapy, but don't stop." Thirty days after that, my therapist said, "I don't think we can get any better than this. You're done; but if you need me later, call again." Two weeks later, when a friend from a previous assignment, visited the church I served on Christmas Eve, he asked me, "What happened to you?" When I asked him what he meant, he said, "You were our priest for five Christmases; but you're very different now. What I saw this Christmas was a man totally at ease and in your element as you led the congregation in worship. Something has happened in the five years you've been gone."

The answer to that question was EMDR, preceded by my work at the Vet Center and the writing of *Unchained Eagle*. It is my hope that our current war veterans will make these discoveries in their own lives a lot faster than thirty years, and that post-adversity growth will become their prevailing experience. This book is the story of how I came out of Hanoi with a residue of psychological baggage that would take years to release. In the meantime, I became a Christian clergyman, successfully led congregations from Maryland to California, served as a reserve chaplain until retirement as a full colonel. In 2007 I led the funeral services for former President Gerald R. Ford, becoming one of fewer than forty men to preside at such services in the history of the republic. By most judgment, I had a successful career in both the Air Force and the Episcopal Church. For twenty-eight of those thirty-nine years I also struggled with post-combat stress. Perhaps, with modern tools and the assistance of their friends, families, and supporters, the current generation of young troops will be able to pan for the gold in their wartime experience with greater speed and success. Perhaps people who have suffered through natural disasters and acts of violence will also find positive "gold" in their own experience of trauma.

Unchained Eagle can be more than a window into the life of one American and his family; it can also provide the reader with a method for examining their own life, a technique and a tool for panning for gold. As you read the book, ask yourself where I missed the signs that my life was continuing to be affected by my wartime experience; see if you can identify where I missed the offer of help; and ask yourself how you can make a difference in someone else's life by observing, intervening, assisting, and pointing that other man or woman in the direction of a new way of living in the world.

A word about the subtitle

When first published, the subtitle "From Prisoner of War to Prisoner of Christ" was prominent on the cover. While I thought the Biblical references were clear (Ephesians 3:1, Philemon 1:23), many people found it incomprehensible. St. Paul referred to his discipleship as being a prisoner, playing off the existential fact that he was also a prisoner of the Romans at the demand of religious authorities in Jerusalem. His image also shows up in a prayer in the Episcopal Book of Common Prayer: "O God, the author of peace and lover of concord, to know you is eternal life and to serve you is perfect freedom ..." The intention of the subtitle was to infer that being a "prisoner of Christ" is to be truly free, a journey that took a very long time from the deprevations of Hanoi.

ACKNOWLEDGMENTS

The writing of this story has been a long time in coming. For years, my wife has urged me to put down my memories of the terrible events recounted here as a gift and legacy to our children and other members of our family whose lives were also changed by what happened to me in the winter of 1972-1973. Little did I suspect the size of the population who fell into that second category. While writing this narrative, the family grew – the families of other crewmembers, the friends and associates who shared parts of this event or parts of the lives of people more directly affected.

I am grateful to my family members who finally shared their experience of having a brother in enemy hands; to Bill Buckley, who survived the night only to return to our quarters, now empty of the men he had flown with for four months; to Marshall Michel for providing me with the Vietnamese account of the shoot-down of our B-52; and to the many people who helped with proofreading, asking questions for clarity, and otherwise jogging my memory of events and emotions. First among them is Dr. Rita Kohl, a counselor for the VetCenter in San Bernardino, California who insisted that I look at the war story as a place to find the hand of God.

As I finished writing the first ten chapters, I thought I was finished. However, members of St. Margaret's Episcopal Church in Palm Desert, California began asking for the rest of the story. It was then that I decided to recount God's hand at work in the years since as I have sought to be a faithful husband, father, and priest.

That task posed a number of difficulties. The first was that nothing in my life stands out in my memory as clearly as does the story of combat and imprisonment. If I tried to be as detailed in the telling of a quarter century as I had been with a quarter year, the work would have been incredibly long and definitely boring. As I prayed over the idea of a more complete memoir, I was led in the direction of composing a spiritual autobiography.

The inspiration for this turn came from a line in the Episcopal Book of Common Prayer's Eucharistic Prayer C: "Open our eyes to see your hand in the world about us." While I thought I was pretty adept at doing that in the events of life, my writing exposed tremendous gaps in my ability to reflect theologically on what I consigned to the categories of "circumstance," "coincidence," and "evil." Those were areas where I did not look for God's hand at work.

The task of writing became one of choosing stories from my life whose themes were common to others even though the details were quite unique. In order to fulfill the prayer, those stories needed to include both the obvious and the hidden activity of God. Twenty-five years as a priest in the Episcopal Church had taught me that Jesus Christ was present in the midst of both joys and sorrows *in other people's lives*. While I knew he was present in all my joys, I would consider his presence only in some of my sorrows. I am indebted to Avis Attaway, a Christian family counselor who helped me become reconciled with the sorrows and terrors of my distant past. As she helped me find peaceful calm in the most horrific events of my life, so this book is intended to open for others the door of all of life to the redemptive hand of God.

In the work of redemption and reconciliation, I am indebted most of all to my wife, Robbie Wade Certain, for providing the love and support necessary to live my life, and finally to share it in some detail with others. It is to her that I dedicate *Unchained Eagle.*

Table of Contents

Introduction iii

Acknowledgments xi

About the Author xiv

Preface xv

1 – Not Again 1

2 – Bullet Shot 7

3 – The Final Flight...19

4 – Captured 43

5 – Interrogation..55

6 – The Hanoi Hilton 71

7 – The Zoo 93

8 – Operation Homecoming...113

9 – Trauma and Grace 131

10 – A New Chaplain 163

11 – A Retreat from the USAF 177

12 – Learning the Ropes 189

13 – Stress Upon Stress..213

14 – Challenges and Disappointments 245

15 – A Time of Refreshment 267

16 – A Golden Opportunity 281

17 – New Challenges and Old Ghosts 301

18 – A New Direction?..307

Glossary 313

Bibliography 316

About the author ...

Robert Certain was born in Savannah, Georgia in December1947. An alumnus of Bethesda-Chevy Chase High School in Maryland, he attended Emory University in Atlanta, Georgia, graduating in 1969 with a BA degree in History and a commission in the US Air Force. As a combat aviator, he flew 100 missions over Southeast Asia in 1971 and 1972.

Following the Vietnam War, he attended an Episcopal Church seminary in Tennessee, was ordained as a priest in 1976, and served as a chaplain in the Air Force Reserve. Father Certain has served parishes in Texas, Mississippi, Tennessee, Arizona, California, and Georgia. As a reservist, he served as chaplain to the Air Force in basic military training, at the headquarters of the Strategic Air Command and Air Mobility Command, and at the Air Force Academy. He retired from the Air Force Reserves in 1999 at the rank of Colonel.

The Certains currently live in Roswell, Georgia where Robert serves as pastor of an Episcopal Church. He also serves on the Defense Health Board and on the Veterans Affairs Advisory Board on Former POWs. Robert is married to the former Robbie Wade of Blytheville, Arkansas. They have two grown children and two grandsons.

Preface

Contrail, *n*. the smokelike trail of water droplets or ice crystals that sometimes forms in the wake of an aircraft flying at a high altitude; vapor trail. [< *con*(densation) + *trail*]

Persistent contrails can be seen crisscrossing the United States on any humid day as airliners move thousands of passengers from one place to another, leaving behind their tell-tale tracks in the sky. In warfare, persistent contrails can prove deadly, since fighter pilots and missile operators can find an invading bomber without using radar, and can aim their defensive weapons without alerting the invader.

As the aerial version of the wakes left behind by ships and boats, contrails can be seen more clearly than the craft themselves and point to the plane's location on the journey. Rarely can the traveler see his own contrails, but if he knows he is pulling them across the sky, the combat aviator will change altitudes trying to find drier air. There have been times when those maneuvers were as desperate as a dogfight.

I grew up in a Christian home in the Old South in the 1950s. Some of my earliest memories feature the white clapboard Garden City Methodist Church, with its steeple, white pews, and florescent cross behind the pulpit. My family attended worship twice on Sunday, once on Wednesday, and I participated in Sunday school and the youth fellowship. As a young teen I was convinced of God's love for me and of my place in his Kingdom.

In the 1960s, with the advent of the Civil Rights movement, the War in Vietnam, and facial hair, life became infinitely more complicated. The church seemed weak, the nation fractured, and the clear voice of faith and reason cracked into a cacophony of internal and external conflicts as I stumbled through high school and college. I was swept into an eddy of the tide of American life that led me into chains in Vietnam at the very time the United States was disengaging from the war under the pressures of a disenchanted society.

After the war, I thought I left behind the tragedy of death and destruction, chaining its traumas behind doors as secure as those behind which I had been imprisoned in Hanoi, and expecting those terrible memories to disappear like contrails on a dry afternoon. But those memories did not dissipate, and I ran from them as from a pursuing missile.

> I fled Him, down the nights and down the days;
>   I fled Him down the arches of the years;
> I fled Him, down the labyrinthine ways
>   Of my own mind; and in the mist of tears
> I hid from Him, and under running laughter.[1]

The opening words of Francis Thompson's poem *The Hound of Heaven* set the stage for the story of a man who runs away from God, not out of disobedience but out of fear. It is a story that is written only after the Hound has caught him and the fear is removed.

The interesting thing about a labyrinth is that, unlike a maze, you cannot get lost within it. There are no dead ends, short cuts, detours,

---

[1] Thompson, Francis, *The Hound of Heaven.* Boston: International Pocket Library, 1936; p. 11.

or false leads. The labyrinthine path twists, turns, and doubles back on itself. It seems at first to approach and then to move away from the center. But it leads always to the midpoint, the place where God waits with all the good that the pilgrim fears is lost.

The twists, turns and movements of *Unchained Eagle* chronicle in prose what Thompson described in verse. For nearly thirty years I strove to avoid the pursuing contrails of my worst memories as though they held a deadly MiG fighter or surface-to-air missile. In the turbulence caused by the collision of new upheavals with old memories, I finally began to see my own contrails as nothing worse than the track of my journey, a labyrinth leading me inexorably toward God. Each person, each event, each memory of my flight through life began to show itself as part and parcel of the sound of the hound's bay pursuing me toward freedom in Christ, not the final destruction of my soul.

While the course I followed may be unique in its details and in the contrails I have left behind, the intricacies of the themes of dark nights and glorious days are common to us all. As such, this story may very well be a key to open the locks of a thousand other chains that prevent the soul from rising to the warmth of Divine grace. By looking back at the stories in the persistent contrails of life, perhaps we can all see more clearly where we are heading in whatever future God has granted us, can break the chains that hold us prisoner and can soar like eagles lifted high on the winds of freedom.

Chapter 1

Not Again

Psalm 13
How long, O LORD? Will you forget me for ever?
  how long will you hide your face from me?
How long shall I have perplexity in my mind,
  and grief in my heart, day after day?

Springtime in the southern California desert is like heaven-on-earth. The spring of 2000 was one of those times, at least until April third. Easter was three weeks away, the climax not only of the Church year, but also the end of a major capital campaign for the parish I serve as rector, the 2000-member St. Margaret's Episcopal Church in Palm Desert, California.

Chapter 1

I arrived in the parish on Memorial Day 1998, following a very popular and beloved rector of thirteen years, who had tragically died from cancer the previous summer. As a result of his final illness and the death of the parish's largest benefactor, the parish had been operating on deficit budgets. Several major projects were nearing completion and they, too, were over budget: a new pipe organ in the church, rebuilding of the chancel, and remodeling of the parish office building.

That first summer, I signed a note for one million dollars, with no pledges and no money to pay it back, and faced another deficit budget on top of it. In order to repay the bank, it was imperative to raise the money to retire the loan, to balance the budget and to fulfill the parish's vision as articulated by Father Brad Hall, as well as to support the bishop in an expansion initiative in the Diocese of San Diego. The total goal was set at $2.55 million. Our consultants told us we could raise $1.9 million; the campaign chair thought we would be lucky to raise the loan money. But if we stopped at either place, we would not have been able to move the parish ahead for another seven or eight years.

The previous fall, I had gauged the amount of energy I had for "high season" when all of our winter residents would migrate south as the snow descended on their other homes. I was confident that I could handle those pressures and the additional ones brought on by an effort to raise capital funds equal to two-year's annual budget. I didn't know at the time that the bishop would start recruiting Father Sean Cox, one of my associates, to move to another parish. For that, I didn't have reserves, and I began to feel an old and very dangerous rage build within me. I also underestimated the way in which the old wounds of Vietnam would begin to haunt my soul.

The campaign was going well, though, and I was just a little more edgy than I considered normal. On Monday morning, April third, I drove to the office to a morning of meetings.

First was a delightful time with the Altar Guild to discuss Holy Week and Easter services. That gathering lasted a bit longer than I anticipated, so my senior associate had begun the parish staff meeting before I arrived.

As I came into that meeting, the staff was discussing two events related to the capital campaign scheduled on the same day at the same time, one in the parish hall and another in a parishioner's home. I observed that they were not on the same day, one was scheduled for Tuesday evening, and the other on Wednesday. The Tuesday event, in a home, included a guest list of people with the capacity to make gifts of $50-$100 thousand and was critical to putting us over the top. The other, for members of less financial capacity, was to be the day following in the parish hall at the church.

I looked at my secretary for confirmation, and she said, "The invitation for the home event says the 12th." *What is she talking about?* I thought. She passed down the invitation, which I had personally proofread a half-dozen times, and sure enough, the date was wrong. *Fire everybody! This is a disaster. No, it's not. You're overreacting! Better get out before you do something really stupid!* I turned to my senior associate, Father Dan Rondeau, and said in a controlled voice, "Dan, take the meeting, I have to leave."

Picking up my notes, I went first to the campaign office to tell the consultant what had happened. "We'll have to call the event hosts to see if they can switch days, and if not, call the invitation list to see if they can switch to the intended date. I'm so angry about this, I've got to get out of here."

From there I headed to my car, noticing that the choirmaster had come out of the staff meeting. *Oh, great, what's that about? The meeting can't be over yet.* I drove home, changed into workout clothes, and headed to the gym to exercise and clear my head. *I can't believe this is happening again. I thought all that anniversary trauma around imprisonment and release was behind me.*

At the gym, I felt good pushing my body and sweating up a storm. It sure beat taking it out on someone else, and gave me a chance to think through the next step. As I showered and changed, I could feel a huge weight settle onto my shoulders and into my heart. It had been twelve years since I felt that badly. By the time I grabbed a little lunch, I was exhausted and very depressed. Then, when I returned to the office, it really hit hard.

The first things I saw were two pieces of e-mail from key staff members castigating me for my behavior in the staff meeting and threatening to quit. Just as I finished reading the second, Dan Rondeau and my other associate, Sean Cox, came into my office and closed both doors. *Oh, no! I know I've told them to do this if I ever made a major screw-up, but I really don't want to hear this.* Sean was very angry. Dan was very concerned. "OK," I said, "I've screwed this up today. As soon as I can get the campaign complete, I'll resign and leave. I'm not up to this anymore."

"No, you're not going to resign, but you are going to get some help. When you left, the whole staff dissolved and you have some major amendments to make. But you're still the right person for this ministry."

I collapsed, sinking deep into my oversized chair. "So what do you want me to do?"

"First, you're calling your doctor; then you're calling Bill Mahedy at the VA; then you've got to apologize to the staff."

I was surrounded again, not qualitatively different from that night in North Vietnam so many years ago. The situation felt hopeless, I was out of options, and the only decision I could make was to follow instructions from these two men. "I'll do it tomorrow. I can't today. Besides, I don't have a doctor."

"Pick up the phone and call Brad Smith," Sean said, "he'll see you."

Resist. Who does he think he is ordering me around? "OK." I picked up the phone book, looked up his number and dialed.

He was not in his office, so I left a message with his nurse to call me when he got the chance.

"I'll e-mail Bill," Sean said.

You jerk, who asked you to bring in the VA chaplain? "OK, suit yourself."

"Dan, I'm going home to rest. I feel awful. Call a staff meeting first thing in the morning." The three of us prayed together, or rather they prayed over me, and I drug myself back to the car and went home, thoroughly humiliated and bone tired.

When I arrived home, I called Dr. Smith's home number, and left a message for him to call me when he got in. When my wife, Robbie, came in, I told her what had happened while we had a light dinner. My appetite was gone. As we finished, Dr. Smith phoned.

"I got your message, and you sounded desperate. What's going on?"

I filled him in on the morning, told him it felt like a recurrence of Post-Traumatic Stress Disorder, and I needed help. He made an appointment for the next day.

The following morning I met with the staff to apologize and to tell them about my propensity to have bouts of post-traumatic stress disorder (PTSD) as a result of having been a prisoner of war in Vietnam. Twelve years earlier, the precipitating event had been my wife's sister's diagnosis with Huntington's Disease. This time it was centered on the danger of the failure of our capital campaign. They took it well, and I left for my doctor's appointment.

Within the next twenty-four hours, Dr. Smith had referred me to a psychiatrist to get set up with an anti-depressant. Bill Mahedy had called and set an appointment with a Vet Center in San Bernardino for psychological counseling with a person trained and experienced to help Vietnam veterans.

* * *

5

Chapter 1

The Vet Center psychologist was a young and very beautiful woman, tough as nails and gentle as a lamb. In the first session, I told her that I had been marked for life by the combat of twenty-eight years earlier. My inner being would not let the memory go; it was as fresh as yesterday, and I felt tattooed by it for life. It seemed to me that you can take the warrior out of the war, but no one could take the war out of the warrior. As I related the details of that story, she pressed me to get behind the "facts" to the "truth" – to my inner soul. The cross hanging around her neck indicated her good intentions, but I had no clue as to how to go where she was leading.

As we parted, I suggested that I write the story down and that she probe from the written word so we could get there more quickly. From those first fledgling pages, she assisted me to reflect theologically on the surface story to find the hand of God working in the past and in the present in ways I had never noticed. John Katzenbach's closing words in *Hart's War* rang true as I began to think, write and pray over the story of my own life:

> "Sometimes I think we live in a world so obsessively devoted to looking forward that it frequently forgets to take the time to look back. But some of our best stories reside in our wake, and, I suspect, no matter how harsh these stories are, they help tell us much about where we are heading."[1]

---

[1] John Katzenbach, *Hart's War.* New York: Ballentine Books, 1999; p. 551.

Chapter 2

Bullet Shot

"They've got the Pilot! They've got the Pilot!" The voice was that of 1st Lieutenant Bobby Thomas. The time was 1313 Greenwich Mean Time on Monday, 18 December 1972; the altitude was 34,000 feet.

++++++++++

The weekend had been one of great tension, dread, excitement, and anticipation at Andersen AFB, on the island of Guam. On Friday, we had been notified that all crew rotations stateside had been suspended, and all combat missions on Saturday and Sunday had been cancelled.

Since we had been scheduled to return to Blytheville AFB, Arkansas on Monday, the six members of our select, all-instructor crew took the news pretty hard. Five of us had wives, two had children, and one was divorced. All of us wanted to get home to our families for Christmas. Robbie and I had been married for only six weeks when I left, so I was particularly eager to get my marriage underway and to start a family.

The crew was finishing its tour of duty in support of air operations over South Vietnam and Cambodia.

Having arrived in July on 180-day temporary duty (TDY) orders as part of Operation Bullet Shot, we expected to return to Blytheville in early December. Bullet Shot had moved several wings totaling over 150 B-52 Stratofortresses bombers to Andersen AFB, Guam to augment the bomber force at U-Tapao, Thailand. By mid-December I had completed 51 missions, flown over 500 hours and dropped more than a million pounds of bombs.

It was another setback to our end-of-tour trip home, first scheduled for 4 December, my twenty-fifth birthday, before a scheduled return to Southeast Asia in January 1973. A first delay occurred when our replacement crew from Loring AFB was snowed in and unable to get out of Maine. When they did arrive on the fourteenth, they had changed two "critical" crewmembers and would have to fly three supervised thirteen-hour combat missions over the next six days before being allowed to take our place on the "line," moving our rotation to the eighteenth.

B-52G Stratofortress

We had already suffered some losses from the crew since our arrival on Guam on 7 July 1972. The original make-up of the crew had been Flight Control: Capt. Mel Polek (Aircraft Commander), Capt. Casper "Cap" Nordic (copilot); Offense: Maj. Richard Johnson

(Radar Navigator), Capt. Robert Certain (Navigator); and Defense: Capt. Tom Simpson (Electronic Warfare Officer), and MSgt. Walter Ferguson (Gunner). On Guam, Cap was judged to be too small in stature to fly the B-52. While that had been true in the D model (built between 1954 and 1956) because of the way the seat worked (full up, full aft; full down, full forward – Cap needed up and forward), it was not true in the G model (built between 1957 and 1959), which had a 6-way fully adjustable seat and which we were flying this year. In September, he was reassigned to EC-47s, a World War II era cargo aircraft converted to an electronic jamming mission. After training, he was sent to Ton Sun Nhut, South Vietnam. His replacement, First Lieutenant Bill Buckley, was from Seymour-Johnson AFB in North Carolina, since all Blytheville crewmembers were already in the theater and assigned to other crews. Bill was fresh in the operational (as opposed to training) side of the Strategic Air Command. He had just completed B-52G training; and was in awe and fear of flying with a Select crew.

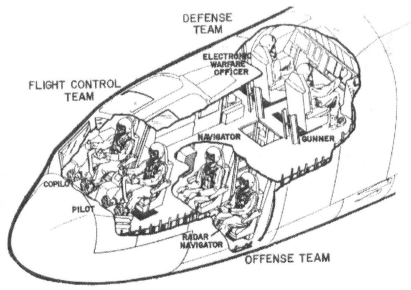

B-52G Cockpit Layout

In late July, Mel Polek, frustrated with constant rotations with no end in sight, and with his fourth child on the way, confided to me that he had resigned his commission effective the first of December. A couple of weeks after arriving on Guam, he and I were talking about our futures. He told me he had put in his papers before we left Blytheville and asked me what my plans might be. I said, "I don't think I can make this a career. I really feel called to go to seminary."

He responded, "I was wondering when you would make up your mind." I was startled by the phrase because an Air Force nurse I had dated at Mather AFB during my bombardier training had spoken those same words to me. In both cases, the subject had not been previously discussed. Mel accompanied me to the personnel office where I tendered my resignation for the following summer.

I wrote Robbie about my decision in late July. The letter contained a number of surprises for her – my thoughts about seminary and my choice of churches. We had met and married in the Baptist Church and I wanted to return to the Episcopal. I explained the decision, and apologized for the surprises, "We should have gone over this a long time ago, Honey, but I've just been trying to ignore it, hoping it would go away." About ten days later, I received her response saying that had she known this, she never would have married me.

In my reply I apologized again for announcing this in a letter, "I realize what a shock it must have been to you… I wish that I would have waited until I got home to tell you." We continued to struggle through this new crisis for the next several months, by letter and by phone.

Throughout the summer and fall of 1972, there were two places I would go to relax, think, and pray about the ministry, my marriage, and the future. The first, shared with Mel and Cap, was the ceramics hobby shop on base. Learning the ins and outs of Michigan slip, molds, paints, glaze and kilns was very far removed from combat

and served as a kind of "mantra" within which I c
the big issues. In the years ahead I would return to
hands whenever my soul was troubled.

The second place, shared with a Lieutenant Colonel Earnhart, a staff officer from Blytheville, was St. John's Episcopal Church in Agana, Guam. The nave had a glass wall behind the altar, looking west out over the Pacific. While the sun left the priest in silhouette, it also juxtaposed the celebration of the Eucharist with the approach pattern of Andersen, with B-52s flying by as they recovered from missions over SEA. As a result, I found my mind wandering to think about the crews on those bombers and how they (we) dealt with the dichotomy between our motto, "Peace is Our Profession," and the execution of war orders. I also wondered why the chaplains didn't address that conflict with the crews. Many of them were visibly present and usually engaged with us at briefings, hobby shops, clubs and other places frequented by the crews; but no one ever seemed to address in any meaningful manner the horns of that dilemma. Would that become my calling?

It would be several years before I would know enough about the Christian theory of a just war to begin to categorize the conflict in Vietnam. In the fall of 1972, I kept a quote in my wallet that I had copied off a wall at Castle AFB and attributed to John Stuart Mill, "War is an ugly thing, but not the ugliest of things: the decayed and degraded state of moral and patriotic feelings which thinks that nothing is worth war is much worse. A man who has nothing for which he is willing to fight or nothing he cares about more than his own personal safety is a miserable creature who has no chance of being free, unless made and kept so by the exertions and blood of better men than himself." In the two years that I flew combat in Southeast Asia, I never thought I was fighting for either patriotism or the defeat of communism. Instead, I was willing to fight to end the war; and I cared for the release of the POWs more than my own personal safety. With those two goals in mind, I began to understand that war is more than the story of horror; it is the story of love among men.

When we flew Mel's last mission on the twenty-sixth of October, typhoon Olga precluded our return to Guam; so we were diverted to Okinawa. From there, he caught his "freedom flight" back to the States on the twenty-eighth. Mel and I had become very close friends and our families enjoyed each other immensely. Before he left, he asked me to serve as Godfather to the child due in November. We had now lost both members of our Flight Control team. A scheduling officer from Guam, Capt. Howard Rose (also from Blytheville) flew us from Okinawa to Andersen on the twenty-ninth.

For the next couple of weeks, we flew with a variety of pilots from other crews. Flying with strangers always meant that crew coordination suffered, since each crew had their own style of communication and could anticipate their crewmates' actions.

One of the scarier flights we had during this period was our very next combat sortie on 31 October. The pilot-for-the-day was Captain Ken Hope from Mather AFB in California. He had spent a year in Vietnam as a forward air controller and was now on his second Stratofortress tour.

Our originally assigned aircraft was broken, so we had to "bag-drag" (move all our gear to the ready spare as quickly as possible) to 58-0575. Taking off forty-five minutes behind the rest of the cell, we could still catch up with them before they reached the bomb run, providing everything went well. But as we leveled off at about 30,000 feet, we had a near total electrical failure.

Circuit breakers popped and could not be reset. We lost radar (except for the stabilizing gyroscope), all electronic heading indicators, autopilot, and who knew what else. The radios were working, so we could communicate with Guam.

I was aware we were over the spot where another Stratofortress had crashed on the same day we arrived on the island. That heightened both my anxiety and my determination to do all I could to help the pilots get this one back to Guam safely. I knew Bill had not experienced a real in-flight emergency, and had no knowledge that Capt. Hope would be able to handle it, either. However, the safety of the flight was entrusted to them.

Captain Hope called back to Charlie Tower (the ground controller who also assisted in solving in-flight problems) for guidance, and they brought in maintenance personnel to help. We tried everything they suggested to no avail. The aircraft was wallowing through the air without an operable stabilization augmentation system, making it very difficult to keep the wings straight and level. Tom Simpson attempted to get some heading shots off the sun, but they were useless because of the unstable flight.

After a half hour with no success in solving any of our problems, Charlie Tower told us to stay with the other two planes visually! Apparently they didn't understand that they were about 400 nautical miles ahead of us and we had no navigation equipment and no way to control the yaw. Contrails, if there were any, would never persist for that many miles. If we encountered clouds, we would have no instruments to assist in keeping straight and level, and no accurate way of finding an emergency base should that become necessary. Someone on the ground clearly did not grasp the situation.

I advised Ken that I was no longer willing to navigate west bound and suggested he return to Guam. He called for clearance and was told to stand by. I said, "Pilot, you're the aircraft commander, not Charlie. Turn this thing around and tell them what you're doing."

He began the turn and reported, "Blue 3 returning to base." Tower then cleared us "Red Alpha Route inbound."

I was disgusted! Getting on the radio, I said, "Charlie, this is the Nav on Blue Three. I've been ded (deductive) reckoning for forty-five minutes with preflight winds. We have no heading indicator except the whiskey compass, and it's written up as being 5 degrees off, but it doesn't say which direction. The only stabilization gyro we have is in the BNS (Bomb/Navigation System). The only navigational aid possible is a sun line, and the E-Dubya won't get out of his ejection seat long enough to shoot it. We're turning in the general direction of east. When you find us on radar, give us vectors!"

The response was swift, "OK, Blue Three. You're cleared direct Guam." I was pretty confident I could get the bird to close radar range of Guam, well within their ability to direct us to a safe landing.

Another departing BUFF (Big Ugly Fat Fella, a pet name for the B-52) read our APN-69 (rendezvous beacon that transmitted a coded identification to other aircraft similarly equipped) and gave us a revised heading to follow. I was surprised it still worked. What else could we get going?

When Guam picked us up they began vectors and an altitude step-down to 4,000 feet. We could not dump fuel, so we had to fly until we were light enough to land, about four-to-five hours total. The lower we were, the more fuel we consumed. When level, we lowered our gear and flaps and raised spoilers to put out as much drag as possible to burn fuel faster. As we approached 50,000 pounds of fuel remaining, we were told to fly to the northernmost island in the Marianas chain and to drop our bombs on that unpopulated pile of rocks. By then I was confident enough in the integrity of the plane that I went upstairs with a low altitude chart to direct the pilots to the island. Throughout the ordeal, I was in constant conversation with God, asking for direction and insight to do my job well.

Counting islands and checking ahead, I noticed a thunderstorm sitting directly over our drop island. When I told the pilot, he asked,

"What are we going to do?"

"See that opening in the clouds to the left? Let's descend to 2,000 feet so Guam will lose us on radar, then we'll go below the clouds, clear it of ships, and drop the bombs in the water. When Guam loses us, tell them we're over the island and must be below their radar."

"We can't do that!"

"Sure we can!" I returned to my station to assist the Radar with bomb-drop checklists. When the bombs fell away we could feel their explosions as they hit the water.

At last, we were on final approach to Guam. Another cell was checking in at the high fix for approach from a strike mission, and it was getting toward dusk. Since we did not have electrical power, I was concerned that we get down before the recovering cell and before dark. On short final, Charlie asked for our fuel. Before I could speak, Bill reported 25,000 pounds. "Go around." *Man! Why did he have to be honest with them?* They wanted us at 15,000 pounds or less. *Those jerks were trying to kill us.*

"Co, Nav," I said. "When we get back on final we will be at minimum fuel."

"I'm working on that now, Nav."

"That was not a question."

"Oh, OK." He quickly grasped my meaning. After all, he wanted to get down, too. After nearly five hours of exceptionally tense flying, we landed. Both the crew and the airplane would fly again.

Over the next several days, Ken and I spent some time together to talk about what happened, and what we might have done differently. He had gone to complain to the operations deputy about the go-around; neither of us had liked his response at the time. All of the crew thought we were close enough for a safe landing, but the deputy did not. Apparently an electrical bus had short-circuited, causing the problems with the electrical system, but the engines, flaps, spoilers, and landing gear had all continued to be normal. He concluded that we could safely fly long enough to get even lighter. He had failed to understand that we didn't have lights to safely land in the dark.

Capt. Hope and I spent some good time in conversation about personal lives and dreams, and attended the outdoor theater together on at least one occasion. It was a relationship that would resurface many years later, showing again how God binds people together in various ways through shared crises.

On the fourth of November, a new pilot, Lt. Col. Don Rissi, who had been selected to become the squadron commander of the 340th Bombardment Squadron at Blytheville, joined us to fly our last few missions and to bring us home. Following two tours in-country in F-4 Phantoms, he had been transferred from Tactical Air Command (TAC) to the Strategic Air Command (SAC) and reassigned to fly the Stratofortress. Dick Johnson, with whom he had flown B-47s at Davis-Monthan AFB, welcomed him and spent the next several days catching up on old times. Don flew his over-the-shoulder (supervised) missions with other crews before flying with us for the first time on the seventeenth.

On fifteen December, all rotations and flights were cancelled. Our first thought (and hope) was that the war was over and we were being held on Guam to bring all the planes back to the US. Why else would the weekend sorties be cancelled? We managed to check out a crew truck and take a tour of the flight line on Saturday morning. What we saw dashed all hope for the end of the war. All BUFFs were being refueled and loaded with bombs. Some enormously important and probably dangerous mission was clearly in the works. We suspected we were going "down town" to Hanoi.

When we returned to quarters, I called the scheduling officer, Howard Rose, and reminded him that the crew was due to leave for home on Monday, that all of us had flown ten missions totaling 115 hours in the preceding twenty-five days, and that we were near our maximum flight time for the month. I said, "I don't know what's going on Monday, but I would appreciate it if you would make us a spare."

I then remarked to Don that I doubted the overseas phone lines were working. He disagreed with my assessment, so I tried to dial home. He was right, the phone started ringing, but I hung up before it was answered. The security risks were too great in my mind, and I didn't want to worry my wife unnecessarily.

The flight schedule was posted on Sunday. Twenty-seven B-52s on the base were going to war on Monday morning, and we were scheduled to fly as Charcoal Three (three aircraft flying in formation were known by various colors), the twelfth G-model in a train of eighteen behind nine D models. Twenty-one D models out of U-Tapao Royal Thai Airbase in Thailand would precede us. President Nixon was finally going to unleash a war-ending strike against the heart of North Vietnam, but where?

Later that morning, while Don and Capt. Steve Smith (a Blytheville aircraft commander in the quarters adjacent to ours) were attending mass in Agana, Bill Buckley and First Lt. Bobby Thomas (Steve's copilot, whose crew was not scheduled to fly on the eighteenth) went to a briefing for the ACs to find out what was going on and to protect the crews from surprises. They were challenged upon entry, but convinced the colonel that they were representing the crews. Reluctantly, he allowed them to stay. Of course this was the briefing where it was all presented – we were going to strike Hanoi in a series of unprecedented massive bombing raids. After the briefing, Lt. Col. Al Dugard, our Squadron Commander, approached the copilots, and asked Bill what he was still doing on the "Rock." He thought we had rotated on Friday. He said, "I was going to fly as the co-pilot on the lead B-52G with Major Robbie Roberson (Barksdale AFB) because his copilot had to go on emergency leave. Bill, since you're still here, I want you to fly on the lead aircraft, and Bobby, I want you to fly in Bill's place with his crew."

"Okay, sounds good to us." Little did they know what destiny would befall us the next night.

The emotions I felt that weekend had been enormous and varied – fear, anger, sadness and elation. Once again, my prayers reflected these emotions as I alternately railed at God and sought his protection. I was fearful of the probable danger of a B-52 strike over the capital of North Vietnam, with more defenses than any city in the world other than Moscow. We would face anti-aircraft artillery, Russian-built MiG fighters, and surface to air missiles (Soviet SA-2s), both going in and coming out. I was angry because we had been scheduled to fly the mission rather than being given spare status on this scheduled day of our return home. I was sad over yet another extension of the separation from my new wife. But I was elated at being able to be part of an effort that was designed to force the government of North Vietnam to sign a treaty and to release the POWs. Finally, B-52s would be used for their original purpose and we were going to be a part of history. Since 1970, I had seen our primary goal in SAC as bringing the war to a conclusion and to free the prisoners. Now I was going to be part of that long-sought event.

I turned to the Lord in prayer for skill, wisdom, insight, and calm as I prepared myself for the Monday's flight into the jaws of hell.

In the World

In mid-November, Margaret Wade, mother of my wife Robbie, had a dream. In it, I walked into her bedroom wearing a striped pajama-like outfit and carrying my helmet tucked under my arm. She was very disturbed by the dream and shared it with Wally Willoughby, the assistant at their family-owned business. She didn't understand the significance of the dream until Christmas.

Chapter 3

The Final Flight

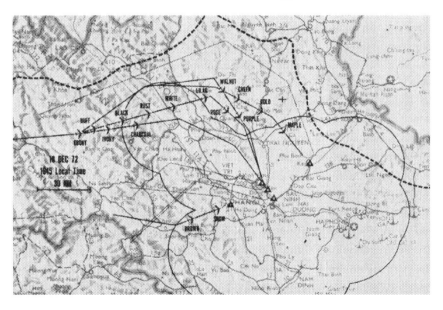

As we entered the briefing room on Monday morning 18 December 1972, instead of the usual three to nine crews (eighteen to fifty-four people), the room was packed with over a hundred pilots, copilots, bombardiers and navigators. Col. Russ McCarthy, commander of the 43 Strategic Wing (D models), came to the podium and announced, "Gentlemen, your target for tonight is Hanoi" as a slide of North Vietnam with a target triangle over Hanoi lit up the screen behind him. Linebacker II was beginning.

Chapter 3

Linebacker II was the code name for the campaign against military targets in the cities of Hanoi and Haiphong. *Linebacker I* had been conducted in the spring that year to mine Haiphong harbor.

A serious quiet settled over the men in the room, ranging in age from twenty-four to about forty. Duplication of mission materials were not yet complete, so they would be delivered to us at the planes. The eight hours it would take to fly to the target would be enough time to get ready, as most of it was over water. The Electronic Warfare Officers were being briefed separately about the kinds of threats we would face and the detection and countering measures they would have to protect the aircraft. The gunners were briefed on MiG tactics and then they picked up our in-flight meals, personal weapons and survival vests.

Arriving at Stratofortress number 58-0201 an hour before engine start, we carefully completed the preflight checks on the entire aircraft and its systems and then sat in the shade under the wing for another fifteen to twenty minutes engaging in quiet chatter and reflection. I carried on a quiet conversation with God, asking for protection for all of us and for our families at home.

My mood was a mixture of somber, anxious, and excited anticipation as I focused on the challenges and the danger that might await us in the next seventeen hours and twenty minutes. We had flown a lot of missions, but almost all of them had been over the friendlier skies of South Vietnam and Cambodia where there were no enemy air defenses capable of reaching our 30-35,000 foot bombing altitude. Lt. Col. Rissi said on one of our first missions together bombing the Delta of South Vietnam, "It's more dangerous flying an approach to O'Hare on a Friday at 5:00 p.m., than flying combat over South Vietnam. The most dangerous thing that could happen would be the copilot spilling hot coffee on himself during the bomb run!"

One mission on twenty-five November over the airfield at Vinh in the southern part of North Vietnam (NVN) had brought no credible threat against us. But Hanoi was a different story. Their anti-aircraft artillery couldn't reach us, but their MiGs could, and their SAMs would find the slow moving (475-knots) and sluggishly maneuvering B-52s a fairly easy target. The briefer had suggested a ten percent loss of aircraft that night. Those were not good odds. Being young, I considered the possibility of being shot down remote; but the likelihood of being hit was higher.

Each of us prepared ourselves in different ways, physically, emotionally and mentally. Bill had stuffed eleven sets of batteries in his flight suit. He decided that if he got shot down, he wanted to be able to talk "forever" on his survival radio. He also carried a small Bible that had been given to him by his best friend in high school. Mentally, he really hadn't considered what was about to happen. We both suffered from that "invincibility syndrome" that so many crewmembers had.

Forty-five minutes before take-off we climbed aboard to start the eight engines and to begin the mission. Engine start was normal; equipment all came on line and appeared functional. Fifteen minutes later we pulled out of our parking stub and joined the long line of BUFFs on the taxiway leading to the south end of the runway. We were on the move, and I was feeling elated and businesslike as I made additional checks of my equipment.

A few minutes later, while stopped on the taxiway, I was standing up in the offense cockpit in the lower lever of the aircraft, when I felt a vaguely familiar rocking. Within seconds, the controller in the Charlie Tower broadcast, "B-52 aircraft do not taxi, do not taxi. Earth tremor in progress." An ominous sign had reared its ugly head. We laughed it off and the pilot joked that maybe if we lined everyone up facing north and went to full take off power, we could crack the runway and stop the mission. Gallows humor took the edge off the underlying anxiety I felt.

Chapter 3

As we resumed our movement to the takeoff end of the runway, we were notified that one of the aircraft ahead of us had been taken out of line because of an equipment malfunction, and we would move up to Charcoal Two, the eleventh G model in the queue. That was not a rare event, and was a part of the contingency plan. I quickly checked the flight plans in my bag and discovered that instead of having the plans for Charcoal plus Buff and Black cells ahead of us, we actually had the plans for the two cells behind us, Ivory and Ebony. Someone in the navigation shop had made an error that potentially threatened the success of the mission. I was concerned by such an error, but welcomed moving up in the line.

Because of the flying time and distance involved in the flight, the bombers were loaded slightly over maximum gross takeoff weight. We had burned a good bit of fuel during engine start and taxi, and would use about 3,000 more pounds of water (water was injected into the eight engines on the takeoff roll and initial climb to augment thrust by thirty percent) and a couple of thousand pounds of fuel in the early moments of the takeoff roll; so we could expect to be down to our maximum takeoff weight of 488,000 pounds by the time the pilot rotated the nose. Very heavy gross weight and a reduced interval takeoff – ninety seconds between the start of takeoff rolls – added another challenge for the pilots.

A few seconds into the roll, Charlie Tower called to say yet another aircraft ahead of us had aborted and left the runway, moving us into the Charcoal 1 position. Major Dick Johnson copied the call, and relayed it to the rest of the crew after we were airborne. Once the takeoff checklist was complete and we were safely climbing out, I notified the aircraft commander that we could move no further because of the flight plan screw-up. "OK, Nav, write it up." We were now in the lead position where we normally flew, and I felt a lot more comfortable being there rather than back in the line.

Crew feedback was important to correct any problems or unexpected challenges that arose from executing the mission as planned.

Normally the gunner took down aircraft malfunctions for the maintenance debriefing following each flight. The navigator wrote up mission problems for debriefing the planners and controllers. The electronic warfare officer (EW), because of the secrecy of his equipment, kept his own write-ups for the intelligence debriefing.

I gave the pilot a heading of 090 degrees. "Wrong way, Nav," he replied.

"True, but it was worth a try. Left turn to 270." We were on our way!

Arriving at 10,000 feet on the climb, the copilot attempted to pressurize the plane – but it didn't work. Quickly, the Radar pulled out the "dash 1" (*1B-52G-1: Flight Manual B-52G USAF Series Aircraft*) and searched for the location of the air outflow valve. Unstrapping, he crawled into the front of the console and found some debris holding the lower valve open, and cleared it. The valve closed normally, but the airplane still did not pressurize. He found the location of a second outflow valve on the upper deck and went upstairs to work on it. Two paper coffee cups were lodged in the valve, and when cleared, the valve closed normally and the pressurization system worked. We were showing our professionalism by quickly analyzing and repairing problems; but this was yet another bad omen. "Write it up" was an uncomfortable common refrain; and I began to wonder if this mission was becoming snake-bit.

From there, we proceeded normally for several hours. I studied the mission, routes, and target, took fixes (positions) every half hour, ate, slept, and chatted with other crewmembers. During the over water portion of the mission, I had plenty of down time and found my mind going back to my wife and our short times together.

I met Robbie Wade on Saturday morning, July 19, 1971. She and I went out that night for dinner, and over the course of the next ten days dated eight times. Each of us was smitten by the other, and believed God had given us our future life's partner.

Chapter 3

Fifteen days later I was on my way to Castle Air Force Base in California for B-52D training as the crew was being transferred to U-Tapao, Thailand for a combat tour that was expected to last around 149-150 days. We caught a KC-135 Stratotanker out to Castle, did the two weeks of training in the D Models and the tour of duty in Thailand. Throughout the fall, Robbie and I corresponded almost daily by letter, card, and an occasional phone call.

When I rotated back to the States, I proposed marriage, and she accepted. On December 31, Robbie and I joined Mel and Elise Polek at the Officers' Club New Year's Eve Party. As we prepared for the clock to strike midnight, Mel and I took the wires off the Champaign bottles to make cork removal easier at the beginning of the year. At 11:59 the corks blew out with a loud pop, startling all of us and giving us a good laugh. I gave Robbie her engagement ring at the stroke of midnight, January 1, 1972. We joined the other couples in an embrace and passionate kiss. At that moment I experienced a profound gratitude to the God who had given us each other, and experienced the peace of knowing that this marriage would weather any storm.

On December 18, as we flew west toward Vietnam, the first storm was brewing. As we approached the Philippines, we were to rendezvous with a Stratotanker (the military version of the Boeing 707, capable of refueling other aircraft in flight) to receive a nominal onload of 50,000 pounds of JP-4 (standard military jet fuel) needed to get us back over Guam with a minimum load of 15,000 pounds. The tanker was to have its APN-69 set to code 2-2-1 (‖ ‖ |) to facilitate the rendezvous. As Dick and I searched ahead, we found a beacon approaching the refueling track. I asked the navigator on the tanker to cycle off his beacon for positive identification. The signal went off, and on my request, back on again. Don contacted the tanker pilot to discuss the hook-up. It appeared that we would complete the line up without the usual turn and would be able to get together earlier than planned.

As we rendezvoused with the tanker, it was off our port bow and in visual as well as voice contact. We requested that he speed up a bit, while we slowed down to swing in behind him. However, the tanker stayed off our wingtip. As tempers began to flare between the pilots, the tanker pilot said he was turning down track. That was bad news because I knew we were fifty miles short.

B-52D ready for refueling from KC-135A

I asked Dick to increase our radar range to fifty miles, and there, at the edge of our scope was another beacon set to 2-2-1. "Pilot, we've got the wrong tanker. Give me all the airspeed you have to catch the right one." We caught the tanker, took our fuel, and proceeded on the mission. We were refueling directly into the sun. Don could not see the boom as we approached until he had contact. Bobby was leaning way over to the right in his seat, calling position. By the time we had our fuel, Ivory cell had closed to five miles behind rather than ten. At least they hadn't passed us, but we were five minutes behind schedule. "Pilot, give me all the airspeed you have and take up heading 250 to rejoin course. We'll deal with overflight problems later."

Chapter 3

Between the Philippines and the coast of Vietnam, there was a lot of chatter over the radio – all on open channel. Anyone listening would begin to get an idea of just how many B-52s were in this raid and could guess where we were going. While it made me very uncomfortable to hear poor radio discipline, I had more important matters on my table – making sure we caught up with our timing and returned to our flight-planned course.

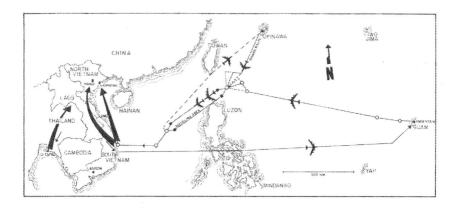

The compression point (where we were to close the wave of nine B-52s from five to one mile separation) was over Laos just beyond the western border of South Vietnam and just southwest of the demilitarized zone (DMZ). As we turned north, Ivory and Ebony cells discovered they were scheduled to be at that point at the same time and altitude. Those six airplanes had to maneuver in the deepening twilight to get into proper formation and to avoid one or more midair collisions.

As things straightened out and calmed down, the copilot came to the lower deck to the urinal. He stopped by my station, tapped me on the shoulder, and shouted above the noise, "I'm scared, Nav, are you?"

I shared his fear; but shared terror could create disaster under fire. I judged that Bobby needed reassurance, and so did I. "I'm too busy to be scared right now, Co. Besides, you and I have more important things to do than to die out here tonight. Just stick with me and we'll be OK." Those were the last personal words I would ever exchange with Bobby Thomas. In the months before, we had often talked about our future goals. I felt called to become a clergyman; he felt called to become a physician because, as he put it, "My people (African-Americans) need good doctors." Bobby's crew was quartered next to ours, so the two crews often socialized, going to movies, the Officers' Club, or just sitting at an outdoor table for conversation.

About a half-hour later, as we approached the Laos-China border west of Hanoi, Bill Buckley, the co-pilot on Rust 1 (the lead G model), called down the line to get fuel status reports from the seventeen BUFFs behind him. We were supposed to be maintaining radio silence, and such information read in the clear would tell anyone listening how many B-52s were on the way and where they were going. Our crew was incensed, especially since Bill had been on our crew for the past three months and knew better than to pull this stunt. We made another write-up for our debriefing. When it was our turn to respond, Lt. Col. Rissi said, "Charcoal 1 is on the curve." Bill came back with a demand for numbers of pounds. What we did not know was that Lt. Buckley had argued the wisdom of this call with both the aircraft commander and the airborne commander (ABC), Col. Thomas Rew, the 72 Strategic Wing commander. He had been ordered by the ABC to make the call.

Chapter 3

SA-2 Surface to Air Missile

Now that the sun had set, the pilots could see SAMs streaking into the night sky from hundreds of miles away. The tankers in orbit over the Gulf of Tonkin as fueling stations for our fighter support were watching and listening as the drama began to unfold. Thirty-nine support aircraft were in the zone to lay down chaff, suppress SAM and AAA sites, jam enemy radar, and escort the bomber fleet against MiGs.

A sign of a professional combat crew is the ability to take things in stride. We had overcome earth tremor, mechanical problems, flight planning errors, rendezvous mistakes, and disappointment at being delayed in our return. Now we had to overcome what we considered to be a breach in security over enemy territory, one perpetrated by our own wing commander. Be that as it may, we were pressing on. I knew we had what it took. But I did pray a lot.

As we turned eastbound out of Laos to enter North Vietnam for the bomb run, we were all focused on making this the best, most accurate mission we had ever flown. We would be within lethal range of SAMs for about twenty minutes, and we couldn't be distracted by the threats. The bombardier and I turned off our exterior radios so we could concentrate only on our checklists and crew coordination. I became all business, super-organized and aware of where we were and what we needed to do in the next several minutes. Any fear I had felt earlier was now gone. We were headed downtown to break the back of enemy transportation and warehousing and there was no doubt in my mind that we could do that.

For a variety of reasons, we had been ordered to take no evasive action from the initial aiming point to the bomb release point, and to restrict any post-target evasive maneuvers to no more than thirty degrees of bank. If we could not guarantee that our bombs would fall in the target, we were to withhold release and bring them home. Those orders seemed to become increasingly suicidal as the pilots reported multiple SAM calls from the bombers from U-Tapao, Thailand that had entered the target zone 30 minutes ahead of us. Colonel Rissi told Captain Simpson (the EWO), to refrain from making threat calls that might interfere with the bomb run. We weren't allowed to take evasive action, so why clutter the interphone? Hold them until after bombs away.

One reason given for maneuver restrictions in the briefing was concern over the calibration of the bombing system. Bombers in Southeast Asia were normally led down the bomb run and given the release order by a Ground Controlled Intercept site. Hanoi would require synchronous bombing using internal systems. Those systems were not checked regularly to insure accuracy. Another reason given was that the waves of B-52s were giving each other electronic counter-measure protection, and evasive action and steep banks would degrade or negate that mutual advantage. Political sensitivity to dropping bombs in civilian areas was another high consideration.

The thing that insulted me was the suspicion that the commanders did not trust the crews to drop bombs accurately while maneuvering. It seemed that the safety of the enemy was taking precedence over our own. We would show them by flying it their way and putting the bombs in the bull's-eye. But we would also recommend major changes in the tactics when we debriefed eight hours later.

About 110 nautical miles from the target, the D cells (Rose, Lilac, and White) and G cells (Rust, Black, and Buff) out of Andersen turned ten degrees left, while Charcoal, Ivory, and Ebony continued straight ahead at 33,000 feet. At 1945 (times are in 24-hour military clock and are stated in local Hanoi time) Snow and Brown (Ds from U-Tapao) struck the Hoa Lac airfield in southern Hanoi. At 1949, more Ds from U-T (Maple, Gold, Green) struck the Kep airfield northeast of Hanoi. At 1955, Purple and Walnut (Ds from U-T) struck the Phuc Yen airfield near our target on the northeast side of Hanoi. Four minutes later the D and first G wave (a wave consisted of three cells) from Andersen struck the Kihn No Complex just to its southeast, followed by our wave flying against the Yen Vien Rail Yard, about another mile to the southeast.

As we made our turn at the initial aiming point, about seventy-five nautical miles from the target, the Radar easily found the target and all four offset aiming points (OAPs). The crosshairs were steady, with no drift. Our initial heading was 147 degrees, with a dogleg turn to 152 for the final run. The wind was a slight quartering tailwind, giving us 7 degrees of drift compensation. I calculated the time to target, and confirmed that our bombs would reach the ground at exactly 2014:00 local time, or 1314:00 Greenwich Mean Time. We were on time (even with a 90-knot jet stream on the final run), on target, and with the best bombing system possible. But there was a problem.

"Radar, where's the chaff?" We had been briefed that we might have difficulty finding the target and/or OAPs because of chaff the

F-4s (primary fighter laying down chaff, small strips of aluminum foil to confuse enemy radar) would lay down for our protection; but there was none on our scope. Dick ran his bombing system through several frequencies, and there it was – at a single frequency and running between the turning point and the target. The sight reminded me of the large green highway signs with reflective letters common on U.S. interstates. *Why didn't they just send the route maps to Hanoi? It looks like our own Air Force has set us up!* I had been puzzled when I realized we couldn't see any chaff. Now I was alarmed that it had been laid in such a way as to further endanger our lives and our mission. This flight was definitely snake-bit; and my heart was racing with anxiety. But for the next few minutes, we had to be all business. Dick tuned away from the chaff frequency, and we once again concentrated on the bomb run checklists. I made a mental note to add that to our long list of mission write-ups when we were safely out of the lethal area. My prayers for safety were more frequent, sandwiched between the tasks that were vital to our bomb drop and to our escape.

As we made our final turn toward the target we entered the 90-knot jet stream, boosting our groundspeed to 560 knots. At least our time in the area was being reduced by a few minutes, and our groundspeed might make it more difficult for the SAM crews to hit us at least until we made our steep, long post-target turn to the west to exit the area. That turn, which would blank out our SAM jammers for nearly two minutes and then reduce our groundspeed to about 400 knots, was another insane feature of the worsening tactical situation.

The EW, Capt. Tom Simpson, reported 100-millimeter anti-aircraft artillery (AAA) radar was locked on, but would be ineffective at our altitude. What we didn't know was that our ALT-22 Modulated ECM Transmitters could be countered by the SAM crews. The D models and some Gs had ALT-6B Unmodulated Transmitters that were more effective.

Chapter 3

With our outside radios still off and the crew maintaining only checklist and bombing instructions on the intercom, the Radar and I were able to concentrate on this critical offensive phase of the mission. By this time I was aware of no emotion other than dogged determination, no words other than checklist items, and few thoughts other than prayers. Thirty seconds before bombs away, Dick opened the doors, and twenty seconds later I was to restart my stopwatch as a backup to the drop should anything go wrong. Just short of ten seconds to go, time seemed to stand still and speed ahead, all at the same time.

At SAM Site VN-119 on the ground below, Thang Nguyen was commanding the 59th Missile Battalion. By using a "three-point" technique with *Fan Song* tracking radar, they were able to find glimpses of our BUFF on their *Spoon Rest* radarscopes. This is his account of the battle:

> The guidance controllers began to track a line of jamming returns on their separate screens. Using the correlater to gather the line of returns into a small area and into a single return, the fire control officer cautiously checked to make sure each of the guidance officers was looking at the same target.
>
> But the B-52 was "invisible" in the dense jamming on the screen. Where to look for the target? That is perhaps the most difficult thing in the three-point technique. Thang Nguyen counted on the ability of his guidance officers, thinking that the B-52 is big and they could break him out of the jamming. They picked up a B-52's jamming strobe on the *Spoon Rest* radar scope, then turned on the *Fan Song* radar, hoping that they could recognize and break out the B-52's radar return in the jamming waves.

Bombs were exploding at intervals in the direction of Uy No and the command van swayed back and forth, but Thang disregarded the bombing and gave the launch order and two missiles were fired at the B-52. After a minute the crews saw the radar return break down and then become dull and eventually disappear. The bombing of the B-52s suddenly stopped at this time. The sky was suddenly quiet. There was only Quang's yelling from the "bird house" on the roof of the van: "It's burning already! It's a big fire! There is one big cloud of smoke like the one in the atomic bomb explosion."

At 1313 GMT, the radar screens went blank and other instruments lost power and the aircraft shuddered and yawed slightly left. My first thought was that the copilot had accidentally knocked the generators off line. Before I could speak, though, he was shouting over the intercom, "They've got the Pilot! They've got the Pilot!" I thought, *Who has the pilot?*

The EW was also shouting, "Is anybody there? Gunner, gunner!" His cockpit had gone black, his equipment had major electrical shorts and explosions, and the gunner was covered in blood and slumped in his seat. Tom had also lost his earphones but not his microphone. We could hear him, but he couldn't hear us. Dick and I had intermittent intercom.

My internal voice was saying, *This can't be me. We haven't been hit; or have we?* Then the voice silently whispered, *Yes, this is for real.* Then, that last internal "still, small voice" took over, and everything went into slow motion. From that point forward, I was truly on auto-pilot, reacting in the way I had been trained. That training was for the worst-case scenario, and now all of a sudden, we were cashing in the "training-chit" with every last ounce of our energy! We are performing and reacting on autopilot. Thank God it worked!

SA-2 Detonation

I pulled out my small Sanyo flashlight to check the altimeter and noted we were in a 400-500 feet per minute descent. I then laid it on my desk to check my personal equipment; and Dick picked it up and aimed it upstairs toward Tom. Tom's voice could be heard briefly, "Is anyone alive up front?" It was then very quiet, and I suspected we had lost the four port engines, and maybe more.

The first SAM had exploded to the left front of the aircraft, scattering hot shrapnel like a shotgun blast at a velocity of 8000 feet per second. The plane flew at 490 knots true airspeed through the burst, and thousands of pieces of hot metal shards ripped through the plane, wounding the pilot and killing the gunner.

Some of it was sucked into jet engines (which destroyed them and the engine-driven generators), and others cut hydraulic lines and set the oil on fire. We probably had ruptured fuel tanks on fire, but there would be no major explosion unless the JP-4 lit off in an intact tank. That might come in a few seconds.

Over the Gulf of Tonkin, my brother, Capt. John Neal Certain, the pilot of a Stratotanker in the refueling orbit, saw the SAM hit the B-52 and the explosions and flames as it began its death spiral toward the ground. He knew I was to have returned home that morning, but a sick sensation in his abdomen told him that I was probably in the middle of that conflagration.

I looked over my left shoulder and saw a fire in the forward wheel well through the porthole in the bulkhead door behind the offense cockpit. First I thought of the twenty-seven 750-pound bombs in the bomb bay right behind the fire, and turned to the Radar, "Drop those bombs!" He safetied them (we didn't know where they would land, so we did not want them armed since we were under orders to avoid POW camps and civilian areas), and hit the release switch. They all seemed to drop away from our now-crippled BUFF. Oddly, though the indicator lights went out, I felt no shudder or lurch as they left. My next thought was that the fire was also directly below the main mid-body fuel tank, loaded with 10,000 pounds of JP-4.

"The pilot's still alive," Don's voice came weakly over the intercom.

"Co, Nav, escape heading is 290." The Tonkin Gulf 60 miles to the east would have been a better place to go for bailout; but there were too many SAM sites and MiG airfields in that direction.

"EW's leaving!" In a controlled ejection, the navigator went first (to make a hole for manual bailouts if any other seats failed), then the Defense Team, the copilot, the Radar, and finally the pilot. In an uncontrolled escape, it was every man for himself. This was definitely an uncontrolled event!

Chapter 3

With that, about ten seconds after the first of two SAMs hit the plane, the first crewmember ejected. I heard the explosion of his hatch and seat as it rocketed up and out, but felt no decompression. We had been at combat pressurization (17,000 feet), but the holes in the airplane had caused that to rise to over 30,000 feet by the time we ejected. I looked at the Radar. Our eyes met, and we both started preparing for ejection. I threw my flight case as far to the rear of the cockpit as I could, cleared my table, tossing pens, dividers, and charts to the back (I didn't want any of that stuff being drawn out the hatch when I ejected, possibly causing injuries), stowed my table, pulled down my visor, cinched up the oxygen mask, pulled the "green apple" to activate the flow of O_2, kicked back into the leg restraints. I discovered the restraints had already tripped; so I had to bend down and reset them before kicking back again. I grabbed the ejection handle between my knees – incorrectly, with palms facing me. Instantly, I remembered that my elbows would extend past the hatch opening if my hands were placed that way, reversed my grip, looked at the Radar again, turned to face forward, saw the ejection light come on as the pilot ejected, and pulled. I thought the seat had failed. The ballistic activators were supposed to blow the hatch below my seat and fire me in the seat out the bottom of the plane, all in three-tenths of a second. But fear gripped me and expletives filled my mind as the panels in front of me seemed to move up exceptionally slowly. *Was this thing jammed on the rails? I'll be beaten to death by the wind!* It was an illusion brought on by the state of shock induced by the extreme danger of being in a burning and likely to explode bomber directly over the enemy capital. Everything from the first call from the copilot to ejection had appeared in exaggerated slow motion, like a movie depiction of an automobile crash. In actuality, it was probably about ten seconds.

The next thing I knew, I was in the cold air of the troposphere. At 31,000 feet, the temperature was –55° centigrade. As I tumbled around all three axes, I thought, *That was a dumb thing to do.*

I'll bet the plane was still flyable. Where is it? Perhaps I could crawl back in. Dumb thoughts from a lingering sense of invulnerability, I suppose. *Now what do I do? OK, God, it's you and me.* My prayers for the next few minutes would remain blunt and somewhat profane.

Next, I checked to make sure the 350-pound seat had separated from me. It had. One second after clearing the hatch, more ballistic activators had blown seat belts and shoulder harnesses loose and activated the man-seat separator, a strap on an inertial reel running behind and below me. When it tightened, I was pushed out and away from the seat, arming the parachute for automatic deployment passing 15,000 feet. I carefully checked to feel my parachute harness. Had I remembered to connect all the clips? I had only checked it about two dozen times on the way in. It was there. Then I concentrated on stabilizing my fall. My oxygen mask was being forced up over my eyes. I pulled it down to my mouth, tightened the connections, repositioned my visor and tightened the lock nut. But still, the force of the tumble kept pushing it up. My mind was racing through checklists and training manuals and all those boring safety lectures I had sat through for the last four years. I was amazed and calmed that I seemed to be remembering so much.

I tried to get into the sky diving position to stabilize in a facedown fall, but that only made matters worse. I doubt that I tried that for more than a few seconds, though it seemed longer. Grabbing my mask, I held it in place with both hands, pulled my legs together, bent my knees, and bent over slightly. Right away, the tumbling stopped as my personal center of gravity was shifted to my lower body, and I was falling feet first toward the earth, now about 20,000 feet below. I began to look around for signs of Charcoal One. Above me I could see a long trail of smoke – wide, thick, and dense – turning slightly west, then looping around and descending before disappearing into the clouds below.

Chapter 3

I could feel the effects of the wind, but I had no sensation of falling. I slipped two fingers of my right hand into the T-handle to manually activate the chute should I enter any clouds (briefed to be solid at 2,000 feet). *Just wait. A high-altitude opening shock could damage the canopy and injure the jumper.* After ejection I was traveling initially at the airspeed of the plane. As I freefell I slowed to terminal velocity (when the wind resistance is equal to the force of gravity, about 120 knots). In a moment, I felt the parachute opening as I passed through 15,000 feet and fully deploy a few hundred feet below. I felt each fold, one at my shoulders, one at my buttocks, as it began its deployment out of the pack. So far, all my emergency equipment was working properly.

With the opening shock I was swinging like a pendulum in a wide arc below the canopy. First, I checked for a good and complete chute, then reached up and pulled the red daisy-chained line on my right riser to release four lines and create a small spillway. That accomplished, the chute stabilized, and the undulations ceased. Finally, I looked down for the first time. There, between my boots, I saw the inferno that made up the three targets that had been struck over the last twenty minutes. As I watched, I saw a series of explosions walk though the target – the twenty-seven bombs from Ebony Three had found paydirt. The time was 1315:50 when Ebony Three's bombs started exploding. I had been falling for two minutes and forty seconds.

Was that the last of the bombs, or were there others falling all around me? Am I really going to land in the target and be burned alive? Grabbing two fists full of right risers, I pulled them down to my ankle, tilting the military canopy and steering it to the west. My heart was racing as fast as my mind. Somewhere around 10,000 feet, the wind shifted out of the east, aiding in moving me west and away from the target area. This nightmare was going exceptionally well.

The solid undercast turned out to be broken to scattered clouds. The moon was full, and I could see the ground clearly all around. Panic was beginning to replace concern. White panels in the canopy, and a white helmet were not going to be assets as I slowly descended into enemy territory no more than ten kilometers northwest of Hanoi. I was going to have to find a wooded area to land in if I was to have any chance of evasion. I looked around the sky above and below for other chutes, but spotted none. Somewhere out there were Tom and Don for sure, and I hoped Dick, Bobby and Fergie were somewhere above me.

As I was beginning to feel relief drifting about thirty degrees west-northwest away from the target, in my right peripheral vision I caught another series of explosions – right in line with my drift. *Oh, God, now what? There shouldn't be another target over there; that was our escape route.* As I looked down through a break in the clouds and drifted past this new blaze (and through the mushroom cloud of smoke), I realized that this fire was shaped like an arrow – Charcoal 1 had plowed in flames into a field below at approximately 21.07N, 105.52E. My watch showed 1317 GMT. Ejection hadn't been such a bad idea after all. *Look Lord, it's you and me. If I'm gonna die down there, just go ahead and let me die right now. I'm ready to go. I would just as soon not have those people down there get me and kill me. I don't care if they capture me. But if they're gonna kill me, you take me now.*

It was time to concentrate on the landing. I tried to slip my chute in the direction of tree lines for cover and possible escape or rescue. But I could see rooftops in every clump of trees. I crossed over a river below, noting a railroad running up to its edge, but there was no bridge connecting it to the other side. I thought I might be able to land in the river and hide out along the bank; but I was still high and continued to drift.

Chapter 3

The situation was becoming clearly hopeless. We had been told back on Guam that search and rescue would not be available. The apparently populated farm country below me offered no place to hide. I had heard horror stories of how wounded aircrew had been killed or left to die, with medical care being offered only if they lived for three days. Being captured with a major injury was not a pleasant thought. I needed to make my fall a good one.

I had some static ground training in the harness, a few dozen parachute landing falls from a platform, and two parasailing rides behind a pickup truck. The cable was about 300 feet long, so we were towed up about 200 feet, cut loose and drifted to the ground. The theory is that falling the first 30,000 feet doesn't hurt – hitting the ground does the damage. The big thing to learn is to land properly. I hoped I had learned it well.

I opened the 60-pound seat kit to string out all of the survival equipment it contained on a tether below, and to decrease my chance of injury on landing. Then I faced forward keeping my eyes on the horizon, grabbed my risers, put my legs together with my knees slightly bent, and waited. When my toes began to touch the earth, I executed a parachute-landing fall (PLF), rolling to the right into a dry ditch. The point of touchdown was approximately 21.07N, 105.50.5E. To the east side was a plowed field, to the west side a railroad. My injuries to this point consisted of a few bumps, bruises and abrasions from the ejection, fall, and landing. The PLF had gone perfectly. Everything continued to work according to the book. But there was no time to relish in this small success. It was time to evade.

Hearing the voices of locals approaching me, I knew I had to get away from my equipment. As I rapidly opened buckles and removed excess items, I found that my dog tag chain (with my dog tags and wedding band) had wrapped around the oxygen hose. I yanked the hose away from me, breaking the chain and scattering the items on it. All could be replaced when I went home. I rolled over, broke the antenna off the emergency beacon and turned the switch off. Because of their ease of locating me (and others after me), I suspected the Vietnamese had direction finders to home in on our beacons. Tom Simpson would report later that, as he crawled out from under his canopy, he was already surrounded. Dick Johnson had turned his off in the air, and managed to evade for about twelve hours.

I pulled off the white helmet, tucked it under my arm and crawl-ran about fifty yards down the ditch toward a culvert under a bridge. As voices grew louder, I hit the deck, tucked the helmet below me, and pulled my two-way radio out of my survival vest. The vest contained the minimum amount of gear—radio, flare kit, knife, strobe, matches, compass, snare wire, and shells for my pistol—needed to survive any environment. The seat kit, strung out over the plowed field, contained heavier equipment—raft, rifle, and other items for water and jungle survival.

CODE OF CONDUCT: Article II

I will never surrender of my own free will. If in command, I will never surrender the members of my command while they still have the means to resist.

I made a quick call in a muted voice, "All B-52 aircraft, this is Cobalt, no. Make that Charcoal One-Delta ('Delta' was the navigator indicator). I'm on the ground, uninjured, surrounded. Will be captured shortly." I could only hope that someone had heard the transmission and reported it; but with all the noise of SAM calls and emergency signals from other crewmembers, I doubted it. I then broke off that antenna and turned the switch off. Breaking off the antennae was a small attempt to render the beacon and radio useless to the enemy. I didn't have time to remove the batteries or to otherwise damage them. Had I remembered my weapon, I could have shot them; but that would have given away my position and could have led to my own death.

By this time I was feeling more like an observer than a participant. Still hoping to make it to the culvert, I lay over the helmet and tried to make myself blend into the shadows of the ditch. Next time I looked, I could see two figures standing on the bridge above the culvert. Small explosions (grenades, firecrackers, tracer bullets?) were showing all around my abandoned parachute harness. Strangely, no shrapnel was flying in my direction. What *was* that? I could see silhouettes of people on the bridge over the culvert, and my hopelessness began to mount. Momentarily a woman eased up to the edge of the ditch, standing directly over me, but looking in the direction of the harness. As she turned to her left to move away, she spotted me in the ditch, sounded the alarm and ran away.

I remembered the loaded Smith & Wesson .38 caliber Combat Masterpiece. I pulled it from its holster, opened the cylinder, ejected the bullets, and threw them as far down the ditch as I could. Then I jammed the barrel into the soft earth to clog it and to make sure it would have to be cleaned before firing, and hastily buried it. I thought, *I can't win a war with a six-shooter; and if they're going to kill me tonight, they can use their own weapon.* Death was a distinct possibility.

Chapter 4

Captured

CODE OF CONDUCT: Article III
If I am captured, I will continue to resist by all means available. I will make every effort to escape and aid others to escape. I will accept neither parole nor special favors from the enemy.

I was quickly surrounded by over fifty civilians wielding rocks, farm implements, and sticks and by several militiamen with automatic weapons. With hundreds of rocks flying in my direction, I pulled my helmet on for protection. Four uniformed militiamen appeared at the edge of the ditch, yelling and motioning for me to stand up.

Because of the full moon, they had spotted me coming down. In that climate I judged that I no longer had the means to resist, that rescue was not possible, and that my only possibility for life was surrender, and that possibility wasn't a probability. Within a few seconds, I was captured, ordered up to the tracks, stripped to my skivvies, and roped.

The civilians began to pull at my survival vest in an attempt to remove it. I remembered the box of shells for my pistol, and the switchblade in my left thigh pocket. My helmet was jerked off my head.

To prevent being injured, I assisted by showing those who were stripping me how the zipper worked on the vest, flight suit, and quick-don boots. I was shoved to the ground while they removed my clothing, save for my skivvies. After they were all off, my wrists were tied behind my back, and the rope was used like a leash. Someone spotted my watch and quickly removed it. I was cold, standing on a railroad bed in bare feet, and helpless. I was completely at their mercy, but could not show any of the terror I was feeling inside.

The North Vietnamese account of this event was published a couple of days later.

SURVIVORS OF B-52 CREW CAPTURED OUTSIDE HANOI

[Article by Ahn Chinh: "Capture of B-52 Pirate Crew"; Hanoi, Nhan Dan, Vietnamese, 20 December 1972, p. 4. Excerpted from Translations on North Vietnam, No. 1327, Joint Publications Research Service, Air University, Maxwell AFB AL, 20 Mar. 1973]

The B-52G, the latest version of the B-52's, was flying exposed in the night sky which was lit up by the fire of missiles and the long range anti-aircraft artillery of the army and people of Hanoi and Vinh Phu. It was hit at approximately 2015 hours. It was dealt a blow which corresponded precisely with its imposing size. It instantly broke up and burst immediately into a flaming torch. Throughout both of the periods when Johnson and Nixon have waged air wars of destruction against North Vietnam, never has there been such a torch in the skies around the capital, caused by the large orange U.S. plane. The healthier and more thundering, the more tragic does something seem in death; the flaming torch plunged and its impetus carried it several kilometers before it fell into a field belonging to hamlet D, township P., Kim Anh District. The pieces were strewn for several square kilometers. The nose of the plane was buried in a fifth-month rice field along Route 3; the fuselage was laying in a subsidiary crops field west of the road.

In the morning we and a number of people, militia and army troops climbed upon the fuselage. The long, wide, and high section of the B-52G made us dizzy. There wasn't anyone in the vehicles going up and down the road below who didn't slow down in order to gain further satisfaction from staring at the wreckage. The letters "B-52G," "United States of America" were painted in black, not only in one but in many places on the section of the plane followed by such annotations as "six-man flight crew," "it is necessary to use oil type JP-4," etc. And above all of this, large, bright, arrogant, and hooligan-like was the insignia of the United States Strategic Air Command "STRATEGIC AIR COMMAND" with a steel fist thrust up hideously through a blue sky and white clouds grasping three thunderbolts and an olive branch! The interior of the plane bristled with electronic lights intertwined with wiring of all sizes and colors. There was even a bottle of perfumed water, several tubes of toothpaste, pieces of clothing caught on the bottom of ejection seats, and dried blood.

Where did the six-man crew of this B-52G go? Only the bottoms of the ejection seats were there, all six of the crew had parachuted. Several of them had been hit by shrapnel with the plane and when they hit the ground they were even further dazed and died of their wounds. Two of them came down in the rice field

of township D. close to township P., where they were
rounded up by the militia of township D under the
command of township unit leader Nguyen Zuan Lam.
One, Richard Thomas Simpson, a 31-year-old captain,
surrendered docilely. Another, Robert Glen Certain,
a 25-year-old captain, hastily grabbed for his pistol, a
Smith and Weston special, but in just a wink of the eye
he lowered his head before the guns of our militia.

The two persons who directly escorted the pirates
back to the detention camp were Tran Quoc Thai, 20
years old, and Ngo Thi Thuan, 19 years old. The father
of Thuan held one of the four old fashioned muskets
used by the guerrillas of Township P. when they first
began fighting the French in the Resistance, just 26
years earlier. The father of Thai, like all of the rest of
the guerrillas in the township, district, and province
during that time, only used the sword. Their family
tribute was being passed on; 26 years ago it was at this
place that their fathers had ambushed trucks filled with
goods for the French aggressors. And today, at the
very moment, they were leading the B-52 pirates over
that road, and this U.S. gang had not yet stopped their
trembling. One of them raised his thumb and began to
speak to our interpreter: "This was the first time that I
flew in to Hanoi…"

During the first few minutes of capture, some of the people kept
asking, "Russki? Russki?"

*Oh, sure. Just take me to an airport and I'll take another
airplane up and kill some Americans!* "Nyet. No." Some civilians
were fascinated with my red hair and pale skin; others made it past
the militia to strike me with fists and rocks, knocking me off my
feet.

The militia chased them off and lifted me up. One of the civilians tore my tee shirt off the left shoulder. Oddly, the guard tied it back up, as though it was a matter of modesty. That was surprising and confusing.

We began walking to the southwest. After about fifty or sixty yards, we turned right onto the levee and walked about another hundred yards to a nearby village where I was shown off to the residents. The locals gathered all of my gear and brought it with them to the village. Strangely, I felt no discomfort from walking on the railroad rocks or the dirt trail. My very pale and freckled skin and my bright red hair fascinated the children. Like children anywhere, they eased up to me to touch my legs and to feel my hair. I smiled at them and tried my best to appear friendly. In the background, though, there was loud talk in what sounded like an angry argument.

Vietnamese monument at the crash site of Charcoal 1

Chapter 4

Wreckage of Charcoal 1 in Hanoi Army Museum

After a few minutes, I was placed in what appeared to be a small brick silo or barn. The door was only about three feet tall, so I practically had to crawl through it. The floor was dug out lower than the door and had trenches in it. About ten feet above, there was a ledge of some sort. I was ordered to sit against the wall, and a guard sat next to me. A local man came in with a flashlight and pair of pliers. Tugging at my jaw, he clearly wanted me to open my mouth so he could do a little gold and silver mining. With two gold crowns and several silver fillings, I clamped my mouth as tightly as I could and tucked my chin into my chest to avoid being mutilated. He seemed to give up and leave, but there was a loud argument outside, perhaps about getting help opening my mouth. After he was gone, others were allowed in one at a time to look at me. Again, I concentrated on stuffing all fear, despair, and panic as far down as I could. With every passing minute it became more important to resist, but to show no emotion. I was now an American fighting man in enemy custody. I had a Code of Conduct to uphold.

After about fifteen or twenty minutes, I was brought outside and the rope was removed from my wrists. It was then used to tie my elbows behind my back, separated by about four inches, then around my biceps and wrists, and finally around my neck. My shoulders, shoulder blades and arms were in a very awkward and painful position, and circulation to my lower arms and hands was substantially reduced. Snare wire from my survival vest was used to tie my thumbs together, and the guard showed me the package it came in. I told him I would show him how to catch squirrels with it, but he obviously didn't understand me anymore than I understood him.

Before long, I was moved on foot to another village. We left the village the same way we had come in; but about half-way to the railroad, we turned left (north) and walked about a quarter mile to a second village.

As I approached another long building I could see that it was separated by a stand of trees from the rest of the town. I also noticed a white sheet on the ground in front of the building we were entering. They pulled the sheet back, revealing the body of Don Rissi, stripped down to his briefs. He had a gaping abdominal wound, but his body seemed to have been cleaned up and I could see no sign of blood. He had apparently died of the wounds sustained in the SAM strike, the ejection sequence, or later on the ground. The people were laughing and shouting as they pointed alternately at Don and at me. My initial impulse was to go to him to render aid; but the looks on the enemy faces made it clear that that was not an option, and the condition of his body made it clear that aid was no longer possible.

Oh, Don, go with God. Joan and the boys will be in my prayers. I've never met them, but I grieve for their loss. You were quite an officer and a patriot, so you must have been a wonderful husband and father. It was a fluke for you to have been here to start with. You should have lived.

Chapter 4

They again covered his body with the sheet, and escorted me into a building with a couple of long tables and some chairs. The captors indicated I was to sit at one end of a table, while an officer at the other end bundled up Don's flight suit, boots, dog tags, ID card and wallet, and made notes about him in a blue book similar to those I had taken tests in during college. About six feet to my left were two windows with wooden bars and open shutters. A couple of nurses came in to check me for injuries and to offer water and a cigarette. They carried green canvas medical bags marked with red crosses, and seemed disappointed that I did not require their nursing. I accepted two glasses of water and a cigarette with a nod and a smile.

As the officer finished his writing, people began crowding about the windows, tugging at the wooden bars and making threatening gestures. When he left, they began throwing rocks and bits of plaster at me. The four or five militia guarding me took a couple of tables and benches and barricaded the windows to protect me. One of them, however, kept opening and closing his hand to show me an AK-47 round – meant for me? I felt like an observer in a surrealistic drama. Offering no protest and doing my best to show no emotion, I sat tied in the chair and watched it all unfold. Was I being protected because of what I flew? Was there a bounty on my head, making me more valuable alive? Did they actually observe the Geneva Conventions relative to the treatment of POWs?

Protection, kindness and consideration were not the treatments I had expected. Charcoal One was the first Stratofortress lost to enemy fire in all the years of the war and I was the first B-52 crewmember captured, unless Tom had been caught already (it never crossed my mind that he might have died; I hoped he was evading capture). With the terror of the bombing continuing through the night, I was anticipating severe treatment as punishment for what our nation was doing to theirs. My understanding of what might be in store was shaped by military briefings and by my reading of U. S. Army Major James (Nick) Rowe's autobiography of his five years of captivity at the hands of the Vietcong in South Vietnam. So far, I had not faced the worst of my fears.

As we left that place I was blindfolded with gauze. We walked down a country path, turning left, or north, through the trees to another destination. The blindfold was not completely effective and I could see below it. At one point, we rounded a curve in the path just as the guard to my left fixed the bayonet on his rifle. To the right I saw a clearing with a mound of dirt at the back. My heart raced and I gasped in terror and contemplated the likelihood that I was to be executed; but we kept going. Rain had begun to fall, making life a bit more miserable. I pleaded with God to give me a clear head and some understanding of what was happening.

A few moments later, the column stopped and someone behind me started poking the back of my right knee while two others held my arms. Thinking they wanted me to sit, I tried that, but the men on either side pulled me back up. After a couple of additional tries to get me to understand their intentions, the man behind me went in front, knelt down, took my right ankle in his hands, and gently tugged forward. I relaxed and let him have my ankle. He placed my foot on the ground about eighteen inches ahead. They wanted me to step over a small ditch without stumbling. Confusion was mixing into the fear, terror, and sense of impending doom that was churning inside me. *Show no emotion; stand aloof from events; try to think this through and understand what is going on. These guys are not going to let anything happen to me out here.*

Soon, the distinctive rumbling of falling bombs and the earthquake-like explosions as they hit the ground returned to the night. That wave of BUFFs began at midnight. I had been a prisoner of war for almost four hours. Immediately, the column moved into a ditch and sat still until it ended fifteen or twenty minutes later.

Chapter 4

While I couldn't see any benefit of sitting in a ditch since the sounds of the bombs indicated the targets were many miles away, it was a relief to rest, listen and to collect my thoughts. There were three distinct waves of bombers, each separated by about fifteen minutes. Between bombing strikes, I was moved in stages to a highway where I was placed in yet another ditch. I leaned back against a concrete pipe. Apparently the footpath we were walking on crossed the ditch and intersected with a road. Trucks and motorcycles could be heard passing by. I could also hear another American voice on the opposite side of the footpath, that of my EW, Tom Simpson. "Tom, is that you?" Before he could answer, we were told to be quiet. After another round of bombing in the distance, a flatbed military truck with a canvas top arrived and Tom and I were put in the back, along with four guards for transport east toward Hanoi.

Even with the guards in the back of the truck, I tried to have a quiet conversation with Tom. He had bandages on his head, his hands and left arm, with bloodstains showing through, and was stripped, blindfolded and roped similarly to me. Apparently Tom couldn't hear me, and I could raise no response from him. The guard next to me kept patting me on the shoulder and talking softly to me, as if to offer some comfort. I said, "If you're asking me if I want to go home, the answer is 'yes.'" I then began to talk louder in the guard's direction, but addressing Tom. He still didn't answer.

After about twenty minutes the truck stopped and we were moved to the back seat of a Jeep-like vehicle with a canvas top. Tom was placed in the right rear, and then I was taken to the left side and forced into the left rear. The regular army guard started yelling at me, and struck me with his rifle butt with some force on my left leg. I took the hint and moved to the middle of the seat so he could climb in beside me. Two other guards climbed in the front. We raced down a narrow paved country road, barely missing the oncoming traffic, and barely able to see them with blackout headlights or none at all. The full moon provided what visibility the drivers had. A collision on this road could mean painful injuries or death. Because of the gaps at the bottom of our blindfolds, Tom and I noticed great crates stacked under the trees along the road: stacks of supplies, earthmoving equipment, etc. The crates were an important item of intelligence for our side – too bad we couldn't get the information out. They would make a great target.

As we traveled, Tom began to talk with me, indicating that he was OK except for a puncture wound in his left arm and some scrapes on his head and hands; he then asked about my health. I was in a lot better shape than he appeared to be in. I told him about Don; he told me Fergie had died in his seat from multiple shrapnel wounds. Neither of us knew about Bobby or Dick.

Master Sergeant Walter Ferguson had fought in two wars and had a wingtip shot off his plane in Korea. With a number of Arclight (B-52) tours under his belt in Southeast Asia, he had voluntarily grounded himself effective the day of our return to Blytheville, and planned to retire in January 1973 after thirty years of service to America. Fergie was long-since divorced and remained estranged from his family. He had served well and should have had a peaceful retirement. Grief over another friend's death sent me into deeper sadness. Again, I offered a prayer to God to receive the soul of yet another friend and crewmate.

I could not grieve for Bobby and Dick yet. *Surely they got out. We'll see them soon.*

I managed to untie the snare wire from my thumbs and to stuff it behind the seat. I doubted anyone knew it was there, and I didn't want that much pliable wire around in case the enemy decided to get really nasty. The terror of the previous hours was beginning to wane into resignation. Within twenty minutes, the jeep came to a halt and the guards got out. In front of us I could see a body of water; to either side was a darkened hut. The three guards left the jeep.

"Tom, this doesn't look good. It may be the end of the line." We could hear other vehicles pull up behind us, and loud discussions being held.

Soon, the two guards, Tran Quoc Thai and Ngo Thi Thuan, returned to the vehicle, yelled "No talking!" and took turns beating me with their fists about my head and torso.

Tom protested, "What are you asking? We don't understand you. Why are you hitting him?" But they ignored him. Since he was clearly wounded, they seemed to concentrate their wrath on me. After a while, they tired of the sport and left.

Then the most amazing thing happened. Trucks started driving up from the water in front of us! We were waiting for a ferry to cross the Red River. When it was ready we continued our journey into the capital city. We had been told in the pre-mission briefing that it would take ten to fifteen minutes for the ferry to cross the river. It must have been almost one in the morning by then. As we drove up and off the ferry, we turned south into the city. During the half hour or so that we drove, I could see no lights and no people on the streets. At last we were traveling with a high wall to our left, and turned into a gate in the wall.

Chapter 5

Interrogation

CODE OF CONDUCT: Article IV

If I become a Prisoner of War, I will keep faith with my fellow prisoners. I will give no information or take part in any action which might be harmful to my comrades. If I am senior, I will take command. If not, I will obey the lawful orders of those appointed over me and will back them in every way.

CODE OF CONDUCT: Article V

When questioned, should I become a Prisoner of War, I am required to give my name, rank, service number, and date of birth. I will evade answering further questions to the utmost of my ability. I will make no oral or written statements disloyal to my country and its allies or harmful to their cause.

As we arrived in the Hanoi Hilton (Hoa Lo prison), I recognized that foreboding place from photos I had seen. "Tom, we're in the Hilton." Tom was ordered out of the jeep and taken off somewhere ahead. While that was happening, I pulled the leash around my right arm down, and put my left arm into it to make it appear as though my wrists were tied. When it came my turn, the ropes binding my arms were loosened. *Wow, this is turning out OK.* I tried to stretch my shoulders to relieve the cramping, but two guards tightened them to the point that my elbows touched.

One pulled them together while the other tied the knot. I was then taken into an interrogation room for about twelve hours of intermittent questioning, roped painfully throughout the night and morning.

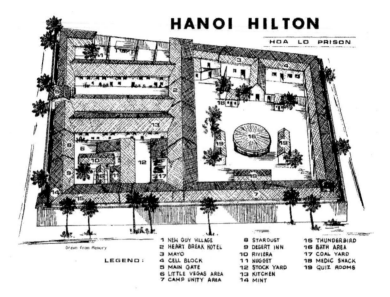

HANOI HILTON

HOA LO PRISON

Drawn from Memory

LEGEND:

1 NEW GUY VILLAGE	8 STARDUST
2 HEART BREAK HOTEL	9 DESERT INN
3 MAYO	10 RIVIERA
4 CELL BLOCK	11 NUGGET
5 MAIN GATE	12 STOCK YARD
6 LITTLE VEGAS AREA	13 KITCHEN
7 CAMP UNITY AREA	14 MINT

15 THUNDERBIRD
16 BATH AREA
17 COAL YARD
18 MEDIC SHACK
19 QUIZ ROOMS

During resistance training at Fairchild AFB, Washington in 1971 I had been taught to have a simple cover story to take pressure off during interrogations. The Vietnamese did not honor the Geneva Conventions on treatment of POWs because the U.S. had never declared war against them. Hard-line adherence to the Code of Conduct was bringing severe punishment to POWs in their custody. We were to remember the acronym KISS – keep it simple, stupid – make up a cover with few details and do not stray from it. If broken, return to it as soon as possible. I had never thought about creating my own cover story because we never flew into threat areas. Now I had to do it on the fly.

After I identified myself by name, rank, service number and date of birth, I was pressed for the home base of our airplane, the organization at Andersen (the names of the Commander, Deputy, Operations Officer), the number of planes stationed there, the type and model of aircraft, numbers of sorties that could be flown in a day, names of other crew members, ingress/egress routes, targets, and a myriad of technical questions about the airplane. My standard response was "I'm a celestial navigator. I guide planes over water using the sun and stars. When we arrive over land the radar navigator takes over. I know nothing about anything else." I gave them fictitious names from Joseph Heller's *Catch-22* – Captain Major, Major Yossarian, etc. When they challenged me (apparently they had heard those names before), I replied that I didn't know – I just flew.

I did admit that Don was dead and Tom was on the same crew with me – rather obvious to them. I hoped they would release Don's name as killed in action so his family wouldn't be tortured by uncertainty. But they did not do that for several years.

The surly interrogator of the pair who questioned me had a scar or burn mark on his left jaw about four inches long, earning him the name of "Al Capone" or "Little Al." He threatened over and over to take me "where the B-52s are bombing if you don't tell us what we want to know." I thought, *I wonder which one of these guys is going to do **that**?* I kept to my simple story and told them they would have to find a radar navigator to answer questions about the bombing system. I totally avoided the use of "bombardier." I figured they might be a little sensitive about that word. Little Al said that B-52s had killed his parents; but when he questioned fighter pilots, he told them that fighters had done it.

They were anxious to know about nuclear weapons and whether we had any at the base of operations. *How can I keep that anxiety at a high level?* "I don't know. I'm just a celestial navigator. I don't handle weapons."

Throughout the night I was forced to remain standing barefoot on the cold concrete floor (the temperature was near freezing).

I hadn't emptied my bladder since the end of the refueling. That was just becoming a problem.

"Did you have any Quail on your plane?"

Good Lord, how do they know about those things? The Quail was a decoy missile carried in the bomb bay. It could be launched outside of enemy radar coverage and programmed to fly a profile similar to the real airplane. On enemy radar, it appeared as large as a B-52, giving enemy gunners additional targets to worry about.

"No. The gunner had roast beef and the copilot had fried chicken; but I don't think anyone had quail."

"NO, NO, NO! In the bomb bay, in the bomb bay!"

"Oh, no! The bomb bay is not heated or pressurized. They would die back there." The butt of a rifle struck me violently on the side of my head. Being blindfolded, I had no idea there were armed guards behind me, did not know it was coming, and was knocked off my feet. Being roped, I couldn't catch my fall and hit solidly next to the wall.

They pulled me back to my feet, placing me back in front of the interrogator's table. Menacingly he said, "Not *bird* quail, *MISSILE* Quail!"

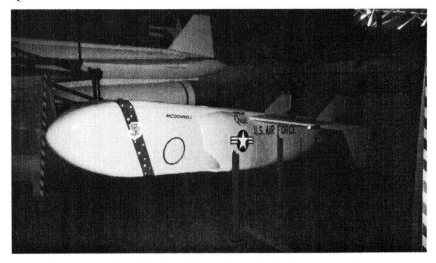

The GAM-72 Quail decoy missile

"I'm just a celestial navigator, I don't know anything about missiles."

"We know you know. You're a young man, plenty smart. If you don't tell us what we want to know, we'll take you where the B-52s are bombing."

Why don't you take me where they're supposed to bomb? I thought, but since they seemed to lack a sense of humor, I kept it to myself. The odd thing was that they never asked how long the bombing might last.

Again they left the room, closing the door behind them. I waited a few minutes, listening for any sound of a guard in the room, before carefully looking around through the opening at the bottom of the blindfold to make sure they were all gone. My legs were swelling and I needed to walk around. A guard was watching through a crack in the door, and came and put me back in place. After a while, I tried again. When I had fallen, I noticed a gallon bucket with a lid next to the wall. Could that be a "honey bucket"? I hoped so, because the bladder was finally becoming a problem. I walked over to it, turned around and removed the lid. Yuck! The fumes made it clear that it was indeed what I thought. Now, how do I do this? By contorting, I was able to reach in front of me enough to free myself from my jockey shorts and to empty my bladder. There was no way I was going to wet myself in front of these people, and I had no idea when I would get more clothes to wear. It was best to keep them as clean and dry as possible. I replaced the lid and pushed myself back into my shorts. Now I could focus and face some more interrogation.

When left alone, I would sometimes lean against the wall, or sit on a low stool and put my head down on the interrogator's table and raise my arms in order to get some circulation going, and possibly to catch a short nap before I heard the door being opened again. During and between quizzes, I was constantly in prayer, seeking God's guidance and direction as I sought to maintain my integrity.

It seemed that they would interrogate me for about forty-five minutes at a stretch and then be gone for about the same length of time.

The next session proved to be very startling. Below my blindfold, I could see laid out on the interrogation desk what appeared to be a B-52 Dash-1, complete with photographs of all aircraft equipment. They could have found it on the ground near our crashed airplane, except for the fact that language of the text was Vietnamese! "Did you have ASQ-38 (B-52G) or ASQ-48 (B-52D) bombing system?"

"I'm a celestial navigator. I know nothing about bombing."

"What is the operational frequency of your bombing system?"

"I told you, I don't know. Find a radar navigator, he can tell you." I felt like a trap was about to be sprung and concentrated on remaining calm and impassive.

"We know you know. You're a young man, plenty smart. If you don't tell us what we want to know, we'll take you where the B-52s are bombing."

Man, I'm getting tired of hearing that. "It looks to me like you have a book on the airplane right in front of you; why don't you just read it?"

"Well, there may be mistakes. We need you to correct them."

Bull. That'll never happen. "I don't have a need to know those things; so I haven't been taught about them. All I know is over water celestial navigation."

During this session, I deliberately collapsed to the floor hoping they'd think I passed out from exhaustion. The guards jerked on the rope around my neck to get me up again. After a couple of such collapses, I decided not to respond to see if they would give up and let me be. After a few minutes, they twisted the rope until I choked and had to respond to get some relief.

Sometime after dawn, and after a few more rounds of fruitless and half-hearted questions, the lead interrogator asked me if I wanted to write a letter home. "That is my Geneva Convention right," I responded. That was obviously a phrase he didn't want to hear.

"You have no rights. You are an air pirate." He stormed out of the room. *Oh, no, I may have overplayed my hand that time. Or are they just playing "good-cop, bad-cop"?*

Shortly, he returned with a piece of paper, a pen and an inkwell. The ropes were taken off my arms and I was directed to sit on a low stool in front of the table. He sat opposite me in a higher chair and said, "Now I tell you what to write."

"OK," I said as I pushed the paper and pen in his direction. "You tell me first, and if I like what you say, I'll write it."

"Write your name. Say you were flying a B-52 over Hanoi and were shot down on this date. Then say you would like to send a Christmas message to your wife. You have to write it to read over the radio."

"No way, man. I'm not going to read it over the radio, first of all." He insisted that I put down my wife's name and home address. "I'll write a letter home, but I'm not going to read it over the radio and I'm not going to put my wife's home address in there."

"Why?" he asked.

"I don't want anybody to bother my wife and I'm not going to tell you where she lives. I'm not going to write that down and put it over the airways because some people might call up and bother her."

That really set him off. "YOU DON'T WANT TO WRITE A LETTER HOME!"

"Yes, I *do* want to write a letter home, but I want to write it using my own words."

Shouting that my family would never hear from me, that I would be killed because of my uncooperative attitude, and that he was going to rope me again, he stormed out of the room, slamming the door behind him. I finally wept. Was this threat serious?

Would the guards be back to really torture and kill me? Over a *letter?* What is happening here? I felt embarrassment and shame at allowing the enemy to see me weep. And I wept for my wife. I should be home in her arms.

The guards returned immediately and roped me for another hour. When they returned the next time, it was to deliver the "clown suit" – the magenta and gray pajamas of the POW, along with "Ho Chi Minh sandals" (made from tire tread for the sole, with strips of inner tube to form an X over the front of the foot to hold them in place). I was told to put them on. *Now what?* A little later, Tom and I were again badly blindfolded, taken from our interrogation rooms, securely handcuffed and put back into the jeep.

We were driven through the streets of Hanoi (the city reminded me of the New Orleans French Quarter) to what appeared to be a hotel. There was a swimming pool, and the rooms had lace curtains in the windows. Tom and I were placed in separate rooms under guard. During the next twenty minutes I heard more trucks arriving, and was then taken back to a jeep for a short drive through a courtyard, and then led into a large room crammed with people with still and moving cameras and instructed to walk to a bank of microphones.

Capt. Certain

Capt. Simpson

Inside myself I was elated. The international press corps was busy snapping photos and taking videos. I walked to the microphones, looked forward, left, and right, but said nothing. In the crowd I spotted an American folk singer, Joan Baez. Questions were being shouted, but I ignored them. Somebody's photograph of me would be on the wire services soon. After that, I was home free. I had no intention of compromising my integrity and sense of duty by speaking to these people. More threats would mean nothing, because the North Vietnamese would never allow an identified POW to be killed or lost.

I looked awful in the photo. After all, I had been up for about thirty hours, and had been traumatized and interrogated for about eighteen hours and had stuffed every emotion I felt as far down into the recesses of my being as possible, including my excitement over being photographed. When I was ushered out of that room, I was going home! I just didn't know when. (The following day, the picture was on the front page of *The Washington Post.* The video was on network news in the States a few days later.) As I was led away I saw four more Americans in the distance in prison garb. But I did not see Tom.

In the War

On his return to Takhli Airbase in Thailand that night, my brother Neal went immediately to Intelligence to get whatever news awaited him about the BUFF he had seen shot down. They had no information for him and he was sent packing.

Bill Buckley had a very pensive flight back to Andersen, knowing our crew had gone down and that he would have been with us except for a chance meeting with Col. Dugard the day before. With the loss of friends, the war became very personal and real, but he didn't know the status of our crew.

Due to an equipment malfunction, his crew had not been able to release their weapons, so they flew out of Hanoi still carrying an extra 22,000 pounds that had not been included in the fuel calculations. Even so, they would not need a refueling to return to Guam. They did attempt to drop the bombs over open ocean east of South Vietnam, getting several to release. Prior to landing, as they descended below 10,000 feet, the navigator crawled back along the "cat walk" and visually checked the bomb bay. Some of the bombs had in fact released, but most of them were still there, some hanging by only one shackle. The crew was extremely concerned that during landing something might shake loose. Fortunately, the landing was uneventful. EOD (explosive ordnance disposal) met them at the end of the runway and checked the bomb bay prior to returning to parking.

By then the other BUFFs had recovered into Andersen. After Bill's crew debriefed, he returned to an empty room with five empty beds. He went next door and knocked on the door of Bobby Thomas' aircraft commander, Capt. Steve Smith. Steve opened the door and was absolutely furious to be awakened during his crew rest. Bill very calmly looked at him and said "Bobby and the crew were shot down." He very quietly closed the door and didn't say a word. The war had just become very personal and very real again.

Bill returned to the room and wanted a drink so bad, but when he opened the refrigerator, all he saw was beer that belonged to some of the other crew members. He couldn't bring himself to drink one of our beers, so he showered and had started to lie down when he got a call to report to Intelligence. When he arrived, they told him that a message had been intercepted with several names of captured flyers. The three names were spelled wrong, but were the names of three of the crew: Major Richard Johnson, Captain Richard Simpson, Captain Robert Certain. He gave thanks to God they were alive, but what about the rest of the crew?

Again he returned to the room hoping to get some sleep, when the phone rang. It was Erlene Thomas, Bobby Thomas's wife, calling from Blytheville, Arkansas. He didn't know Erlene, but she asked a lot of questions. She had been told by another wife at Blytheville AFB, who had heard from another wife on Guam that Bobby had been shot down. What was going on? What did he know? What about the rest of the crew? Bill asked her if the Wing Commander had contacted her? She said that no Air Force officials had talked to her. Bill couldn't tell her much of anything, because the intercepted message was classified, and he didn't want to discuss the missions for fear of compromise. He hung up knowing that he hadn't given her what she wanted. He was infuriated that Bobby's wife found out the news from another wife before she was notified through official channels.

Lt. Buckley stormed out of the room and headed directly to the Wing Commander's office. He was not there, so he walked into the Deputy Commander for Operation's (DO) office screaming about the phone call from Erlene. How could this happen? Does the OWC (Officers' Wives Club) have a better communication and notification system than the Air Force? What were they going to do about this? Bill was tired, confused, angry, frustrated and screaming at a Colonel! He figured that he would either be court marshaled for insubordination or be kept on Guam flying more combat missions. At this point, it really didn't matter to him. The Colonel and his staff finally calmed him, and placed a call to the Wing Commander at Blytheville.

The commander apologized, but said they were trying to insure the accuracy of the information before making notifications. Because Bobby was not flying with his regular crew, they wanted to insure exactly who and what was involved. Bill was assured that everything would be taken care of. Nothing was ever mentioned about his tirade. Everybody was obviously under tremendous pressure. None of them had ever gone through this type operation, so no one had any experience handling the events that were unfolding. Once more, he returned to the room and got some much needed rest.

Chapter 5

At about the same time, Capt. Neal Certain reported for the day's mission briefing at his base in Takhli, Thailand. As he arrived, the squadron commander called him aside. "I have some good news for you. Your brother is a POW." When Neal drew back his fist to punch the guy out, the commander looked surprised and asked what was wrong.

He responded, "He just got shot down last night, you jerk! That was a heck of a way to notify me."

"Oh, no! I'm sorry. I thought he was an old MIA who had just been confirmed." The commander offered to send him stateside immediately; but he insisted on remaining in the theater until POWs were released.

In the World

BLYTHEVILLE, AR (11:00 A.M. CST 19 Dec., 12:00 A.M. 20 Dec. Hanoi Time): Robbie was a Kindergarten teacher, but school had recessed for the Christmas holidays the previous Friday. She was busily cleaning and decorating our home for my return and for our first Christmas together. At 11 o'clock she took a break and drove over to her parents' home for lunch. In a few minutes her father, Robert, arrived from work for his standard lunchtime. The base commander had called Wade Furniture Company to locate Robbie, and asked Wally Willoughby to call the house to request that Mr. Wade remain at home. That seemed a little odd and a bit ominous. Robbie began pacing the floor, suddenly losing her appetite for fried chicken.

Back in July, a B-52 out of Guam had crashed into the Pacific the day after we had arrived. Elise Polek (Mel's wife) had told Robbie not to worry about stories of BUFF crashes until a blue staff car with a white top drove up out front. On this day, that advice struggled to the surface of Robbie's memory as she worried about the meaning of this event. When the staff car drove up, she saw a commander

(Col. Earnhart), a chaplain (Maj. Jones), and a flight surgeon (Capt. Smead) get out and walk toward the door. Behind them was another carload of people, including Mrs. Earnhart.

The Wade family knew instantly that something was very wrong. The mood shifted from curiosity to terror and despair as suddenly as a light comes on when the switch is thrown. Col. Earnhart read the letter, which had been typed (without error or correction in the day before the invention of word processors) on plain paper and in all capitals. The members of the notification team were all well known to the family. Dr. Smead gave Robbie a sedative to calm her hysteria and they sat and talked with her parents. Within the hour, Col. Earnhart received a phone call from the base, informing him that I had been confirmed captured and that my status had been upgraded from MIA to POW.

```
MRS ROBERT G. CERTAIN
804 NORTH 1st STREET
BLYTHEVILLE, ARKANSAS 72315

IT IS WITH DEEP PERSONAL CONCERN THAT I OFFICIALLY
INFORM YOU THAT YOUR HUSBAND, CAPTAIN ROBERT G.
CERTAIN, IS MISSING IN ACTION IN NORTH VIETNAM. ON
18 DECEMBER 1972 HE WAS A CREW MEMBER ON A B-52
AIRCRAFT ON AN OPERATIONAL MISSION OVER NORTH
VIETNAM. THE AIRCRAFT WAS OBSERVED TO CRASH AFTER
APPARENTLY BEING HIT BY HOSTILE FIRE. OTHER DETAILS
CONCERNING THE INCIDENT ARE UNKNOWN AT THIS TIME
HOWEVER, NEW INFORMATION RECEIVED WILL BE FURNISHED
YOU IMMEDIATELY. PENDING FURTHER INFORMATION
HE WILL BE LISTED OFFICIALLY AS MISSING IN ACTION. IF
YOU HAVE QUESTIONS YOU MAY CALL MY PERSONAL
REPRESENTATIVE TOLL FREE BY DIALING 1-800-531-5501.
PLEASE ACCEPT MY SINCERE SYMPATHY DURING THIS
PERIOD OF ANXIETY.


MAJOR GENERAL K. L. TALLMAN
COMMANDER AIR FORCE MILITARY PERSONNEL CENTER
```

Chaplain Jones remained behind to comfort Robbie when she arose from her sedated nap. He stumbled over his attempts to make sense of all this with comments about "God's will," but those words were hard to hear. Robbie assured him that I would be OK, because I wanted to be an Episcopal priest. That announcement was the first her parents had heard of it, adding to their sense of confusion and tragedy.

WASHINGTON, DC (2:00 P.M. EST): A second notification team arrived in my father's office at Southern Railway to notify him that "your son is missing in action." When he interrupted them to ask "Which one?" they were startled and taken aback. The rules were that only one son could be in the war zone at a time. However, since both Neal and I were on temporary duty orders and based outside of South Vietnam, we didn't "count" in the war zone rules. At this hour Neal was flying a refueling mission over the Gulf of Tonkin and had not been able to call home since he heard the news at the briefing. Within a couple of hours, Dad had called the rest of the Certain family with the news, and had called Robbie and the Wades to share in their mutual grief.

ATLANTA, GA: Other family members heard my name being read over the radio (mispronounced as "Robert Rowlin Sirson" but with my social security number correct). My oldest brother's wife, Genie, thought the name sounded a lot like Certain, so called Alan to ask if he had heard anything. He hadn't, so he called our Father in Washington, just 30 minutes after he had been notified.

THE CAPITAL TIMES

HEAVIEST BOMBING IS COSTLIEST EVER TO U.S.

2 B52s, Fighter Downed; 8 More Fliers Are M...

The Washington Post

FRIDAY, DECEMBER 22, 1972

...ilies Turn
Nixon

Flier Captured on Eve of Visit Home

MADISON, WI: *The Capitol Times* reported the loss of two B-52s under the front-page headline "HEAVIEST BOMBING IS COSTLIEST EVER TO U.S." The next day, the paper ran another front-page article along with photos of the six of us who had been before the Hanoi press conference on the nineteenth. Madison was home to my brother, Phillip, and his family.

Phillip and his family were preparing to drive to Washington for a family Christmas. The highlight was to be the reunion with me, and the opportunity to meet Robbie. They had been unable to attend our wedding, so this was the first chance they had to meet Robbie.

The first news they received was from Dad, who, by the time he called, already knew that I was "safe" in captivity. Thus, they were spared some of the shock and grief of the MIA designation that his parents and Robbie first felt on learning of the tragedy. They packed their car and set off on the long drive to Washington.

I-95 BETWEEN SOUTH CAROLINA AND WASHINGTON DC: My sister Glennell and her family were driving up Interstate 95 from South Carolina to be home in Maryland for Christmas. They heard on the radio that the first B-52 of the war had been shot down and that Robert Sirson from Silver Spring, Maryland was among the captured. They listened to the news several times, but because they didn't want it to be me, decided it was someone else.

They went straight to Mom and Dad's place when they arrived in Silver Spring where they learned that the notification team had come earlier in the day to confirm the news to Dad. The next days were awful.

Chapter 6

The Hanoi Hilton

CODE OF CONDUCT: Article VI
I will never forget that I am an American, fighting for freedom, responsible for my actions, and dedicated to the principles which made my Country free. I will trust in my God and in the United States of America

---

I was driven back to the Hilton alone, and placed in a large cell, big enough for three or four men, in the Heartbreak Hotel courtyard near the interrogation rooms. These appeared to be large quarters that may have been offices at one time. Built by the French, they had tall double doors, and a pit in the floor that may have been for a fire or hot rocks for heating. During our incarceration the pits were never used. A bowl of cabbage soup, a half loaf of French bread, and a tin cup of weak tea were brought in and placed in front of me. I hadn't eaten since we came off the tanker near the Philippines, so this meager meal tasted great.

In the cell, there was a bed board lying on the floor. It was constructed from four 1x6 planks nailed to two 2x4s. The planks were of uneven thickness, which would add to my discomfort when sleeping. A rice straw mat (similar to ones Americans used as beach mats) was the "mattress." There were two cotton blankets, a towel and a mosquito net, a set of the magenta and gray striped shorts and short-sleeved shirt, and another complete set of black pajamas.

There was also an aluminum cup, a bowl, and a metal oriental spoon. A tube of toothpaste, a toothbrush and a bar of lye soap were also present. The toothpaste tube was made from lead, with a lead seal over the top that had to be broken with a nail pulled from the wall. My earlier elation was replaced by gloom at seeing what appeared to be provisions for a long incarceration and a life reduced to the bare essentials. I was interrogated two or three more times before I was finally left to sleep. It came quickly, but didn't last long.

Suddenly, the doors were flung open, the light was turned on, and four guards tossed in another bed board, gear, and a tall black man in prison garb. I was immediately on guard and wide awake, my heart racing and adrenalin pumping. *Oh, great! More interrogation. Who is this guy? A Vietnamese ally? A turncoat? Do they really think I'll tell him anything?* I helped him put his stuff together, but became hyper-alert as he introduced himself as Major Alex Alexander, a B-52 crewmember. *Bull! Tom and I are the only unlucky crew dogs to be shot down and captured.* "Did you fly a D or a G?"

"A 'D'."

"I was in a 'G'."

"I didn't know anyone else had been shot down."

"Well, I was."

"Do you know Cusik?"

"I know Steve."

"Where are you based?"

Great. I haven't told the interrogator that yet. Is that important information to withhold? After all, a Russian spy trawler has been stationed north of Guam for months. "Blytheville."

Maj. Fernando (Alex) Alexander

"I mean here. Andersen or U-Tapao?"

"Andersen."

"I was at UT."

"I was there last year."

"Me, too, but I never saw you there."

"I never saw you."

"I play poker in the back room of the Officers' Club every night."

"I just went there for meals."

After a pause, Alex continued, "Do you know where Gilligan's Island is?" (Gilligan's Island was our name for a "roach coach," a snack wagon permanently parked outside the briefing room on Guam. It had a patio with palm trees and picnic benches. Crews often got a hot dog before heading out to the planes.)

"Yep."

"Did you ever go there?"

"No. I don't like chili dogs."

With that exchange, each of us decided the other was an authentic American officer. Alex was the Radar on Rose One, a D model in Wave Three (tail number 56-0608) from U-Tapao and had been shot down at 0245 hours on 19 December. (The same cell color had been used in Wave 1, but that one was from Guam.) Three other crewmembers from his crew were also in custody and had been taken before cameras that day, too. They were the four men I had spotted when I left the press conference.

As we relaxed and talked about our experience of interrogation, Alex told me that whenever he was asked technical questions about equipment, he would reply "I've been operating this stuff for nearly twenty years. I don't remember the technical details. If you want to know that, find a young navigator right out of school." We had been using the same diversion!

73

Chapter 6

The interrogators had been shuttling between our rooms. They would leave me, go to him, and say, "You're an old man, you plenty wise. If you don't tell us what we want to know, we'll take you where the B-52s are bombing." Because his name was Fernando Alexander, the interrogator had asked him, "Are you Mexican?"

"No."

"Are you, uh, are you, uh …?"

"You mean, am I black?"

"Uh, yes."

"Yes I am." It was good to have a roommate and a little humor amid the depressive conditions.

We settled into a restless night, with the awful bed boards, cold temperatures, and uncertain futures. All night long, we could hear tracked vehicles, probably tanks, circling the streets around the prison. The second night of raids began shortly, striking the same targets at the same times as the night before. The wail of air raid sirens filled the air and electrical power to the city was cut off. The rumbling of falling bombs and their explosions as they hit the ground were both nerve-wracking and comforting. We could hear the sounds of AAA rounds and SAM launches reaching up to find other B-52s. That night, they missed. As long as BUFFs were raining terror and destruction on the capital, the sooner their government would agree to sign a treaty and release the prisoners.

The next day we began to get a glimpse of "normal" prison routine. We were rousted out of bed shortly after dawn, and fed breakfast. That consisted of a half loaf of French bread and a cup of sweet reconstituted milk. Lunch and dinner were the same as before – a bowl of cabbage soup, with maybe a piece or two of fatback (including bristles), a half loaf of French bread, and a cup of weak tea. Every day or so we were allowed to empty our honey buckets. For the next few days, Alex and I were subjected to no further interrogations.

On 21 December in mid-afternoon, while Alex and I were lying on our beds, we heard the sound of a US F-111 fighter aircraft patrolling the city. We could hear AAA bursts, but we didn't hear any retaliation from the 111. We thought it might be a reconnaissance bird. However, he dropped a bomb on a Triple-A position about a block away from the Hilton; so he was armed. The over- and under-pressure from the explosion was such that it tore the door off the cell. First the doors were blown into the room (they were hinged to open out); then they slammed shut and, because of the termite and rot damage to the doorframe, one of them fell off as they were sucked outward. Both of us sat straight up in terror. Dust and debris were flying everywhere. Immediately, an armed guard burst in with his AK-47 pointing directly at us, and shouting orders in Vietnamese. Raising our hands, we sat frozen, hoping he would calm down.

(When a bomb explodes, it forces air outward with enormous force, causing it to form a shock wave of high pressure [over-pressure], which in turn leaves a center point of low pressure at the point of the explosion. As the outward energy dissipates, the shock wave reverses itself as it rushes back with nearly equal force [under-pressure] to the area of low pressure.)

Once the camp authorities realized we hadn't attempted an escape (not really possible for a 5'9" redheaded white boy and a 6'2" African American in the middle of an Asian capital), they calmed down a bit. However, the missing door did render our cell unusable.

Alex and I were moved into another cell across the courtyard with Tom Simpson and three of Alex's crewmembers, Hal Wilson (pilot), Charlie Brown (copilot) and Hank Barrows (electronic warfare officer).

As we walked over, the interrogator appeared clearly rattled. "They bomb very near here," he said.

With a wry smile, I replied, "You're right, they sure did."

When he put us in the room with the others, he said, "We let you live together."

When he left, we greeted each other warmly and had a good laugh about the explosion. The guys had pulled themselves up to look out a transom window to spot the aircraft. When they saw the bomb fall free of the F-111, they jumped down just in time as the wooden bars in the transom and a rear door were blown into the room. They had quickly replaced them before their guard came into the cell.

  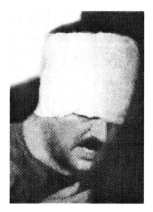

Capt. Hal Wilson   Capt. Charlie Brown   Capt. Hank Barrows

Within an hour, the guards returned and took all six of us to the Heartbreak Hotel section of the Hilton, in order to give the new arrivals a place to be interrogated. Brown and Barrows were placed in room 2, Wilson and Simpson shared room 3, and Alex and I were tossed into room 4. The Heartbreak Hotel of the Hoa Lo was a particularly nasty and unsanitary part of the prison. In that place, where the floors were covered with at least an inch of rat dung, we had rats crawling over us every night as we tried to sleep.

The room was 7'x7' with 2½ foot wide concrete bunks on either side and with a 2' wide aisle to the door. There was a drain hole in the back (easier for the rats to come in). Each bed was equipped with leg stocks, which could be closed over our ankles, then a flat iron bar pushed in from the corridor to secure them in place. Fortunately they didn't use the stocks, but their presence reduced the effective length of the bunk to about 5½ feet. That wasn't bad for me, but it was difficult on the taller Alex.

The straw mats were wider than the bunks by about six inches, further adding to our sense of discomfort, as they tended to slide off. There was a bare light bulb hanging from the ceiling, which could not be turned off from inside the cell. The first night, we tried to save some of our dinner bread in case they didn't feed us the next day. I placed it between the wall and the leg stocks. The only effect was to attract a number of large rats that stood on my blanket-covered feet while feeding on the bread. I was disgusted and terrified. I had no idea what kind of infection would result if I provoked a rat to bite me. So I forced myself to lie very still.

The Heartbreak Hotel wing of the Hanoi Hilton

Chapter 6

That night, B-52 bombing of Hanoi was in fairly close proximity to the prison, and as we discovered over the next few days, six BUFFs had been shot down. Lt. Col. Jim Nagahiro commanded one, Olive One. He and his navigator, Capt. Lynn Beens, were taken prisoner; the ABC, Lt. Col. Keith Heggen from Blytheville, was taken into custody, but later died of his wounds. The same night Tan Three, another Blytheville crew, commanded by Capt. Randall Craddock, had been hit. The gunner, SSgt. Jim Lollar, escaped before the plane exploded, but the others perished. The losses had been awful, but the sounds of fury continued to give me encouragement that President Nixon was not going to back down. Of course, it was also scary, giving me widely divergent emotions at the same time: terror, elation, bravado, hope, and despair. The following morning, we could see new prisoners, some on stretchers, being brought into the camp and distributed around the courtyard cells.

Each day for the next week I was taken out for daily interrogations. Again they wanted to know about Quail missiles, "Why did you not carry decoys?"

"I don't know."

"What is the range of your radar?"

"I'd say about thirty to forty miles."

"What's an APN-69 for?"

"What's an APN-69?"

"Did you have ASQ-38 or ASQ-48 radar?"

Oh, great, I haven't told them whether I flew Ds or Gs yet. "I'm just a celestial navigator." I was caught giving all kinds of wrong information during the week, and hoped the interrogator would assume that I really was as ignorant as I claimed.

The next morning the camp authorities brought in some kind of anti-war manifesto and demanded that Alex and I sign it. We were also given a blue book with about a hundred biographical questions, including both personal and military history, wife's name and address, etc. We both refused when we saw what they were. The punishment was a tongue-lashing, but nothing more.

Periodically a guard named Liet, from the South Vietnam town of Quangtri, would come to the cell for an English lesson. He would ask us the English name of something and would write it down in Vietnamese, and we would write the English beside it. One word he went over and over was "teapot," which quickly became his nickname.

The night of the 23 December we had an undisturbed sleep. That was not a good sign. Had the bombing stopped already? Were they concentrating on Haiphong for the night? Has Nixon declared a cease-fire like Johnson had, only to see the war prolonged and the North able to replenish its supplies? Bombing close by and no bombing at all raised our anxiety about the future and our eventual fates.

But a quiet night did allow for undisturbed sleep and dreams of home. My mind drifted back to May 21, 1972, the day I was notified that the wing would deploy to Guam, and the week that followed.

That week, our crew was standing alert at Blytheville. We had taken charge of our nuclear bomb laden Stratofortress at the alert facility on May 18, and would be relieved on May 25. But events began a major shift. Col. Bruce Brown, our Wing Commander, arrived at the Alert Facility on Sunday morning for the daily briefing on scheduled routes should WWIII break out. After the briefing, he called me aside.

"Lieutenant, aren't you planning to marry Robert Wade's daughter in June?"

"Yessir. The twenty-third."

"Well, you're not going to be here. The wing leaves for Guam on Saturday."

When Robbie arrived for the afternoon visitation hour, we sat in her car in the parking lot, where I told her about our imminent departure. She was terribly upset, sobbing that her mother had just mailed fifty invitations. We hugged and wept for some time before I suggested that we get married as soon as I could get off alert, which would be Thursday at the latest. We decided upon Thursday, May 25. When we parted an hour or so later, we began to notify our families.

My parents and my oldest brother and his family arrived on Wednesday, just as I was coming off alert and the planes were being disarmed and prepared for the flight to Guam. We had already purchased the rings and wedding gown, and the pastor of the First Baptist Church was able to set the big event for 2:00 Thursday. That morning at the departure briefing, I learned that my crew, along with one other, would not be leaving with the rest of the wing. With everyone gathered, Robbie and I decided to proceed with the wedding.

A good number of our local guests were able to attend, along with my pilot and copilot, as well as my friend Bobby Marshall, a KC-135 navigator who had been my flying partner in navigation training. Bobby served as best man. As we waited at the chancel rail, Robbie and her dad appeared at the back of the church and began the long walk to join us. I was light-headed and filled with excitement as I thanked God that this day was happening.

Following the ceremony and a brief reception in the Wade home, my new wife and I drove to Memphis for a weekend honeymoon before I was to report back to duty on Monday. That night we celebrated our new marriage; but the next day, I came down with food poisoning and spent the remaining hours close to the toilet.

As I wakened in the early morning quiet of Christmas eve, I thanked God for our safety thus far, for the gift of Robbie as my wife, for her comfort and our swift release.

That day Alex and I were taken to a little washroom down the hall where we were able to empty and scrub our honey bucket, bathe, and wash one set of our clothes. Algae was growing in the sink and other perpetually damp surfaces, the water was cold, the lye soap didn't lather, but it was a bath. We also heard Americans speaking to us on the other side of the wall. The old prisoners were trying to tell us to keep the faith and continue to resist. There had been no torture since Ho Chi Minh died in the fall of 1969.

Alex and I also washed the dishes for twelve POWs in that same nasty room. As a result, we frequently were able to speak to them quietly. It was the only direct contact we would have with them until release. We called the older prisoners FOGs (Freaking Old Guys) and ourselves FNGs (Freaking New Guys).

In the next cell, Tom Simpson was beginning to get delirious from a growing infection in a puncture wound in his left arm. On ejection, a pen in the arm pocket on his flight suit had caught on the hatch and been jammed into his triceps. His arm was now infected and swollen, and he was running a high fever. Hal Wilson, Alex and I asked the guard to send for a medic to take care of him. But nothing happened. Again that night, we heard no bombing, only a distant rumbling that could be in the area of Haiphong, and Tom's fevered moaning in the next cell.

On Christmas Day, we had a couple of nice surprises. First, the medic came around to check on us for the first time since our arrival. They gave Tom a shot of penicillin. When they came to our cell we first said we had no needs. But then Alex said, "Do you have anything for piles?" The interpreter looked puzzled. Alex was standing in the aisle; I was sitting on my bunk facing the door. "You know, piles, hemorrhoids," he said, and pointed to his backside.

Chapter 6

The interpreter still did not understand, and said, "Show him."

Alex turned toward me, and we made eye contact, finding a moment of amusement at what was coming next. He faced the wall, dropped his pants, and bent over, spreading his cheeks. The medic and his companions looked shocked and disgusted. It was all I could do to keep from laughing. The medic reached out his index finger, spread Alex's cheeks a bit farther, took a turned-up-nose look, and left. The door closed and locked. That was the last we saw of any medical treatment for a long time. As a substitute, Alex found that the fatback in the soup could be used as a salve to help ease the pain. When he ejected, he had landed on the roof of a village house and fell on his buttocks, aggravating his condition.

The second surprise was a "gourmet" meal. Instead of the usual cabbage soup, we were given scrambled eggs, BBQ pork, and some greens, along with a cup of coffee (very sweet and half grounds) and some kind of red liqueur that had the nasty flavor of Mercurochrome, but gave us a nice alcohol buzz. While serving the meal, the officer took the opportunity to say they had arranged for us to attend a Christian Mass, but the B-52 attacks had made it too dangerous. However, while they could control our bodies and dangle imaginary carrots in front of us, they could never withhold Christmas. The bread and the liqueur, even with the lack of a priest, reminded me of the Supper of the Lord that is so central to the celebration of Our Lord's Nativity.

On 26 December, the BUFFs returned to Hanoi with a punishing vengeance. Forty cells of B-52s (120 planes) struck ten targets in fifteen minutes. Twenty-five of the cells had targets in the city of Hanoi, the rest in Haiphong. The bombs, SAMs and AAA caused the building's two-foot thick stone walls to shake, and sent Alex to cover beneath his concrete bunk to avoid the danger of falling ceiling sections. "Alex, what are you doing?"

"I'm afraid the ceiling will fall on me if I stay up there."

"Alex, if the walls or ceiling fall, they will break the bunk and you'll be injured. If you stay up here, you'll probably be killed. I think I prefer death to injury in this place! Besides I'm not sitting in that rat dung." Nothing fell. The old place held together pretty well.

The one thing that changed after that night was the diet – instead of bread, we were served rice for the next week or so. Apparently the bakery had been damaged or destroyed.

The next day, while we were emptying the honey bucket and washing our faces and brushing our teeth, we asked for and were allowed to take a broom back to the cell to sweep the dung and dust out. Conversing through the wall with Tom, we discovered he was much improved.

Again that night, thirteen BUFF cells returned to bomb five targets within a five-mile radius of the Hilton. Fifteen cells went after four targets on December 28; nine cells bombed one target on the 29th; with that, Linebacker II ended.

After ten days in these conditions the six of us in Heartbreak cells 2, 3, and 4 were moved to a larger cell in the interrogation area known as Heartbreak Courtyard and placed with five more prisoners, the other four members of our crews plus Terry Geloneck, another G aircraft commander. This cell had the usual French doors. There was an anteroom where we kept the honey buckets, a larger room that would sleep five, and a back room where Alex and I bunked. During the day, we all huddled in the large room for shared warmth and for camaraderie.

Five of seven POWs had festering wounds (Alex and I were the healthiest). We figured that the wounded guys needed each other's body heat to help them stay as healthy as possible. The temperature was below freezing at night and the rooms were quite drafty. Not only were there cracks in the cell door, there was a glassless window in the back room covered only with wooden bars and wooden shutters. Alex and I made a pad out of our mosquito nets and one of the blankets and hung it over the window to cut the draft somewhat; and we kept the door between the rooms closed at all times with a towel rolled up and wedged into the bottom gap to cut the draft down further in the main room.

New Year's Day was marked by another special meal similar to the one on Christmas. However, in place of the red liqueur, we had a warm Vietnamese beer. I didn't care much for warm beer, but the buzz was a nice relief after the days of terror. That night, we heard no bombing, nor for the next several nights. We became worried that a futile bombing halt was once again being tried to coax the government back to the Paris Peace table.

Tom Simpson was taken out for daily periods of interrogation about the electronic defense systems. They showed pictures of his equipment; but he gave them no information. Instead he drew them into tangents and lies, talking about one-hop sky waves, actually used in LORAN navigation. When asked to draw an Alt-21 SAM jammer, he sketched his FM radio tuner.

Sanitary conditions did not improve. There was no medical care. Baths were only allowed once a week. Toilet buckets were in the anteroom and were emptied daily, except on Sundays. Rats visited nightly, crawling over us in search of dropped food. Meals consisted of bread made with rat-dung-and-insect-contaminated flour, and the usual cabbage soup containing similar contamination and undercooked pork fat and skin. The morning beverage continued to be the sweet reconstituted powdered milk that came from Poland. We had to eat to maintain our strength; but the meals were becoming boring, repugnant and hard to swallow. Nevertheless, I always offered thanks to God for the food and for life.

Vietnamese cigarettes were provided for all prisoners at the rate of two per day; lights were provided at mealtime. Since half of the men in our cell did not smoke, those of us who did had four. In order to keep them lit as long as possible through the day, one or two would be lit at each meal by the guard, and the rest would be lit one at a time from the butt of one that had been smoked down. The cigarettes were very strong and unfiltered. One or two would leave a brown stain on our fingers; there is no telling what they did to our lungs.

Another problem we had was the construction of the cigarettes themselves. The entire leaf, stems, veins and all were cut up into the tobacco, resulting in a number of problems. Sometimes the smoldering ash would simply die or drop off and roll under a bed board, extinguishing before it could be recovered. Sometimes, the fire would follow the line of least resistance around stems and veins, and come out the side of the paper, often where the POW's fingers were. The surprise usually led to the sudden tossing of the cigarette with the result that it would go out in flight or when it hit the wall or floor. Perhaps the most nerve-wracking problem was that the stems held a small amount of moisture. As it heated up, it would cause the cigarette to explode, sending all of us for cover thinking a weapon was being fired.

Terry Geloneck, shot down several days after Charcoal, had dislocated his shoulders when his arms became entangled in his shroud lines on parachute deployment. One day, they took him to the hospital to repair them. While he was sedated, they interrogated him. When he came back to the cell still groggy from the drugs, he reported that they had asked him whether the exhaust from the engines went straight back or angled down. He said he could not imagine why they would want to know that, and answered that he had never even thought about it. Several of us answered Terry, "that's so they will know how to aim heat-seekers." It's a good thing he was too groggy to remember the significance of their question.

In the cell next to us were another seven men with various injuries. Whenever they were allowed into the rear courtyard to wash the dishes for us all, Navy Lt. Commander Al Agnew told us what was happening in that cell.

Chapter 6

One of his cellmates, John Anderson, an F-4 pilot, had broken both arms. The medics had set them in a cast with his arms pinned to his chest. He could do nothing for himself, from bathing, to toileting, to eating and smoking. His cellmates had to do everything for him. During bath sessions, they avoided a large dark spot on his back, assuming it was a terrible bruise from a broken rib sustained in his ejection. After a couple of weeks, they gently washed over the area, and it came off! It was dirt! We all had a good laugh over that. His back seat crew member had one arm broken, which never was properly set, and who was forced to remain behind until the last release, even though the injured were supposed to go out with the longest held.

Our clothing was inadequate to keep us warm. We could not wash our clothing because we could not spare the time needed to dry it. The stench was so bad in our cell that at one point the kitchen boy refused to enter to bring our soup in at lunch. He took one step into the room, gasped, put down the soup bucket, covered his face with his hands, and said, "Open the window! Open the window! You need fresh air." Of course, having been in the cell while the aroma had built up, we hadn't noticed anything. We came outside to get our soup, looked around, made sure anyone watching from the other cell doors around the courtyard could see us, returned to the cell and had a good laugh about his reaction.

A couple of hours later, two guards with weapons stormed in, threw open the door between the rooms, pulled our curtain down, pushed the shutters open, returned to the main room where we were all watching in shock, said "leave it alone" and left, leaving the front doors open. Amazing! We puzzled over how badly we must smell, and stayed near the front door both to observe and to be observed by others.

After the room had plenty of time to air out, the camp commander came in to give us a lecture on personal hygiene, "You must take care of yourselves."

Unafraid at the moment, several of us challenged him. "Your guards haven't let us empty the toilet buckets in four days."

"We haven't had baths or washed our clothes in ten days."

"We have guys with festering wounds, and your medics refuse to treat them."

Following that event, medical care was provided for wounded prisoners, we emptied and scrubbed the toilet buckets, and we were allowed to bathe. During January, the temperature dropped below freezing at night, making a bath somewhat painful. We were led across the courtyard and through a breezeway to a corner of New Guy Village. There we were shown a large vat, like a water trough, about 6'x4'x4'. We had our small towels and our lye soap. There were a number of rubber buckets with wooden bottoms and handles.

The procedure became painfully obvious. We stripped, broke the thin layer of ice off the water, dipped a bucket of water, and poured it on ourselves (or our buddies). The buddy system worked better for me because I couldn't bring myself to pour ice water on my own body. We scrubbed as best we could with the soap, rinsed off the same way, and dried ourselves. We all put on the set of clothing we had been wearing furthest from our bodies and washed the other set.

When we returned to our cell, the stench had abated some more. A medic then appeared with cotton swabs and iodine. He called over the five with infections one at a time; picked opened the wound with his fingernails, squeezed the puss out, then scrubbed it with the iodine. It made me hurt just watching the process, and I felt sick in my abdomen. I was also very grateful that I had escaped that "medical" treatment.

Lukewarm water and razors were brought in. The blade's trade name was Mephisto (i.e. "The Devil"), fit into a Gym-style double-edged blade holder. I hadn't seen one of those since the 1950s. As they brought one blade for two prisoners, one used one edge, the other the opposite. The warm water and lye soap didn't create much lather for lubrication. The blades were not very sharp, either. The technique we discovered rather quickly was to saw the whiskers off, rather than shaving them as we normally did at home. With a twenty-day growth it was no easy task. The blade was sharp enough to hook the whiskers, but not to cut through them; so it would rip the hair out. The sawing method helped, but our skin was left pretty irritated by the experience. Following the shave, a camp barber arrived to give us all haircuts.

2   SECTION 1   THE COMMERCIAL APPEAL, MEMPHIS,

Maj. Dick Johnson escorted into Hanoi Hilton

One of our biggest battles was against boredom. The toilet paper was sheets of very coarse rice paper. We took one sheet, tore it into squares, and made a deck of cards for games, marking the symbols with cigarette ashes. We told stories of our backgrounds, talked about our plans when we were freed, and speculated and worried over the apparent bombing halt. We compared notes about what we knew or suspected about lost BUFFs. The radio broadcaster insisted they had shot down fifty; but given their penchant for super-exaggeration, we figured it was more like twenty-five. Some of the later shoot-downs had witnessed planes explode in mid-air and assumed no one got out alive. Some of the guys captured on the twentieth thought that Charcoal One had exploded before anyone got out, and were surprised that we had survivors. Someone had seen Dick Johnson in another cell, but Bobby Thomas was still unaccounted for, so at least three of us had made it out safely. We could account for survivors from only ten BUFFs.

During this time, Tom Simpson and Hal Wilson were moved to another cell, and were replaced by Jim Condon and Dave Drummond. Jim Gough and Henry Hudson were also put in with us.

On 28 December a group of POWs were given civilian attire, taken to the Bac Mai Hospital (which had been damaged, apparently by stray bombs falling from a crashing BUFF), and filmed looking at the wreckage. Early in the second week in January 1973 all the POWs in the courtyard cells were brought flight suits, both Air Force and Navy styles, and ordered to change into them. They gave us Dien Bien cigarettes (their premium brand), and a warm beer. Now what? We hadn't had direct guidance from the older prisoners, and we worried about the prohibition against accepting favors. Some buses came and took us out of the Hilton to a war museum, where they proceeded to film and photograph us as we walked around looking at F-105 tail sections, B-52 cockpit sections, and other debris from crashed US aircraft. Throughout the tour armed women guarded us, another propaganda stunt. Inside we were shown displays holding the wallets, ID cards, and helmets of some of us. At one point we were brought together for an official photograph, but most of us, including myself, held our hands in the classic "bird" gesture to ruin the picture.

Chapter 6

When we arrived back to the Hilton, we were again filmed, this time removing our flight suits and receiving the very supplies and clothing we had been using for the last month. The funny thing was that as we removed our flight suits, the film caught the fact that we were all wearing the magenta and gray prison underwear. We were treated to another bottle of warm beer, which I promptly vomited up in the courtyard as I returned to my cell. While that had not been intentional, it did serve as an indication of what I thought of the day's activities.

Every few days, the camp commander would gather his staff on a porch near the cell for political instruction. Like GIs anywhere, the first couple of rows sat appearing to pay attention to his droning. The next couple of rows were picking their fingernails or toenails, and those further in the rear read the Hanoi newspaper.

One Sunday, a North Vietnamese guard we called "Lt. Sheisskopf" (a character from Joseph Heller's *Catch-22*) came into the cell. As usual he appeared in the door and waited for everyone to stand before proceeding. Once we were all on our feet, Tom Simpson and I were told to put on long shirts and come with him. Outside we were told to "reenact an air raid."

"Do what?!" we answered.

"Stand over there, and when I tell you, run and jump in this wooden bomb shelter."

This was ridiculous; there had been no bombing in weeks. We sauntered into place, looking around for cameras, but saw none. When the siren blew, Tom and I walked over to the shelter and jumped in. Only then did we finally spot the camera hidden in the shadows. Other prisoners were tapped for propaganda films showing them getting haircuts or sweeping the sidewalks, very much like other prisoners in earlier years.

In the World

WASHINGTON, DC, 22 December: *The Washington Post* carried a front-page article with my photo, "Flier Captured on Eve of Visit Home." In the article, my sister Glennell was quoted as saying the family was "split" in our views of the war. Her husband said, "Part of the family is university-oriented and part is business-military oriented."

The Madison, Wisconsin Certains were the other part of the "anti-war" branch of the family. Like the Vanns, the most radical things they did, however, were to work in the Presidential campaigns of Gene McCarthy and George McGovern. At the same time, they were proud of their brothers, Robert and Neal, for the jobs they were doing. "If somebody has to fight this war, we are glad that people of the intelligence and integrity of our brothers are the ones doing it." Phillip, just three years older than Neal and 4½ years older than Robert, escaped the difficult decision about serving in the war through student and married student deferments.

ATLANTA, GA, 22 December: A reporter for *Time Magazine* called my brother Alan at his home in Atlanta to ask him about the *Post* article. His response was, "We are a middle-class family. We all live on our salaries. We work for a living. The family is all very close. When things of this sort happen, when a crisis period occurs, we rally around each other." Alan took umbrage at the press report that the family was split on the war. "I was not aware we had a split of any kind," he commented. "We are split by distance. But I know of no other split." The article appeared in the January 1, 1973 issue of *Time*.

WASHINGTON, DC: The family was gathered at my parent's home in suburban Maryland for a very somber Christmas celebration, grateful that I was alive, but with awful speculations about my treatment. Mother decided to defer opening a box I had sent her for her present. In it was a porcelain figurine of a soldier hugging his mother, his luggage on the ground by his feet. When she finally opened it on my return, the soldier's head had been broken off in shipment.

Before Christmas break was over, the family planned to gather in Atlanta and to have Robbie come in to be with them. While they were at Alan's and Genie's home, one of my fraternity brothers from Emory called to say that I was on the WSB-TV news from a Hanoi news briefing. Alan called WSB and arranged for the family to go the station to see a rebroadcast of the news.

During the months that followed, our parents stopped watching television, because the Washington stations would show my picture with a reminder to remember the POWs. It was a really rough time for the family trying to deal with the unknown and speculating about my treatment.

Chapter 7

The Zoo

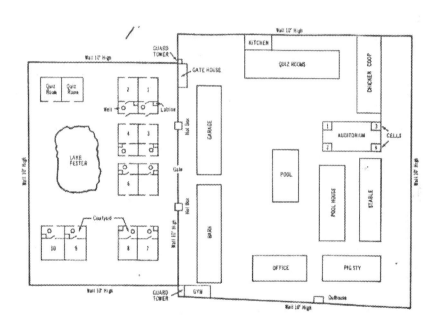

On January 19, 1973, one month after entering the Hilton, we were told to prepare to move. Before we left the Hilton, Hal Wilson and I each were allowed to write a twenty-line letter home, but the letters never made it out of North Vietnam. As we were to discover, the healthiest of the December shoot-downs were moved out of the Hilton and transferred to the Cu Loc ("Zoo") prison.

93

Because of the size of the trucks, we were taken in shifts. One group from New Guy Village was moved after breakfast, and most of the men in my cell were moved after dark. Alex and I were the last two, left alone in the cell. We feared the captors had something special in mind for us. I felt a sick foreboding in my gut as we discussed the various unpleasant possibilities that occurred to us. Fortunately, it was just a matter of room in the truck rather than the sinister plot we had assumed.

Finally we were loaded in a truck with ten more guys from other cells. During the trip, leg shackles and torture cuffs were placed on us, with our hands and arms twisted and circulation restricted. Arriving at the Zoo, we were moved into a cell in the Pool Hall, and quickly determined there were eight guys in two rooms at one end of the building, and four more in a cell at the other end. No association was allowed between cells, but we managed to communicate easily; and we hoped that interrogations were over.

When we first arrived at the Zoo, it was a mess. Ceilings had collapsed and there was shrapnel from exploded bombs all over the ground. We were told that fighter planes had dropped high-drag bombs just outside the walls, causing the damage. A few days before Christmas, the locals had tried to break in, necessitating an evacuation of the prisoners. The Vietnamese said the locals wanted to kill the Americans, but we figured they were trying to get in where it was safe. They knew the Americans would never drop a bomb into a known POW camp. The target outside the wall had been a large tract with communication antennae, AAA and SAM sites; they had been hit to clear the way for the BUFFs. Phantoms had dropped high-drag bombs at extremely low altitude to destroy the target without injuring prisoners or locals. (High-drag bombs were equipped with four large fins which popped out as they fell and acted like speed brakes, making the bomb fall straight down rather than in the usual arc which would have resulted in them exploding under the fighters flying at 200 feet or less.)

CAMP REGULATIONS

American servicemen participating in the war of aggression by U.S. administration in Viet-Nam and caught in the act while perpetrating barbarous crimes against the Vietnamese land and people, should have been duly punished according to their criminal acts; but the Government and people of Viet-Nam, endowed with noble and humanitarian traditions, have given those captured American servicemen the opportunity to benefit a lenient and generous policy by affording them a normal life in the detention camps as practical conditions of Viet-Nam permit it and conforming to the situation in which the war is still on.

Detainees are to observe and carry out the following regulations of the camp:

I- Detainees must strictly obey orders and follow instructions given them by Vietnamese officers and Armymen on duty in the camp.

II- Detainees must be polite towards every Vietnamese in the camp.

III- Inside the detention rooms, as well as outside when allowed, detainees must not make noise or create noise. Quarrel and fighting between detainees are forbidden. In time of rest, total silence is imposed.

IV- Detainees must not bring back to detention rooms any object whatsoever without the camp authorities permit it.

V- In case of sickness or sign of sickness if felt, detainees must immediately inform the camp for the medical officer to check and cure.

VI- Detainees must assure hygiene of the camp, take care of personal items provided by the camp as well as of any other thing for collective use.

VII- In case of air alarm, detainees must keep order and silence, and follow the camp regulations on security.

VIII- In need of something, detainees should address themselves to Vietnamese armymen standing nearby by announcing two words "BAO CAO" (means "report"), and should wait if no English speaking people was available yet.

IX- In the detention rooms, every detainees are equal with each other. Anyone does have the right to free thinking, feeling, praying, etc… and no one is permitted to coerce any other into following his own opinion.

X- Violation of the regulations shall be punished.

THE CAMP AUTHORITIES

Chapter 7

The December group was the first to be moved back in after the evacuation. The first four or five days, we cleaned the cells and filled "shelter holes." Once we had the Pool Hall in order, we were moved to a similar cellblock we called the Stable to clean that area; older prisoners from the Hilton were brought in behind us.

Posted on the walls in all of the rooms were the camp regulations. We accepted those regulations as challenges to defy. We "misunderstood" every order given, gave defiant and rude nicknames to each of the guards, sang loudly, talked incessantly, sneaked things into our cells and insisted on observing our own strict military discipline and authority by rank. The camp authorities wouldn't respond to us if we used our rank, but they recognized it anyway. They knew who were the senior ranking officers (SROs) in each cell and went through them to disseminate information and instructions.

We did follow their rules about hygiene and illness, since it was important to us; but we suspected that BAO CAO really meant something that probably indicated our subservience. The phrase did lend itself quite nicely to mispronunciation: "Bow, Cow!" – as did the name of the leader of China, "Mousy Dung."

At first, quizzes continued for the senior officers, lieutenant colonels and above. The interrogator there was known as Plato or Alpha, a very knowledgeable officer who spoke very good English. He told the senior officers about the progress of talks in Paris. He also claimed to be the officer in charge of releases when the time came.

In the Zoo, we began to be given time outside our cells with other prisoners. We could talk, walk, and exercise. Every few days a load of coal dust would be brought in along with some water. Our chore was to fashion the dust into orange-sized briquettes for the kitchen.

At first the diet remained the same, but towards the end of January, there was a noticeable change for the better. We began receiving more protein in the way of canned fish, beef, and pork from Russia, as well as tofu and other soy products. Occasionally, we had "sewer bass" – a particularly bony fish that took a long time to de-bone and eat. We were allowed to play volleyball from time to time, take showers whenever we liked, and wash our clothes at will.

From the day of our arrival, we would receive a communication every morning from Eagle (Colonel John Flynn), the senior POW at the Hilton, giving us our instructions for the day, and informing us of any news that he might have heard. How it arrived, I never knew. Someone from the Vietnamese side must have been delivering it. That really puzzled me (and lent a sense of pride that the older POWs had won allies among the Vietnamese), but I was not in the "need to know" loop.

On 1 February, we were told to bathe and to shave. All facial hair had to be removed; and we were to put on clean clothes. About noon, we heard over the camp radio news of the signing of the Paris Peace Accords. That was not supposed to have happened; in the afternoon all the POWs in the Zoo were brought into a large theater or auditorium. One man turned around and said, "Hi, Bob." Though I recognized the voice, I couldn't place the face. "It's me, Tom. Tom Simpson." It was the first time I had seen him in weeks. His mustache was missing, and his upper lip was bright red from the shave. His arm had healed, and he looked much better than he did at the Hilton. When we were all assembled, the camp commander made the official announcement that the Paris Peace Accords had been signed on 29 January. All prisoners were to be released on both sides within sixty days of the agreement.

We were elated! Linebacker II had been successful, and the lack of bombing for the last month had not signaled a failure after all.

We would be going home no later than 29 March. We were now officially SHORT, and could start a real countdown to release (i.e. fifty-seven days and a wake-up.) There were a few attempts to interrogate us after that, but we all refused and the North Vietnamese did not hassle us further.

The following day, we made our final move to the Pig Sty, where we would remain for the duration of our captivity. The guard said, "You go home now." As the twelve of us moved in, we found fourteen already there. Most of us were B-52 crewmembers, two were from the Tactical Air Command, and two were from the Navy. Tom Simpson was added to the cell with me. Dick Johnson was next door.

From what we saw, we assumed that this prison had been a compound for the French army. The floors were terrazzo; there was a pool, showers, and a European-style toilet (a hole in the floor with a place to situate your boots on either side to squat over the opening). The long narrow buildings had windows and doors on both sides. In each cell, a riser had been built to hold six bed boards. The riser had been constructed by building a concrete wall about eighteen inches high and about six feet from the longer wall. Then it was backfilled with dirt, and a thin layer of cement was poured to make a top.

Block walls had been built around each building to convert it to a prison. As we communicated around the compound we discovered that everyone had been down less than eighteen months, and that the most severely wounded were still in the Hilton with the longest held prisoners. The middle group – those shot down following the resumption of air raids through mid-1971 – was in the Plantation.

One of the two guards in the Zoo was Radio, a South Vietnamese communist, and a nice guy. The other was Tank, a surly individual who clearly didn't like Americans very much. These two men were a study in human nature. Radio had a family he hadn't seen in several years and longed to be reunited with them.

He was trained as a radio operator, but enjoyed trying to cultivate a citrus tree in the harsh prison environment. He went about his duties as a prison guard with ease and was gracious and kindly disposed toward us. As a result, we found it easy to cooperate with his requests and instructions.

Tank, on the other hand, was seldom pleasant to anyone, prisoner or Vietnamese. He kept his tank insignia polished and his uniform neatly pressed. Because of his harsh attitude, we went out of our way to make his life difficult, responding slowly or not at all to his orders and instructions. When he discovered that some of us had marked in the propaganda magazines, drawing coal balls in the hands of applauding Chinese peasants, he became irritated and took the evidence to the camp commander. That gained us a lecture from the senior Vietnamese on showing respect and taking care of the reading material provided by the lenient government of the Peoples' Republic. Tank's actions also resulted in the Americans seeking new ways to irritate him in the future.

Within days, we could see C-130s from the USAF flying in and out of Gia Lam Airport, about five miles distant. Were they bringing CARE packages, picking up KIA remains, evacuating the wounded, and repairing the runway for the C-141s that would eventually fly in to pick us up? Our minds were ripe for speculation, and we engaged in it freely.

On Tet, the Vietnamese New Year, we again received a special meal similar to the ones on Christmas and January first. The Vietnamese also began to provide us with reading material, mostly propaganda magazines from China and Russia, but written in English. The magazines were filled with photographs of beautiful landscapes and smiling people. They gave us a Bible, which we eagerly passed around. The most amazing thing, however, were clippings from *Stars and Stripes* pasted to cardboard sheets. *Stars and Stripes* is the overseas military newspaper.

How it came to Hanoi, I do not know. I suspect that a couple of collaborators clipped the articles. I had seen one of them, dressed in regular clothes and tennis shoes, on my way to an interrogation session. While intended to demoralize us with stories of the losses of B-52s during the campaign, they actually had the opposite effect. The articles told us that only ten had been lost over the city, with five more escaping to eject over friendly territory to be rescued. We knew we had at least one crewmember from each of the ten downed aircraft. Sixty-one men had been aboard, thirty-two were known to be prisoners. The loss rate was not the fifty the NVN had insisted on; nor even our "optimistic" estimate of twenty-five. Ten out of 900 was surely an acceptable loss rate for such a massive campaign. Of course, being one of the ten was no comfort; but being part of a successful campaign gave me a great sense of pride and accomplishment. We had ended the war and freed the POWs even though some of us had become prisoners in the process.

Because we had all missed Christmas at home, we began to wonder if we would be home in time for Easter. When was Ash Wednesday? Several of us wanted to know so we could begin the Christian season of preparation, fasting, and denial. I was not sure when it began and initially tried to calculate from the phase of the moon. Since Easter is the Sunday following the first full moon following the vernal equinox (21 March), and since Ash Wednesday is forty days (plus Sundays) before Easter, it takes a little math and astronomical knowledge to figure it all out. But it was very important to us young men to be able to establish a "free-world" routine in order to help us resist the enemy. We knew we would be released on 29 March and be home by April first, but when was Easter?

The navigators huddled to make the calculations. There had been a full moon within a day or so of 18 December. How long was a lunar month? Twenty-five days? Or was it twenty-nine? Since we were never quite sure about the lunar month, and since the full moon is not always visible, we made a mistake in our calculations, and at first thought Easter would be in March. For a few days, I felt sad that we would miss Easter, too.

However, one of my cellmates, Jack Trimble, was an Episcopalian. In mid-February he received a *Book of Common Prayer* in a package from his mother. I knew the prayer book had a table of Easter Days, so I quickly looked it up. Easter would be on 22 April and Ash Wednesday on 7 March. We *would* be home in plenty of time. So, we solemnly marked our heads with coal dust on Ash Wednesday and selected some very tiny, but enormously important, prison "luxury" to give up for the remainder of our time in captivity. That year, Easter would truly be a celebration of the Resurrection for each of us as we returned to our new lives of freedom and restored relationships back home.

Our captors never understood why we did what we did, though Radio inquired with apparent interest. We were men of Christ, whose Lord had paid the ultimate price for us – a price spared us. Giving up a cigarette a day or an extra bit of cabbage soup was a small but significant reminder of the blessing of life and liberty that Christ had won for us so many years earlier.

We did continue to be harassed in a few irritating ways. They still ignored us when we used our military rank. One cell was left unlocked and open all day; but the men refused to come out as long as the rest of us were locked down.

With the war over, and the prison routine reduced to practically nothing, I had time to think again about how I had come to this point of acceptance of the sense of call to ministry I was feeling:

It had all begun in the early summer of 1963. I was fifteen and in high school. The idea of ministry seemed terribly uncomfortable to me; so I went to discuss it with the pastor of Garden City Methodist Church where I had grown up.

He was very pleased and supportive, but made the awful decision to announce it to the congregation the next Sunday. That was my announcement, not his. The doting of the adults, the teasing of my peers, and the discomfort in my own soul caused me to rethink the whole thing. In August my Dad was transferred to Washington DC, and I was grateful for a new start where I could be anonymous.

Two years later I had an accident – at least, that's what I thought. I was seventeen at the time, living with my oldest brother in Atlanta, and a freshman at Emory University. I had grown up in the Methodist Church, was attending a nice Methodist college, and trying to avoid a recurring sense of call to ordained ministry. I wanted to go to law school.

One Saturday, I borrowed my brother's pickup truck to take my nephew to the barbershop. After our haircuts, I drove around the block to return home. That's when it happened.

There was a stop sign at the top of the hill. And the truck had a stick shift. After coming to a full and complete stop, I couldn't get that thing to move again. As embarrassment and panic began to take hold, I decided to back down the hill and go around the other way, where the hill was less steep and the intersection had a light. Maybe I could catch it green.

As luck would have it, there was a long line of cars parked on the hill; and as I backed down it, I sideswiped one of them, damaging the doors. So, I parked the truck, picked up my nephew, and went into the building on the corner – the Episcopal Church of Our Saviour – to find the owner of the damaged car. Fortunately, the owner was most gracious (maybe the presence of the nephew in my arms helped), and my brother's insurance covered the damage.

Because of the kindness and warmth I felt from the people in the room, I returned the next day to attend an Episcopal service for the first time in my life, and discovered I was home! Maybe here I could be a good layperson, though I knew deep inside that was not to be. That accident started me on the journey again. In my sophomore year, I again felt a strong sense of call. The Air Force offered me a two-year full scholarship which carried an active duty commitment, so I took it. That way I could once again dodge the bullet of seminary. When I graduated and was commissioned, I went to Navigator training, which added another year of commitment to the USAF.

When I was in Bombardier training, I was dating Capt. Sarah (Robie) Robertson, a nurse at the base hospital. We had met at Trinity Episcopal Cathedral in Sacramento. One night we were discussing our futures when the subject of careers came up. She was contemplating returning to civilian practice, and I found myself saying, "I don't think I can stay either. I want to become a priest."

"I was wondering when you would make up your mind." Since we had never discussed this before, I was startled. Her transfer to Elmendorf AFB in Alaska was a good excuse to break from this woman who knew what I was thinking before I did.

I began visiting other denominations, looking for a safe place where I could worship without being called to ministry. When I was assigned to Blytheville, I joined a Baptist Church. Surely God would leave me alone there. Then I met Robbie Lee Wade, a member of another Baptist church in town. We dated for two weeks; I went to U-Tapao, Thailand, for four months, carrying on a furious romance by daily letters. When I returned in December I proposed and she accepted. We planned to marry in June, but Bullet Shot moved the date up to 25 May 1972.

In July, I was on Guam, when Mel Polek spoke the same words to me in the same conversation I had had with Robie Robertson two years earlier. Even when I was resisting God's call, my soul hungered for him and my heart was marked with a hole that only he could fill. It took an accident to get me into the Episcopal Church; it took a war to get me back and to decide to accept this nagging demand from God to go to seminary. But I had agreed to that in July. So why was I lying here in this damnable prison? Didn't God trust me to follow through? Come to think about it, I didn't have a very good track record there. But couldn't he have found a less dramatic way to bring me to obedience? What was the point of all this? What could I learn? What meaning would emerge? And why did Don, Bobby, and Fergie have to die? Those questions defied immediate answers.

The camp authorities allowed us to assemble for worship on Sunday mornings. With the Prayer Book in hand we had worship services and prayers already designed and suitable for what we needed. Because my fellows knew I was planning to attend seminary when we returned, I was asked to lead the services and to serve as their chaplain. Each Sunday, we would gather in the end cell to read Morning Prayer, sing hymns from memory, and listen to scriptures read. "God Bless America" was one of our favorites, and we learned that the old guys sang it every Sunday, along with the National Anthem. We prayed freely for families, our fallen crewmembers, for a swift and safe return, and for our captors, especially Radio, our favorite guard. While not everyone in the cellblock participated, choosing instead to exercise, read, have personal quiet time, or to engage in conversation with someone from another cell, everyone benefited from the worship services.

The first Sunday we noticed that while the guard would check on us periodically, he never made us quit until we were done. Therefore, the longer the worship service, the longer all of us were able to stay out of our cells.

Slowly it began to dawn on me that everything I had learned before I was captured seemed to be part of a divine composition that was beyond human or scientific explanation. There was a heavenly plan that was in motion all the time and nothing would or could prevent the plan of God that was to unfold over the decades that followed. I knew that I was not alone and that I was where I was supposed to be at that given time and space in my life. Even so, I had no idea how far reaching that experience would be in my life, nor did I realize how many people I would reach and help in their lives. I didn't see the war, my captivity, or the deaths of my friends as God's will; but I did know he was working to bring good out of the tragedies that surrounded us.

When 10 February rolled around, we were all on edge. We had speculated we might be first, since we were in the best shape; but the prisoners code insisted that it would be first in, first out. I had argued in vain with the camp authorities that two of our guys needed bone and tendon repair and should go home with the first group. That morning, we knew they were going nowhere. During the afternoon lockdown, we heard in the distance the distinctive whining of C-141 engines. Immediately, we were at the windows watching it make its approach to the airport – a beautiful gray and white transport with a big red cross painted on its tail. At the last minute it made a missed approach, turning right toward the Zoo. As he approached, he waved his wings in salute to us and reentered the landing pattern. We were shouting and jumping for joy. The guards tried to quiet us down, but it was no use.

Chapter 7

Over the next few days, I thought again how circumstances had converged to get me to this place.

When Robbie and I returned from our honeymoon the previous spring, I reported to the 340 Bomb Squadron to check the flight schedule for 30 May 1972. The crew was scheduled to fly the next day, but I was no longer on it. I asked the commander what was going on, and he told me I had been reassigned to the Standardization-Evaluation Section ("Stan-Board") as an instructor-evaluator. We had two bombers left on the base and a few crews, mostly scheduled to go to D models within a few weeks. I was puzzled why we even needed a Stan-Board, but went in to say farewell to Mel and the others.

About two weeks later, I was informed that I was being reassigned to a crew leaving for D models at U-Tapao. I called Mel and asked if he had heard the news. He said, yes, that the crew was to go to Andersen in mid-July. That was not the news I meant; and I began to think of a way to get back with my old friends.

I made an appointment with the Deputy for Operations, Lt. Col. Andy Pringle, to discuss it. I pointed out that if I stayed on the D crew, and the other navigator stayed with Polek, both crews would arrive in the theater non-combat ready; but if he swapped the navigators, at least Polek's crew would be ready to fly without supervised missions first. He agreed and reassigned me to crew S-18.

Had I accepted things as they were in early June, I would have flown with a crew that returned safely. While lots of evil had resulted, I was convinced that "all things work together for good for those who trust in the Lord."

On February 14, we were given paper and pen to write another twenty-line letter home. I attempted to get information about the rest of the crew out. I told Robbie to call my godson to say I was sorry to hear that the head of the family had died and that I hoped that the two brothers were OK. While Mel Polek was my godson's father and had two other sons, I hoped that he would understand that the head of family would mean the pilot, and that the two "brothers" would be the copilot and gunner, both African-Americans. The letter never made it to the United States.

Throughout our stay in the Pig Sty, only three men received letters from home, although all wives wrote and sent packages. Those of us who received the packages shared their contents with other men in the cellblock.

In a few days, we came to know that we had four "pals" in the camp: three Thais (Chip, Pen, Dale) and one South Vietnamese (Max Dat). We also came to know that Col. Kittenger was now the camp Senior Ranking Officer. About this time, we could see over the wall that massive amounts of heavy weapons, including SAMs and AAA, were being moved and repositioned, but exactly where was a matter of some conjecture.

While we were able to keep our toilet buckets, clothes, and bodies cleaner than before, dishes and hands were still washed in cold water with lye soap. The soup and bread continued to have insect and rat dung contamination, and on one occasion shards of broken light bulb. That led to a spontaneous hunger strike. The camp commander came immediately. We accused his kitchen staff of deliberately trying to kill some of us. I didn't really believe that, but it was good to be able to harass this guy. Col. Kittenger confronted the camp commander about the glass, but we continued to find little shards in the soup for the next three or four days. He ordered another meal brought out, and in a short while we were served tofu soup. That surely wasn't much of an improvement!

Chapter 7

Big chunks of gray tofu floating around in water, tasting a lot like the sole of a well-used Converse All-Star tennis shoe. Throughout the countdown to zero, treatment never improved. Even when we received canned food from the USSR, it was always cold and greasy.

The second release date was scheduled for Saturday, 24 February; but no C-141s arrived. What had gone wrong? Our fears of a new stalemate grew exceptionally large as we speculated and our hope for an on-time release fell into the cellar. An announcement over the camp radio claimed that the U.S. had violated the terms of the treaty by failing to sweep the mines out of Haiphong harbor. That meant to us that the NVN government had probably done something to test the U.S. government. When the 141s appeared on Monday, the crisis was over. We would later learn that NVN had refused to release four men captured in Laos but held in Hanoi, claiming they were Laotian prisoners. With the threat of renewed BUFF strikes, they relented.

As our release date drew closer, food began to improve with the addition of hot peppers (with the idea that they would kill intestinal parasites). Some CARE packages were delivered with dried food of various kinds and American medicines for colds and infections, as well as some packages from families. Each of us was called to the distribution point to receive our allotment of goodies from the packages. We were not allowed to take the outside packaging, so we had to take the medicine bottles out of the cardboard boxes. The Vietnamese couldn't get the childproof tops off the medicine to inspect the contents, so they handed them to us. We would quickly push down and twist, remove the top, show it to the guard, replace the cap, and give it back to try again. It was great fun to watch them get frustrated, especially since retaliation was deemed remote.

When they realized we were toying with them, they gave up on inspecting the pills.

Cases of cigarettes and cigars were included in the shipment.

Every man received two cigars and several packs of American cigarettes. The Vietnamese had two brands, Trung Song and Dien Bien, which I labeled Bad and Awful. They had no concept of the differences between red, green, gold, filtered, unfiltered or anything else about the myriad of American brands and styles. As a result, one cellblock got all the greens, one the golds, etc. We resorted to trading by throwing packs of one kind across the wall to the adjacent cellblock in exchange for another kind. Still, only half of the prisoners smoked, so each of us smokers had twice the intended ration. We also continued to receive the daily supply of Vietnamese cigarettes, enabling us to ration our U.S. brands over the course of our expected stay.

One of the men in the cell next to us had received dried eggs in his package from home, but had no way to prepare them. By this time we had been given a small kerosene lantern to keep in our cells to light our cigarettes. If they could devise a way to build a fire at night, when the guards were gone, they could cook them in a tin cup. When Tank (the guard we detested because of his surly attitude) left his machete and hammer in the courtyard, the guys took them back to their cell. The concrete shelf had been broken in one place. The concrete was only about an inch thick, laid over dirt. They buried the purloined items in the dirt, and placed a bed board over it. At night, they would chop slivers of wood off a bed board, light it with the lantern, and cook their eggs. The guard in the tower couldn't come down to check on the noise. The second or third night, another guard opened the shutters to see what they were up to in their room. All of the prisoners stood between their little fire and the guard, so he did not see. The smoke coming from the fire rose above their heads and billowed out the transom above the door. Fortunately, in the dark the guard didn't notice the smoke.

Some received packages from wives and parents with everything from underwear to books to candy and cookies.

Chapter 7

Those packages were often robbed by the Vietnamese, or split with another prisoner for some reason, probably to start a fight between us – but that didn't work. Prisoners who realized they had another man's items simply returned them to the rightful owner. My wife sent butterscotch and peppermint candies, which I was able to mete out to my cellmates – there was enough for each of us to have one piece a day until 29 March.

The 17 March release occurred on schedule, and we grew increasingly restless, anxious, hopeful, and defiant. More and more we discussed our wives and families, our favorite foods, our dream houses, our next assignments and career plans. Tom Simpson, who shared the cell with me in the Pig Sty, talked constantly of black-bottom pie as his favorite dessert.

On 25 March we were measured for civilian clothes and shoes and told we could carry home a souvenir from the prison. Two days later, we received a visit from the Four Power Commission and the international press corps. That gave us one more chance to demonstrate major defiance to the camp authorities. We had cleaned our rooms and laid out our "personal" belongings at the head of our bed boards as we had been told. Then we huddled with our SRO, Lt. Col. Lou Bernasconi. We knew the camp authorities hated it when we referred to each other by rank, so we took it several steps further. Our plan was to mill about the courtyard as usual, and when the gate opened to let in our visitors, to fall into military formation by cell, with the senior officer in the front, and lined up in file in order of rank. The camp authorities were taken completely off guard; the camp commander was clearly flustered, but strained to make the best of the situation.

The U.S. Army representative on the Commission, a Colonel Roberts, was straight from central casting – head and shoulders taller than the camp commander. Standing beside him, he accepted a salute from Lt. Col. Bernasconi, and instructed him to dismiss his men to their cells. With crowds of reporters all around us and with cameras rolling, we marched into our cells and stood at parade rest at the end of our bed boards. We refused to look at or speak to the reporters, save one – Walter Cronkite.

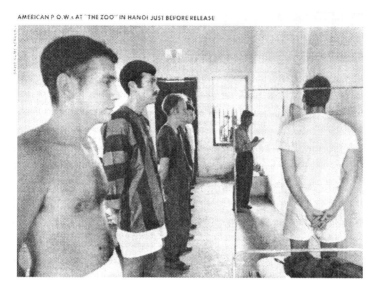

AMERICAN P.O.W.s AT "THE ZOO" IN HANOI JUST BEFORE RELEASE

The Zoo on 25 Mar 1973. L-R: Henry Hudson, Tom Simpson, Robert Certain, Dave Drummond, Bill Condon, Alex Alexander, reporter, Jack Trimble

As the press corps left, we gathered in the courtyard for some good-natured conversation. One of the reporters came back in to take some candid photos, whereupon one of my cellmates turned his back to him, dropped his pants, and mooned him. The tower guard had a lady friend with him watching the events below. She practically flew down the tower stairs, and the guard doubled over with laughter.

The guys in the next cell brought out the machete and hammer they had stolen weeks earlier, and solemnly presented them back to Tank. He was red-faced and angry at being duped by us, and because he had been accusing Radio of stealing them. Tank could do nothing, but Radio had a big laugh out of the presentation.

The next day, we were issued the clothes, dark blue slacks and light blue shirt, belt, socks, shoes and a vinyl tote bag.

Chapter 9

Tomorrow was our day of freedom. March 28 was also the freedom flight for half the camp. As the men in the other cellblocks dressed, we were able to mingle with them for a while. I told one, "Make sure that tomorrow we see either a 141 or a mushroom cloud. Don't leave us here."

He smiled at this gallows humor, and said, "Sure."

That night was very restless for all of us as we anticipated our flight out in the morning. We were up early, dressed in our release clothes, packed our bags and talked nervously as we waited.

Chapter 8

Operation Homecoming

The last release of American prisoners occurred on 29 March 1973, sixty days after the Paris Peace Accords had been signed. We were placed on buses and taken to Gia Lam Airport. A host of spectators were gathered, so we were kept behind the hangars until things were ready and the C-141 was on the ground and prepared to pick us up.

While we waited, men were arguing and placing bets about who had won the Super Bowl in January – Miami or Washington? As I gazed out the window, I saw Walter Cronkite walking up from the rear of the line of buses. I leaned out the window and asked, "Walter, who won the Super Bowl?"

He looked at me with a puzzled expression. Was he trying to remember, or was he wondering why anyone would ask that question at the end of March? After a few seconds, he brightened, smiled, and said, "Miami." Groans and cheers arose from the bettors, and promises made to pay up as soon as we had cash.

A few exceptionally long minutes passed before the bus started moving again. My insides were churning with anxiety, my mind alive with prayers of thanksgiving and thoughts of my wife and family. We were driven to the front of the terminal, where we climbed out of the bus and formed two lines in order of our shootdown dates.

Chapter 9

When our names were called we marched across the tarmac to a USAF Colonel, saluted, and reported in, "Sir, Captain Certain reporting for duty." From there I turned right and walked toward the ramp of the 141 known by now as the Hanoi Taxi, where more officers and NCOs greeted me, and then up the ramp into the aircraft to be greeted by doctors, nurses, and a masseur.

C-141 Starlifter in role as Hanoi Taxi, Gia Lam Airport, Hanoi, North Vietnam

We settled into our seats and buckled in so we could get underway. Quite soon the ramp came up, the doors closed, and the Hanoi Taxi moved out smartly to the runway. Although it seemed like hours, in a few minutes we were airborne. Up to that point we were all quite solemn, talking in soft tones or praying. I was anxious and nervous that something might yet go wrong. When the wheels left the ground and began their retraction, a spontaneous cheer arose. Fifteen or twenty minutes later, Maj. Don Goodin, the aircraft commander, announced we were "feet wet" (over water) and then that we were clear of North Vietnamese airspace. Each announcement brought another cheer and the swift ebbing of the fear and anxiety of prison life. The last one resulted in seatbelts being unbuckled, cigars lit, and general movement, hubbub, and frivolity. U.S. magazines were plentiful. The masseur busied himself relieving the tension in our bodies that had amassed over the previous hundred days.

Capt. Certain approaching Hanoi Taxi

Homeward bound

Chapter 9

We spent three days at Clark AFB Hospital in the Philippines before being flown to the USA. There we were fitted with new uniforms, complete with name tags and updated ribbons, and assigned an escort officer to be our friend, companion and gofer on our flight to the States. Mine was Capt. Bob Kirby. As a phone became available I called home and talked at length to my bride, Robbie.

In the hospital cafeteria we were offered a wide variety of the rich American food we had talked about, dreamed of, and longed for during the prison days. Steaks, eggs, vegetables, salads, desserts, and ice cream were ours for the asking – but with the warning, "be careful, your system may not accept this fare very well." Naturally I ignored such advice and stuffed myself with my favorite foods.

I was debriefed by another Intelligence Officer, Charles Darr, for about four hours, and interviewed by a Personnel Officer who would get me to my next assignment. When he asked me what I wanted, I told him I wanted to go to seminary. I asked about the resignation I had submitted in July. He told me that it had been rejected on 15 December 1972 because of my request for an early out and the fact that I had a regular commission and was in a critical crew position. *Is that why I had been in prison? Did God know I probably would have changed my mind again? And why was I assigned an escort named Robert Kirby and a debriefer named Charles Darr, the same names as the Offense Team on Randy Craddock's missing crew?*

I told the personnel officer that I figured there were three ways to handle this. One, the USAF could accept my resignation as requested earlier; two, I could switch from regular to reserve, go to seminary, and return to active duty in any capacity the USAF wanted; or, three, send me to school under the Air Force Institute of Technology (AFIT) masters degree program and assign me as a chaplain. Two days later, he returned to tell me that the commander of AFIT had agreed to the third plan, providing I could get an agreement from a bishop to ordain me when I graduated.

I was amazed and excited. My correspondence with Atlanta in the fall had not been very promising; and I had never met the bishop in San Antonio who did seem interested. Then, too, I really thought that the issue of separation of church and state would preclude this particular option.

Escort Capt. Kirby, Capt. Certain, nurse Lt. Mikelene "Mickey" Mantel

My crew was sent to the Scott AFB Medical Center in Illinois for another week of medical evaluations. It was there that our families met us for the first time on 1 April 1973. After I made my greetings to the crowd, my wife ran across the tarmac to greet me. On the makeshift reviewing stand, a flat-bed truck trailer, were my parents, my best friend and his wife, Bobby and Beth Ann Marshall, and my second-grade teacher, Miss Lewis. I was introduced to my "permanent" escort officer, Major Rick Dicamillo. Robbie and I, along with family and friends, were taken to a suite in the Distinguished Visitors Quarters, for more conversation into the evening.

The next day, my parents returned to spend the day with Robbie while I began in-depth physical tests. For dinner, Dad took us into St. Louis for a very elegant meal. We had a wonderful time catching up with each other, and enjoying the great food. The next morning I was sick as a dog. My system had finally rejected rich food. I had gotten so used to the meager fare of Hanoi, that the body rebelled against all that protein, sugar, and other nutrients. I was very upset that night that I couldn't join the family for another feast, but sent Robbie on ahead while I lay on the bed in abject misery, much as I had on our honeymoon a year earlier when I had eaten some Mexican food that didn't agree with me.

An intestinal parasite was found and I was treated orally with a poison to kill it. As the doctor explained, anything that will kill a parasite will also kill the host. The powder would not dissolve in any liquid, so it had to be stirred or shaken to suspend it, then drunk quickly to get it down. I had to gag down each dose. Once I poured Coca-Cola over it, resulting in a massive amount of foam rising and flowing all over the counter like something from a mad scientist movie. I also went through the most thorough physical I had ever experienced, including an immersion test to determine total body fat and ideal weight.

At the end of that week, a T-29 was sent in to transport the three returnees from Crew S-18 of the 340 Bomb Wing back to our home base in Blytheville, Arkansas. I was informed that I would need to return in four days for more tests. When I asked the reason, I was told that they simply had not finished everything, even though I had had every test that Dick Johnson and Tom Simpson had experienced.

We arrived back at Blytheville AFB in a light rain, and with hundreds of base and community people gathered, along with video and print media and official Air Force photographers. A receiving line of senior officers awaited us at the foot of the airstairs.

Crowd gathered to welcome Blytheville crew members home

In their number was Capt. Howard Rose. When I spotted him, anger boiled up within me as the memory of my request to put us on standby for 18 December came back, and my first impulse was to strike him. I did not understand my own reaction, but he seemed to be the lightning rod for all the anger, fear, and terror I had been suppressing since the day we were shot down. I stuffed the anger down for future examination, shook his hand, greeted him by name, and made my remarks of gratitude to the base and community. The crew proceeded to shake hands down the line of spectators, and then Robbie and I climbed into the back seat of a Ford to be driven home. After that, I forgot all about Howard as I concerned myself with my mandated return to Scott Medical Center.

I remembered that I had experienced a similar reaction in the winter of 1971. Following Survival School at Fairchild AFB in Spokane, Washington, I was shopping in the BX when I spotted a Technical Sergeant (TSgt) in the next aisle. I instantly felt tension and anger, but couldn't understand why, since I could not place anything but his face in my memory.

I followed him around for several minutes until it came to me – he had played the role of the bad-guy interrogator in the POW training compound at the school. I felt immediate relief, and walked over to introduce myself to him. He acknowledged that I wasn't the first to experience that, and we both had a good chuckle over it. In Hanoi, I was grateful he had taught me so well. In Blytheville, I simply tried to hide the reaction and get out of the rain.

On my return to Scott, my wisdom teeth were removed, and I was given a bone scan and other exotic diagnostic procedures, still without any hint why. After a week of this, I was once again sent back to Blytheville, with orders to return in thirty days.

Capt. Certain arriving in Blytheville

It was time to pick up the phone and start contacting the Bishop of Atlanta to discuss seminary in the fall. The conversation was anything but hopeful, as the person I spoke with told me that Atlanta had a policy that required prospective seminarians to work for a year in a parish before applying for postulancy and theology school. I tried to explain that I would not be staying in the diocese, but returning to military duty as a chaplain. I did arrange an appointment with the Suffragan Bishop, Milton Wood, during the time that Robbie and I would be attending a family reunion in April.

When we met with Bishop Wood, he explained their policy again, saying that Atlanta had too many priests and couldn't send anyone to seminary without a year of trial ministry. Again I explained that the USAF was sending me on active duty, that the cost to the diocese would be zero, and that I wouldn't be adding to the clergy glut because of my transfer to the chaplaincy. I wondered at the time if the Diocesan Bishop's position as president of the Episcopal Peace Fellowship had anything to do with the apparent stonewall. I began to wonder what the Lord was doing in all this.

Robbie and I returned to the family reunion at my brother Alan's house in Decatur. The entire family had gathered, and Alan's wife, Genie, had graciously invited some of my best friends from my Emory University fraternity to join us for part of the time. Surprisingly, I felt exceptionally uncomfortable with both family and friends in spite of my great joy at being with them. I wanted to be gracious, but felt very awkward and out of place. Perhaps it was because of the odd time at the bishop's office, perhaps it was because my confinement had left me wary of and nervous around crowds of people. Then, too, my sister and her husband, having made statements to the press that upset me, were present and I had no idea how to address the *Washington Post* article from December that quoted them as saying our family was divided over the war, an event I was just learning about.

Life had been very simple in Hanoi; now it was almost overwhelmingly complicated. I finally had to withdraw by myself to find calm.

On Palm Sunday, I took Robbie to her first Episcopal worship service at my college parish of Our Saviour. The two-hour service included a Procession of Palms all the way around the block, the rector's knock at the church doors that they be opened for the Lord, and solemn high mass, complete with asperges, incense, and an awful sermon. It was very meaningful for me, but Robbie was in tears the entire time in such a foreign land. I began to wonder if she would transition well into the Episcopal Church at all, much less into the "high" church that I had so fondly remembered from my Emory days. It would take a lot of prayer and conversation to calm her; and I determined then to seek the center of the church in liturgical expression.

As the reunion ended, I flew to New York to meet with Bishop Clarence Hobgood, Suffragan for the Armed Forces, in the national headquarters of the Episcopal Church. He and his executive assistant, Father Charles Burgreen, greeted me warmly. Both were eager to help find a sponsoring bishop soon, before "the Air Force realizes what it has promised and withdraws the offer." We spent a couple of pleasant but inconclusive hours together and I returned to Arkansas.

Back home, the base held a memorial for the nine men from Blytheville who had not been released. They were still missing or known to be killed in action. In no case had any of their remains been repatriated. I remember feeling out of place in the service. Joan Rissi knew from my report that Don had died in December. The Department of Defense would have continued his full pay and benefits had he not been declared KIA. I was surprised by the Government's decision to deny her and the boys any long-term benefits in honor of Don's long and heroic service.

The Base Commander told her she would have to vacate base housing, even though she had a high school senior and junior she wanted to keep in Blytheville to finish school.

During this stay, I finally started going through personal effects from Guam. Some of my things were missing, but I did find the correspondence from the previous fall with Bishop Harold Gosnell of West Texas. I had forgotten all about him.

In the early fall of 1972, Episcopal Chaplain Peter Booke had been stationed at Andersen AFB. When I went to him about the possibility of seminary, I told him I had corresponded with Father Roy Pettway of the Church of Our Saviour in Atlanta and with Bishop Sims. Neither remembered me, nor were they particularly eager to discuss matters further. Chaplain Booke suggested that I write to Bishop Gosnell. Peter had worked for him when he was the rector of St. Mark's in San Antonio, and suggested that if he couldn't sponsor me, he would know someone who would. He also told me that the bishop was a chaplain captain in the Naval Reserves.

As I had corresponded with the bishop, he had invited me to come to San Antonio in January 1973 when I was scheduled to be home on a twenty-eight-day R&R from the war. When I was reading the letters in May, I obviously had missed the meeting, and sat down on the edge of the bed, picked up the phone and dialed the number of the Bishop's office. There was no time to trust this to the postal service.

Expecting to go through a receptionist and secretary before I would ever get to the Bishop, I was surprised to hear a man's voice on the other end of the line. I asked to speak with Bishop Gosnell and was greeted with "This is he."

I was stunned, but managed to say, "Sir, this is Captain Certain."

"Where have you been?" Before I could recover enough to

answer, he laughed and said, "Never mind, I know where you've been. When you didn't show up in January, I wrote Peter Booke to ask why you hadn't appeared and if you were serious or not. The letter was forwarded all over the Pacific before finally getting to him at March AFB in California. He told me you were still interested, but had been unavoidably detained. Anyway, here's the situation. I can only send four men to seminary this year. I've already accepted three and have eleven applicants for the fourth position. Now, do you want it or not?"

"Yessir, I do."

"Fine. It's yours. When can we meet?"

The Good Lord had just opened the biggest door I had ever seen. I explained that we would be coming to Dallas in about a month, so how would mid-June work? He readily agreed. Excitedly I told Robbie what had happened and we were ecstatic about this new turn of affairs.

On May 22, Robbie and I traveled on orders to Washington for a gala dinner with other repatriates, their spouses or significant others, various entertainers, including the entire Bob Hope Show, and governmental officials. We were housed in the Washington Hilton as guests of Conrad Hilton. On the morning of May 24, the ExPOWs went to the State Department for a briefing from President Nixon and the opportunity for him to shake all our hands. The wives, mothers, and girlfriends went to a reception hosted by First Lady Pat Nixon.

On the bus, I ran into USAF Major Keith Lewis, another former POW who had discussed with me the possibility of going to seminary. When I asked him where he was going, he said that his personnel officer had told him no. When I told him I had been approved, he managed to get his orders back to F-4s changed so he could attend the Virginia Theological Seminary in Alexandria.

The days in Washington were filled with great joy. We visited my parents in Silver Spring, my sister in Gaithersburg, and the Poleks in Baltimore, in addition to the grand dinner at the White House on the evening of May 24, the eve of our first wedding anniversary. It was heady to be in the company not only of long-time POWs, but also Bob Hope, John Wayne, Jimmy Stewart, Henry Kissenger, and other famous entertainers and statesmen.

After a few days, we returned to Blytheville to continue convalescent leave and physical examinations. We had a few days for me to pray and to ponder again the labyrinth-like path I seemed to be on.

In June, Robbie and I flew to Dallas to participate in a city-sponsored parade honoring the returned POWs. Ross Perot had organized it, and the festivities began with a big party and barbeque at his home. As soon as it was over, we flew to San Antonio to meet with Bishop Gosnell. The meeting was delightful. Robbie was worried about what it meant to be the wife of an Episcopal clergyman. Her experience of the wives of Baptist ministers suggested she might have to play the piano and sing in the choir. He explained that her role was to be a good wife and to exercise her faith in anyway that made sense to her.

The following day, we again met with the bishop, this time with the Commission on Ministry, too. They quickly agreed with the bishop to support my postulancy. The bishop then said that I would meet in the afternoon with Ben Benitez, rector of Christ Church, and his vestry. They would be my sponsoring parish. And oh by the way, "I want you to go to Sewanee," the School of Theology of the University of the South in Sewanee, Tennessee.

I had intended to go to Nashota House in Nashota, Wisconsin because of my "high church" entry into the Episcopal faith; but I knew the difference between a Navy Captain and an Air Force Captain. "OK, that's fine, sir." It would be years before I would really appreciate just how much red tape Harold Gosnell had cut during those twenty-four hours. The Holy Spirit was really working wonders.

Chapter 9

On my third trip to Scott, I picked up my medical records and read the radiologist's report of the bone scan. In it was the phrase, "uptake of the isotope into the lungs and spinal column is indicative of malignant lymphoma." When I asked my primary physician about that, he responded that it was not confirmed and that other tests would be conducted, including another bone scan and a bone marrow biopsy. For that procedure, I laid on my left side on the bed; the doctor froze my right hip and pushed a large-gauge needle into it. I felt a sharp pain on the back of my knee. "That hurts. How long is that needle?"

"That's just referred pain. We're working close to the nerve endings, and because your hip is frozen, your body thinks the pain is in your knee." After a few days, I was once again released to Blytheville with orders to return in thirty days.

My prayers were pretty blunt. *What on earth is this all about, God? I told you I would be a priest. I've been shot down, captured, survived. The Air Force is sending me to seminary, and Bishop Gosnell has accepted me as a postulant and promised to ordain me. Have I done all this just to die from cancer before I can take another step? Why didn't you just let me die in December and let one of the other guys live? And, oh by the way, is there some little joke in the bishop's name being the same as the hamlet outside the main gate of Blytheville AFB?*

The next week, Robbie and I drove over to Sewanee to look for housing and to complete the formal interviews for admission into the School of Theology. Some faculty members seemed irritated that Bishop Gosnell had more or less instructed them to accept me. As we looked over married student housing, I quipped to the housing officer that I had larger quarters in Hanoi, a comment she didn't take very kindly. A one-bedroom apartment of about 800 square feet simply didn't appeal to either of us. She referred us to a retired couple who had bought the old convent building owned by the Sisters of St. Mary and were converting it into a home for themselves and an apartment at one end.

126

The place was in a serene setting in the country overlooking a bluff. The apartment would take over the chapel on the first floor with living room, dining room, and kitchen, and the library on the second floor for a master bedroom, bath and study along with another large room for a second bedroom. We agreed to rent at their asking price and were promised a move-in date in the middle of August.

Robbie and I then proceeded to take advantage of various vacation offers and journeyed to Florida to see the Kennedy Space Center, Disney World and St. Augustine. We had a grand time, but we needed to return to Blytheville for my final appointment in Belleville.

On the fourth trip to Scott, I was informed that the symptoms that pointed toward lymphoma no longer existed, and I was released to duty. Finally, I told Robbie what all these trips had been about. Seminary would start in August, so I was kept on convalescent leave until then. The experiences of the eight months leading up to that event profoundly affected my view of both life and ministry, in some ways for the good, and in some ways not.

As I drove back to Arkansas along the west side of the Mississippi River, I slowly began to think of myself like the "nearly-dead," a person leading a life that, but for the slightest of circumstances, should have already ended, not only because of battle, but also because of the threat of cancer. How was I going to live my life now? The Lord had sustained me through some very difficult times, some of which had resulted in the deaths of friends. As long as I would live, those lives would have to be reflected in my life and their memories kept alive.

I suppose that anyone who has been in battle has, to one degree or another, almost died and has seen his friends die close by. That fact will continue to alter those of us who shared the experience of battle long after the treaties have been signed, forces have returned home, and weapons of warfare have been recycled into other uses.

Chapter 9

War breaches lives like tornadoes cut across the land and nothing is ever again the same. It was a drive that would begin to set the course for the ministry I hoped to pursue.

Unfortunately, there was another trend at work that would keep me from fully realizing the hand of God working in my life. I began to assign big pieces of my experience to the realm of evil, devoid of any redeeming hope. Many well-intentioned people had commented to me during the first few weeks of freedom that it was "God's will" that my life was spared. It seemed to me, if that were true, it necessarily followed that it was also "God's will" that others had died. I couldn't accept the second proposition, so I rejected the first, and came to believe that while God could bring good from the evil of war, destruction, death, and disease, he wasn't really working within those events and circumstances as they happened.

The reaction of other people against the war in Vietnam exacerbated my exclusion of the harsh pieces of life from the realm of God's action. The difficulty with the Diocese of Atlanta was a case in point. I felt like my participation in the war was a definite black mark in their minds. Letters written to my parents by high school and college classmates pointing out their disagreement with the war, and the general attitude in the nation against Vietnam and our veterans added to the subconscious idea that the most destructive of life's events were outside the possibility of redemption.

With my lingering sense of guilt over the deaths of so many on the receiving end of our bombs, I found it necessary to relegate the most disturbing thoughts, memories, and events to the unexamined and unspoken vault of hidden fears. In 1973, no one seemed prepared to consider the depth of suffering that veterans of the conflict could be experiencing. Some were concerned that asking questions would bring up memories too painful to consider; others saw us as cold blooded and evil men. The message from everyone was that we were damaged goods; but repairs proved elusive.

I was invited to Salina, Kansas by the local Episcopal parish to address the citizens of the community about my move from combat to the ministry. We flew into that town at the center of the state and were well received by our hosts and the people who came to the high school stadium to hear me. It was good to be able to witness to God's love and call to these people of America's heartland.

Back home in Arkansas, Robbie and I continued to prepare for our move to Sewanee. We packed, made plans, worshipped at St. Stephen's Episcopal Church, prayed and attended to details. Every few days I checked with the landlord in Sewanee to make sure the apartment was coming along, receiving each time a confident reply. The traffic management office at the Air Force base scheduled our move, and sent packers and a truck to move us out.

As the men were loading the moving van, the landlord called to say the apartment would be delayed another two weeks.

"What do you mean, you told me a week ago it was finished."

"No I didn't."

Dismayed, I informed him the truck was on the way, and we would be moving in within three days. Now what was going on? The next day we left for the day trip to Sewanee.

Chapter 9

Trauma and Grace

Psalm 61
Hear my cry, O God,
   and listen to my prayer.
I call upon you from the ends of the earth with heaviness in my
   heart;
   set me upon the rock that is higher than I.
For you have been my refuge,
   a strong tower against the enemy.
I will dwell in your house for ever;
   I will take refuge under the cover of your wings.
For you, O God, have heard my vows;
   you have granted me the heritage of those who fear your
   Name.

When Robbie and I drove up in front of the apartment the
next afternoon, we discovered that there was no door, no stairs, no
plumbing, and no carpeting. The landlord had not been forthright
with us, but we moved in anyway. It took several more weeks for
things to be completed, but we were finally settled into our home for
the next three years.

We found it particularly appealing to have our home in a space
that had been used for worship for nearly a century.

Chapter 9

The windows were amber glass; the rood screen, which had once divided the congregation from the chancel and would have had a crucifix (rood) atop it, separated the dining room from the elevated kitchen (the former altar level). We could never cook without thinking of all the Suppers of the Lord that had been prepared in that very place; and, we could never dine without thinking of all the nuns and guests who had shared in the Messianic banquet of Holy Communion over the many years before.

Our Sewanee Apartment

We were hoping for a peaceful and supportive time of preparation for the ordained ministry. The events of the previous year had been traumatic for both of us and we often felt like we were fighting just to keep our noses above water. The Holy Spirit had been swift to move us from repatriation to seminary, so surely good things lay ahead.

When the junior (beginning) class arrived to begin orientation, we were invited to a reception by the upper classmen. As we walked up, Robbie discovered to her horror that it was a keg party. In the next few hours she witnessed one seminarian after another become quite drunk, reminding her of college fraternity parties. For a Baptist, she was sure she had stepped into Satan's training ground. It would take some time for her to come to grips with being an Episcopalian; but she was determined to do so.

A few days later, our class had a potluck dinner to get to know each other better before classes began, and Robbie decided to bake a chocolate cake. In the move from Arkansas to Tennessee something had happened to the thermostat in the oven. Rather than heating to the set temperature, it must have gone to the "clean" setting, and within a few minutes the cake was burned on the outside and raw on the inside. That would provide us with a bit of humor whenever we were feeling low, and we would joke about "burnt offerings" from the altar of the convent chapel for several years.

At the time, the curriculum called for Biblical studies in the first (junior) year, and we launched into Old Testament for the first semester. The professor was outstanding in his lectures and I was able to take copious notes. However, his strong suit was the Torah and we barely made it through Genesis before Thanksgiving. Between then and Christmas we struggled to get to the major prophets and were able to continue a bit into the second semester to scan the minor prophets.

Because of the reading load, many of us formed groups of two or three for study and reading. I invited a couple of young bachelors, Ted Boya and Steve Gideon, to join with me and to study in my den on St. Mary's Road. Robbie and I enjoyed their company, and they quickly became fixtures in the afternoon for study and in the evening for dinner. All four of us assisted with meal preparation and clean-up, becoming more like family than friends.

Chapel offered a time of refreshment, peace, and spiritual formation with daily Morning Prayer and a mid-week Eucharist for the Seminary community. In that quaint little building I found a special place where I could feel the presence of God even when I was alone.

Throughout our time there, I made the services my spiritual discipline, a practice that would carry forward into the ministry ahead.

St. Luke's Chapel

But it wasn't long before troubling things began to surface. The USAF required me to wear my uniform to class one day a week, but it seemed that on that day, I was given wide berth by many of the students and faculty. I was proud of what the uniform represented to me – duty, honor, discipline and love of country – but it didn't seem to have anywhere near that meaning to others. I began to feel like a lightening rod for people's frustrations over the war in Vietnam.

The class was divided into small groups, called preceptorials, to discuss our spiritual journeys. I hoped for nurture, but the discussions were more often times of picking apart our faith rather than building it up. I was very unhappy with the idea that we had to have our faith stripped away and dissected before we could find true adult belief.

It seemed to me that my ten-year struggle with my calling, topped off by combat and imprisonment had already done that. I prayed that I might find understanding and the right words to speak; but the words never seemed to come.

In November, I was invited by a rector in New Jersey to speak to his parish about my experiences and my new course. Always eager to share my faith, I readily accepted. Most of the people in the forum were polite and inquisitive. One woman, however, asked me how I could possibly reconcile being a baby-killer with seeking to be a priest. I was stunned and struggled to explain how other veterans and I had done everything in our power to make sure that our efforts were honorable; but she wasn't interested in understanding. The rector called her down and the forum ended shortly afterwards.

I dropped many bombs in Vietnam, and I wish I could say that they only destroyed military targets. But surely noncombatants were among the casualties. A combatant, who may be a righteous, God-fearing, loving human being, must become inhumane day after day if he is to do what his country has asked him to do. The injunction to love all as we would be loved is the first casualty of any war. William Tecumseh Sherman was right when he observed that "war is hell," and anyone who speaks otherwise is a fool or a fraud. That does not mean that we should forget our humanity. Our experience does not absolve us of our moral obligations, but they can be very hard to keep, given the extraordinarily difficult and conflicting expectations imposed on us: to kill people and destroy on the one hand, and to be good and virtuous on the other. How could I ever explain that concept adequately to myself much less to so many who harbored such animosity toward soldiers?

A gray lining was quickly attaching itself to my silver cloud. How on earth was I going to survive three years of this kind of confrontation? Could it be that a former combatant could not represent the priesthood of Christ to others, and could not bring other sinners through the cloud of unknowing into the conscious presence of God's saving word? I could never believe that I had committed an unpardonable sin by serving my country and her allies in war. After all, hadn't God opened every door necessary for me to walk swiftly through and into seminary? I was convinced that my only course of action was toward the priesthood. What was the problem that others doubted that?

Our return trip to Sewanee became a symbol for the journey I was on with my beloved by my side. We flew from New Jersey into Nashville, picked up our car and drove down I-24 toward Monteagle and Sewanee. The last seven miles is a very steep and winding road as it climbs to the top of the Cumberland Plateau. As we neared the top and entered the clouds, the fog was so thick that headlights were ineffective and the only thing I could see was the solid white stripe on the right side of the road. Robbie watched ahead as well as helping me stay to the left of the stripe. In the dark of the early night, we couldn't see any exit signs or even the neon business signs as we approached the Monteagle exit. We simply followed the white stripe off the interstate and up to US41. Turning left, we crept west toward Sewanee with visibility less than thirty feet.

Somehow we managed to find the turnoffs that took us back to our home, narrowly missing a cow in the middle of the road. The answer to the besetting question was clear. Yes, I could get through the cloud of unknowing just as safely as I had survived the fog and friction of war, providing I put my whole trust in the Lord and did everything I could to follow his lead.

Soon, Robbie began to be ill when she woke up. Morning sickness had struck, and she would be giving birth to our first child sometime in July. We were excited about such wonderful news, but the morning sickness continued unabated. It was as if we were being reminded of all the troubles we had seen in our first year of marriage before we were given a new and joyous start.

Other young couples were experiencing the same joy with the beginnings and additions to their families, providing us with a growing circle of friends.

The Sisters of St. Mary were also thrilled that a new life would inhabit their former home in the not too distant future. Throughout the fall, Robbie and I walked down to the Convent, now housed in their former schoolhouse, for Sunday Eucharist. Father Howard Rhys, the New Testament professor, was their chaplain and agreed to teach Robbie about the Episcopal Church in preparation for her confirmation when Bishop Gosnell came for a regents meeting in February. We learned to love him as a truly holy man, steeped in his faith and kindly in his ways. I served him at the altar for over a year, soaking up his powerful sermons and basking in his holy glow.

In addition to taking classes from Father Rhys, Robbie took up piano and art lessons to keep her interested during the long hours I was reading, studying, and attending classes. She also took a part time position teaching in the early childhood program at the parish church, St. Paul's on the Mountain, or Otey Parish, as it was commonly known.

As academic life became more hectic, we found ourselves left out of many impromptu suppers held in the married student housing area. It was hard to believe that four miles separated us from full fellowship with our fellow pilgrims. So we would invite groups of them out to the apartment for periodic dinners. That seemed to help, but I wondered if it was more than the short distance. Could it be the relatively palatial apartment we had, or the new cars? Being on active duty with the Air Force meant that I was receiving a good salary and that the government was paying all my seminary bills, while some of my classmates were barely getting by.

When I was approached by Christ Church, San Antonio about renewing my pledge for 1974, I told the rector that I was going to cut it to five percent and give the other half to the Dean's Discretionary Fund so he could help some of the seminarians in unhappy financial straits.

Chapter 9

I asked Dean Holmes to keep it in confidence; the Lord had provided us with extra resources and we could help a little bit. We were committed to the Biblical tithe, and five percent of a captain's compensation would provide a good bit of assistance to impoverished seminarians.

Robbie's coworker at St. Paul's, Martha Lowe, took an instant liking to her, as did most people. One evening, she invited us to join her and her husband Jim for dinner at their home. During the cocktail time, she thoughtfully explained that rice was not on the menu. I assured her that she did not need to worry, because rice was a rare part of our diet in Hanoi. When we sat down in the candlelit dining room and returned thanks for the food to be set before us, she presented in elegant fashion the soup for the evening, borsht. *Now what was that?* I wondered. Potato? Beet? It's red; must be beet. Oops, wrong again – red cabbage. I nearly gagged. Gently pushing the bowl away, I explained, "I'm sorry. Cabbage soup was our main staple over there. I just can't eat it." Martha graciously removed the bowl and we completed the meal with our new friendship intact, even finding humor in my unexpected reaction. Not even God's blessing could calm my gag reflex to the tastes of Vietnam.

In January 1974 I was summoned to Dean Holmes' office. He began by saying, "What's this I hear about Robbie being secretly confirmed?"

"What? What are you talking about? She hasn't been confirmed. Bishop Gosnell will be out next month and will confirm her then, at the convent. The service will be public and the seminary is invited."

"Oh, that's not what I heard," he said. As we continued to talk, the Dean told me that the liturgy professor, the college chaplain, and the parish priest had come to him complaining that the confirmation should be held in their respective chapels.

I had no idea that there was any problem and had not been approached by any of them. Robbie wanted to be confirmed at the convent because some of the elderly ladies who lived there couldn't travel even the four miles into town.

I couldn't believe that such controversy had arisen or that I had not been included in it until Dean Holmes called me to his office. After talking with Robbie, we decided to move it to St. Luke's chapel, but I insisted that it be registered on the books of Christ Church, San Antonio.

On February 21, we gathered with nuns, seminarians, faculty and friends in St. Luke's chapel as Bishop Gosnell presided over the Confirmation Eucharist. We had decided to combine it with a blessing of our marriage and prayers for a safe delivery of our first child. It was a terribly important day in our lives, but we came away a little sad that some of our convent friends could not be present.

Lent began the following Wednesday, providing a time for Robbie and me to experience that holy season together. The previous Lent had been very strange in the Hanoi Zoo; 1974 was considerably better. The cycle of the liturgical seasons in a seminary community is a real blessing; filled with worship, quiet days, and celebrations that are rare in a parish setting. Everyone participates and understands at least in part what is meant by each day. The academic load seemed somewhat lighter as we prepared ourselves to celebrate the Lord's Resurrection in April.

The second semester was as multifaceted as the fall. Personality conflicts had subsided somewhat, but one or two continued on a regular basis, particularly in preceptorials, and were rarely resolved. That seemed strange in a place where we gathered to know Christ in each other and to support each other in our callings.

After months of showing no emotion, and certainly no anger to my captors, I continued to try to keep strong negative feelings buried; but in seminary and beyond they would erupt periodically when I was faced with stressful situations – and always out of proportion to the current event.

Chapter 9

I was unable to gain insight from the phenomenon at the time, and would ever so slowly learn in the years ahead. I felt like St. Paul praying for his affliction to be removed. I knew that God could and would bring relief, but how could I open myself to it? The seal that kept God's hand out of the worst of my memories effectively prevented his grace from entering.

I continued to be wracked by internal conflict and nightmares. Throughout seminary, I would have dreams in which my body would suddenly stiffen and shake the bed. Robbie was startled awake many times. When the "jerks" woke me up, it felt as if I had just fallen from a great height and hit the ground hard. Those night jerks returned periodically for many years, particularly after I gave speeches and talks on my experience.

As the junior year came to a close, I was looking forward to returning to San Antonio where I would be enrolled in Clinical Pastoral Education at the State Hospital. Ted Boya, also from the Diocese of West Texas, came along to help drive. We dropped Robbie off in Blytheville to visit her parents for a few days before she flew the rest of the way. Ted and I drove the two additional days into Texas.

Being in San Antonio made it convenient to receive an annual physical examination at Brooks AFB. For the first five years after repatriation the USAF followed the ex-POWs closely to ascertain any delayed physical effects that our incarceration might have had. While it was not nearly as complex as my experience at Scott the previous summer, at least they didn't find any recurrence of the blood problem that had indicated some sort of cancer.

My class at the State Hospital was a group of interfaith seminarians from a variety of backgrounds, and mostly very unsure of ourselves as we contemplated working in a mental facility for the next three months.

After a few days of orientation and a day on a ward as a "patient," each of us was assigned to a ward of our own to act as chaplain for the patients and staff. Periodically we would preach at the ecumenical worship service, where anything might happen from roaming to argumentative patients.

One patient I would never forget was a man with Huntington's Disease. His arms and legs flailed as he walked or when he tried to sit still; and his mental capacity was drastically reduced. He had been quite successful until his genetic disorder took over. I learned that the gene for this disease was always dominant and was passed from parent to child, with each child having a 50/50 chance of getting the affected chromosome.

Huntington's manifests itself in a variety of ways, most prominently by dementia and/or loss of control of the large muscles of the limbs. The latter causes arms and legs to flail around, giving the appearance of a very awkward dance-like movement. The disease is chronic, progressive, and, at that time, usually fatal within ten years of symptom onset.

Typically, Huntington's appears in a person in his or her mid-forties or older, after they have borne their children. There was no confident test to determine its presence so that the person could choose to forego bearing children. I found that my work with this man was both interesting and profoundly sad. Little did I know then how this disease would affect my family in years to come.

Each week the class would meet in the chaplain's office to debrief our experiences on the ward and to encourage and challenge each other as we sought to become pastors and understanding counselors. The group work was much like the groups at Sewanee, but the summer experience was exceptionally more difficult.

In mid-June Robbie and I attended the first reunion of the prisoners of war from Vietnam. Because I was known to be in seminary and living in San Antonio where the reunion was held,

Chapter 9

I was invited to sit with Robbie at the head table and to give the invocation. The speaker for the event was Governor Ronald Reagan of California, an old western actor turned statesman. Robbie and I were thrilled to be in the green room with the Reagans and to be able to chat with them privately.

After the White House dinner the year before, we began to feel like we were moving in some pretty heady company. Socializing with legendary war heroes, ministering to institutionalized mental patients, and serving affluent parishioners of Christ Church, I found the variety of associations to be a source of both wonder and enrichment.

On July 13, Robbie woke up suddenly as her water broke. The day of our son's birth was here. I quickly got dressed, thought she was doing the same, and took the packed bag to the car and started the engine. As I returned to the apartment to help her out, I found her in the shower shaving her legs. "Good Lord! What are you doing?"

"Getting ready." I couldn't believe it. When she finally got in the car, I raced the quarter mile to the emergency entrance, took her in, and returned to park the car. I placed a quick phone call to my parents (who had been visiting for a week and were due to leave that day), then sat with Robbie for another 13 hours waiting for Stephen to make his appearance. After his surprise sunrise announcement, it was nearly dusk before the nurse held his squalling pale body up to the window in the father's waiting room.

What a blessing I saw at that moment. The doctors had sent me out of the room so they could check her progress and before I could be summoned back to watch, he forced himself out into life. Robbie and Stephen were both very healthy. My mother stayed on for a few more days to relieve Robbie while I worked. A week or so later, Robbie's mother joined us to visit her second grandson.

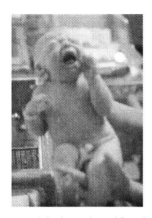

The bishops of the diocese and the priests of Christ Church were very attentive to us at this joyous time, visiting Robbie in the hospital and helping us in any way possible. It seemed everything was beginning to turn out very well as we moved forward to our next year at Sewanee.

On Sunday, August 18, we presented Stephen Wade Certain for baptism at the font of Christ Church. Bishop Gosnell presided, assisted by the rector, Father Ben Benitez, and his associate, Father Tommy Tomlin. As I entered the church that morning, I noticed a lady seated in the back, with a look I recognized from the State Hospital. As the family and sponsors gathered around the font later in the service, she tried to get past us. Mrs. Benitez took her aside to see what she wanted. "They're trying to drown that baby." The story seemed momentarily funny, but then I was struck by the profundity of her concern. Yes, we were going to drown him, return him to the womb of God, and bring him to new life in Christ Jesus our Lord.

Bishop Gosnell with Stephen and his parents at his Baptism

143

How many of the Christians gathered that morning, and how many of those surrounding fonts around the world, understood the true significance of what the Church meant by Holy Baptism? "Stephen, you are sealed by the Holy Spirit in Baptism, and marked as Christ's own forever."

Middler (second) year at the School of Theology was focused on four areas of study: church history, theology, ethics, and liturgics. The courses were quite interesting and effective as they gave substance to my sense of call.

The preceptorials continued as before, but initially with less conflict as we shared our experiences of the summer. With time, though, they became complaint sessions; in some, one member might be "raked over the coals" by another. "Transference" in the psychological sense began to take on new meaning, and before long, the old contentiousness returned.

The tension and sense of anger among the students reached a zenith during the winter and led to some serious questioning of faith. In the wisdom of the School, that was desirable and was touted as preparation for being able to assist other people in their own faith struggles as we entered parish ministry. Perhaps it did, but at the time it felt like a miserable darkness had settled upon us. Even memories of Hanoi sometimes paled in comparison to the interpersonal struggles in the seminary community. In Vietnam, the enemy was clearly identifiable and cellmates always backed each other up. In preceptorials, everything was often upside down. Before the year was out, these group experiences were thrown into my "closet of unredeemable life events."

As pressures mounted, my night jerks became much worse. They startled us and kept us from sleeping restfully. With two-hour feedings for the baby throughout the night, our weariness was compounded.

In the midst of the darkness of the "middler mood" which hit us all, we actually managed to draw closer to one another. New parents spent more and more time with each other, sharing experiences and lightening each other's loads. My study partners were helpful, often caring for Stephen, giving Robbie some time to relax. A new Common adjacent to the School of Theology provided a gathering place to let off steam and to keep us all on a more or less even keel.

Consequently, my prayer life actually deepened as I began spending time before going in for Morning Prayer saying an abbreviated Office with specific prayers for family, friends and personal concerns. These early-morning times with God, frequently with Stephen cuddled against my chest, began to take on a substance of their own. A half-hour with God in the early dawn brought peace to my soul, and became a permanent part of my spiritual journey.

Daily Morning Prayer in St. Luke's Chapel continued to provide a time of divine presence in the midst of trial, and built the foundation for my personal prayer life that supports and nourishes my soul every day. In that place, I learned to be silent, to listen for God's guidance after the reading of Scripture and within the prayers we offered. It was there that I began to understand the example of Our Lord when he withdrew from the crowds to be alone with the Father.

Another saving grace for the year turned out to be my field work assignment to Christ Church, South Pittsburg, Tennessee, about thirty miles south of the University. The rector, the Rev. Dr. Jack Wilson, and his wife Bettie, took us under their wing. Bettie helped Robbie through the postpartum blues that lingered through the fall, and Jack gave me meaningful ministry to accomplish and to balance the sense of pervasive gloom I felt on the mountain. In the warm bosom of Christ Church, our family was nurtured and given a sense of the kind of community that we longed for in the church.

Robbie and I struggled with our emotions throughout the year, finding peace in our remote apartment and in our association with the Sisters of St. Mary. Our son had brought great joy to our lives and we knew him to be a symbol of Christ's promise of new life coming from old death. A hurried wedding, the separation of war, the trauma of imprisonment, and a move to a completely new life in seminary had marked our first two years of marriage. There were enough changes in those years to test even a long-term marriage, but the Lord had seen us through and given us both deep love and a great gift in the life of our son.

In early 1975, renewed war in Vietnam was going badly for our former allies in the south. After two years of relative peace, the Communist north broke out of their various encampments and moved toward Saigon. Without the American presence or military aid the South Vietnamese army was quickly routed and pushed back toward the capital.

In mid-Lent, I sat with some other classmates in the common room of the seminary watching news of the crash of a C-5 cargo jet attempting to evacuate Vietnamese-American orphans from the city. Tears were streaming down my face and I could not talk for grief. In the next few days, a few of us gathered for the news of the evacuations, watching thousands of our nation's friends climbing the ladder atop the American Embassy, trying to board one of the many helicopters being sent in to pluck as many as possible to safety.

I was puzzled by the strange looks and shrugs coming from students and faculty who had opposed American involvement in the earlier war. They seemed unaffected by the tragedy before us, and registered no understanding of why I, a former combatant in Southeast Asia, would be in tears. For my part, I couldn't comprehend their apparent indifference, nor could I account for the depth of my grief.

In the 1960s and early 1970s young Americans had gone to Vietnam, fighting what they believed to be a just war defending a people striving for democracy and freedom from the oppressive Communist regime to the north. Despite the pure motivations of the soldier, airman, marine, and sailor, inept civilian authority had thwarted their efforts, and a hostile anti-war citizenry had condemned them when they returned from the field of battle. They were men and women of honor, hampered in the execution of their duty and disdained by their own countrymen. It seemed to me that every good we had sought to accomplish had been tainted by excessive death and destruction. And now, in one last valiant effort to whisk the Vietnamese children of American fighting men to safety and a new home, we were failing.

On April 30, it was again time to watch the news from Vietnam. As I sat in stunned silence before the television, surrounded by nearly the entire Seminary community, we witnessed the live scenes of the final evacuation of Saigon.

The stairs of the American Embassy filled with human beings stood out as a symbol of the hope of freedom given to us in our very creation. The War in Vietnam may have been a political failure, but I viewed our nation's inability to remove all the people seeking refuge as a sign of our real weakness and moral bankruptcy. Pictures of President Ford agonizing in his office were seared into my mind alongside those of the stairs and the wreckage of the C-5.

I wept unashamedly for those who died half a world away during that April and who would continue to die in that place in the years ahead. I wept for the hardened souls at home who could not see the tragedy of human suffering and the snuffing of a dim light of freedom. By the time the sun went down on April 30, the day Saigon fell, I wept for myself, feeling that my military service had lost substantial meaning.

While the academic year, coupled with the tragedy in Southeast Asia, seemed to be like living in a funnel cloud, there had been enough havens of rest and peace to keep us fairly focused on what lay ahead.

Chapter 9

As Robbie and I prepared to leave the mountain for another summer in San Antonio, this time at Christ Church exclusively, I received a phone call from Bishop Gosnell. "Bob, I understand you're coming to San Antonio this summer."

"Yes sir. Didn't I tell you that?" *Good grief! Did I forget to inform him? Is he going to chew me out?* I was beginning to sweat.

"Yes, you did. I'm calling to tell you that we are giving canonical exams to the graduates in a couple of weeks. I'd like you to take them and, if you pass, I'll ordain you to the deaconate before you return for your senior year. That way, when you graduate, I can ordain you to the priesthood and you can return to active duty as a full-fledged chaplain."

"OK, sir. I'll be there."

Now I was really sweating. After the controversy over Robbie's confirmation, this would likely bring down the wrath of the faculty. I immediately called Dean Holmes for an appointment. Upon entering his office, I told him what was up, and watched him slump lower into his chair. I explained the bishop's reasoning, reminded him that the diocese did not require General Ordination Exams, and promised not to wear my collar or otherwise disrupt the sensitivities of the faculty and student body. We both knew that he would have to handle damage control.

We decided that Robbie and Stephen would fly to Blytheville for an extended visit with her parents. For the next two weeks, in addition to the three-day drive to San Antonio, with a stop in Arkansas to pick up the family, I spent every free moment trying to get enough knowledge from the senior curriculum to have some chance of actually passing the canonicals. Steve Gideon grilled me on the material every afternoon, but I was anything but confident when we arrived in San Antonio in early June.

I had made an appointment to have my annual physical examination at the Brooks AFB hospital soon after my arrival.

Once again, I received a clean bill of health. However, there was never any in-depth psychological review, a lack that might have helped with the nightmares and interpersonal conflicts that abounded at Sewanee.

In the second week of June, I stood for orals with three graduates from the diocese, two from Sewanee and one from the Seminary of the Southwest in Austin. One of the Sewanee graduates failed. I passed. Robbie and I, along with the parish of Christ Church, rejoiced that my first ordination would occur in July. I prayed that God would make me worthy and that he would soothe the faculty of the School of Theology.

Father Tomlin, now the interim rector, served as confidant, minister, and mentor throughout the summer and well into the years ahead. The parish was a warm and supportive community, healing the soreness of the previous year, and building my confidence about my future ministry.

On July 27, the parish gathered for my ordination to the Sacred Order of Deacons in the One, Holy, Catholic and Apostolic Church. Bishop Gosnell presided; Suffragan Bishop for the Armed Forces, Clarence Hobgood, preached; in the congregation were his assistant,

Ordination to Deaconate

retired Army chaplain Charles Burgreen, and General John Flynn, the former senior ranking officer in the prisons of North Vietnam and now the commander of the basic training center at Lackland Air Force Base. My family had gathered to celebrate this day with me and with Robbie and Stephen.

As I waited to process in, I noticed Father John MacNaughton seated near the back. He had just arrived to become the rector of Christ Church, but was dressed in shirt and tie rather than clericals. When I asked him why he wasn't in the procession, he replied, "This is your day. If the people know who I am, they'll want to talk to me. They need to focus on you." I was stunned and humbled by his thoughtfulness, and my devotion to him was sealed from that moment on.

As I took my vows and felt the hands of the bishops on my head in ordination, I felt very much as I had in 1963 when I first perceived God's call to this day. "Take thou Authority to execute the Office of a Deacon in the Church of God committed unto thee; in the name of the Father, and of the Son, and of the Holy Ghost." Pride and fear, mixed with humility and joy filled my soul as I stood to be vested as a Deacon.

The Communion ended with the prayer of the people gathered, "Make him, we beseech thee, O Lord, to be modest, humble, and constant in his Ministration, to have a ready will to observe all spiritual Discipline; that he, having always the testimony of a good conscience, and continuing ever stable and strong in thy Son Christ, may so well behave himself in this inferior Office, that he may be found worthy to be called unto the higher ministries in thy Church."

I had read those words many times in the past two months, but the sound of them spoken by a large gathering of the people of God left me introspective, wondering if I could ever fulfill these words, and grateful that so many people stood in support of this ministry and of my place in it.

After the ceremony and reception, Fr. Tomlin took the extended Certain family to lunch at the King Wah Chinese Restaurant near the church. As we talked, Tommy ordered the meals. The first course was won ton soup. As mine was placed before me, I wondered how I was going to be able to handle this. I took a sip, but that flavor of cabbage soup with pork sent me back to Hanoi and all those bowls of cabbage soup.

I felt the oppression of imprisonment the moment I tasted it. I pushed it away gently, and explained to Tommy what was wrong. By any other name, it was still cabbage soup with pork. A little laughter lightened the tension.

I had been taught that physical senses, particularly smells and tastes, are the most direct triggers of memory. In the early years of freedom, flavors of foods would conjure up memories of incarceration. This was the second occasion in two years when friends inadvertently served cabbage soup flavored with pork. It took about a decade for me to redevelop a taste for cabbage in any form, even though I had grown up eating boiled cabbage, cole slaw, and won ton soup.

Other flavors and smells, the taste of the wafer and the wine of Communion, the smell of musty incense in a church, would remind me of both my entry into the Episcopal fellowship and of my ordination to the ministry. Similarly, the smell of burning kerosene or jet fuel brought back fond memories of life on the flightline. However, the importance of the emotions and memories triggered by these senses did not register. Within the memories, God had been with me; and from those memories he was calling me to new life. But the door was closed and the key was missing.

A few days after my ordination, we departed for our final year on the holy mountain of Sewanee. Perhaps this year it would become truly holy for me, as I knew it was for so many others ahead of me.

The senior year in seminary was focused on the more direct concerns of the practice of parish ministry, now brought into focus by the foundation of Scripture and the building block of church tradition of the previous two years. Ethics, theology, pastoral care, and the leadership of worship filled our time. Preceptorials continued to be an exercise alternating between spiritual insight and emotional strain and frustration. Slowly it began to dawn on me, usually as I meditated in my study as the sun began to rise, that the group sessions might actually be an experience of the church in microcosm.

Chapter 9

As seniors now, our class joined with the middlers to welcome the new crop of juniors to the mountain. The new arrivals reminded me of our introductory experiences two years earlier, and Robbie and I gained new friends to fill the gaps left by spring graduation. Both of us were surprised when I was elected president of the Student Body, and Robbie became president of the Spouses Association. After the rocky days of 1973, we became thoroughly engaged in the overall life of the School and her students.

For the second year, I continued at Christ Church, South Pittsburg, now ministering as a Deacon at the altar in that holy and life-giving place. Father Jack gave me more responsibility for youth, adult education, and preaching, and I began to feel comfortable in the ordained ministry. My prayer life was coming together in a more profound way than during the spiritual turmoil of the middler year. The entire liturgical cycle, both formal and informal, was giving substance and meaning to each of us as we stepped closer to graduation.

Stephen continued to be a source of wonder as he learned to toddle, walk, and speak. He was also a big hit with the nuns, who frequently dropped by to visit him as well as Robbie and me.

Robbie, now fully acclimated to the Episcopal expression of the Faith, audited church history while continuing to take piano and art lessons. We were beginning to get a glimpse of the appeal of Sewanee. Tensions began to subside in the class as we peered over the horizon toward graduation and ordinations.

In the fall of 1975, the seniors were given the requirement to write a major paper about the pursuit of ministry. Because of my wartime experience, I chose to write about the way in which Air Force combat officers and chaplains viewed the moral difficulties of warfare. While just war theory made participation in combat permissible and even necessary under certain circumstances, it didn't do much to assuage the internal turmoil of the combatant when he was sent forth by the nation to "kill people and break things."

With the assistance of my ethics professor, I developed a lengthy questionnaire to test the moral awareness and acuteness of combat aviators and chaplains of the Air Force. Part of the questionnaire also tested the impressions each of those groups had of the other. My hunch was that many combatants would have benefited from moral discourse with and spiritual direction from chaplains, but that neither group would have articulated it in that way.

I spent most of the fall developing the questionnaire, the rationale behind it, and a double-blind procedure to distribute and to collect them. I would first send copies of the blank forms to the command sections of the Strategic and Tactical Air Commands, the Air University, and the Chief of Chaplains office. They would then distribute them down the line to wings, squadrons, students, and chaplains. Completed forms were to be collected by wing educational officers, forwarded to the dean's office at the School of Theology, and finally returned to me for analysis. I hoped by that process to get honest and thoughtful answers that would help point to ways in which military chaplains could be trained as spiritual directors and guides to the people who faced the most severe moral and ethical issues on the field of combat.

I was stunned when the response came back from the Air Force Institute of Technology that the questionnaire could not be distributed without removing all questions having to do with moral or ethical dilemma. The letter stated that the form placed the officer in the difficult place of self-incrimination, even though the process I had devised insured that no one would see the completed forms except for me and that no raw data would ever be released. Historians for the Chief of Chaplains office later wrote, "It was decided that ... the negative reactions to the proposed survey by TAC (Tactical Air Command), operations personnel, Air University personnel, and some SAC (Strategic Air Command) personnel, outweighed its advantage.[1]

---

[1] John E. Groh, *Air Force Chaplains, Volume IV: Air Force Chaplains 1971-1980* (Office of the Chief of Air Force Chaplains, Washington, DC, 1986), 46.

Chapter 9

Unknown to me at the time, three chaplains, working together on a paper at the Air Command and Staff College (ACSC) about the spiritual lives of POWs in Hanoi, had completed a paper late in the year which concluded in part, "The early religious training of prisoners was extremely important. To develop the virtues of patience, courage, perseverance, and hope that were so important in prison life, the POW fell back to the religious training of home and church, to the practices and hymns of early family life, and to the Christian teachings on suffering and pain. ... The debriefings studied contained no mention of any spiritual direction or guidance given by chaplains to aircrew members. Although this establishes no ground for any inference that chaplains have been ineffective, ... it does serve as a point of challenge to chaplains to develop a program and an active ministry for the flying personnel they serve."[2]

Chaplain Groh's history points out that there was an intention to distribute the ACSC paper to senior commanders and chaplains, it was never done because of printing errors. As I look back, it seems that the institutional chaplaincy was no more eager to look into the decade-long pain of the war in Vietnam than I was. I limited my seminary paper to a critique of the official Air Force position, pointing out the need for the thorough discussion of just war criteria and of the moral and ethical issues facing combatants *before* battle was engaged. I received an excellent grade on the paper, but chose not to forward it to AFIT or the Chief of Chaplains. Perhaps an opportunity would present itself at a later date, when the war was more remote and emotions less volatile.

As 1976 appeared on the calendar, a few new clouds began to form. In January, I took the General Ordination Exams, not out of necessity but to demonstrate to the faculty and to myself that I had learned the requisite material to be ordained in the first place. In spite of the occasional dysfunction of my class, all thirteen of us passed all sections on the first effort. The dean and faculty were as pleased as we were.

---

[2] Ibid.

By the end of January, Robbie was once again waking up nauseous. Our second child would appear sometime in October. Another great joy was coming our way, but not before more struggles and trauma.

Vietnam returned again in some force in the early months of the year, surfacing my grief over the loss of friends and over the difficulty of finding reconciliation in the various factions created in our country by the great upheavals of the 1960s. My prayers, beyond daily concerns, turned more and more to seeking the good that God was doing during the winter of 1972-73. How would that experience inform and shape my ministry in redemption rather than sit below the surface like a tumor? The block for answering that question was my insistence that none of it was God's will, that it was a circumstance of war brought on by ideological competition between nations. Would I ever be able to see God in the deaths of friend and foe alike? Or would I simply tell stories whose meaning eluded me?

Fortunately, an emerging discipline of theological reflection taught at Sewanee led me to start looking for how and where God was working in my life. Consequently, I was gaining glimpses of understanding people whenever their lives are out of their own control, or their jobs or relationships have lost their meaning or are in danger of being lost. Like looking "through a mirror darkly" I was beginning to see good things in the various experiences of the months since our arrival on the mountain. The first test of that understanding came in February.

As I entered seminary, Bobby Thomas from my old crew was still listed as MIA, as were most of the members of Randy Craddock's crew. In January, some remains were repatriated and identified, including those of Ron Perry, Randy's defense officer. The escort, Capt. Denny Kono (an old Blytheville crewmember) called me at Sewanee to assist with the funeral. He told me of estrangement between Ron's widow, Kak, and the Perry family.

Chapter 9

There was considerable tension at the mortician's in Nashville and at the gravesite in Alabama. In the fall of 1971, when Ron was stationed at U-Tapao, he had married a Thai woman. His parents thoroughly disapproved of mixed-race marriages and made their feelings known to both Ron and Kak. The fact that she was Buddhist and not Christian raised their upset into the stratosphere. Captain Kono, a Hawaiian, was also of oriental heritage and a Buddhist, and he was concerned that his presence might rub salt into the wounds. Jim Lollar, the only surviving member of the crew and a close friend of the Perry family was also present to lend love and support.

My first funeral as a clergyman was exceptionally difficult. Denny and I talked with Mr. and Mrs. Perry about the Burial Office in the Episcopal Book of Common Prayer, which spoke so eloquently of hope for new life in the Resurrection, as an excellent choice for their son's military funeral. I read the Office in Nashville, and then listened to the sermon from the local pastor who never spoke of Ron's widow, made it clear that Jesus died for the "elect" only, and issued an "altar call" to non-Christians to give their lives to Christ. A second service in Alabama elicited from the same pastor an acknowledgment that Christ died for the sins of the whole world. Could those be two sides of the same story of grace? I couldn't see that at the time, or even frame the question.

Those words from the same pastor on two adjacent days would reappear in my mind's ear for many years, as though God was still trying to tell me something important. After years of experience, my theology would eventually conquer my irritation as I concluded that both were true, Christ did die for the sins of the world, and yes, he does invite all of his creation into the arms of his mercy.

At the graveside, I conducted the service, trembling in the icy wind and trying to maintain my composure during the twenty-one-gun salute. Denny had the diplomacy to change the flag on the coffin between Nashville and Alabama. He presented the flag from the gravesite to Kak, Ron's widow, in accordance with military protocol, in gratitude for Ron's service to his country.

After the ceremony, he presented the second flag, in accord with compassion and care, to the Perrys. So each part of Ron's family received the token of his ultimate sacrifice.

Denny and his wife Sue returned to our home in Sewanee, Tennessee for the night. There we were able to debrief our experience of the war's return – icy winds, gunfire, and alienation between Caucasians and Asians, Christians and others. Denny and I had fought together for peace, not for prejudice and division. It was very disturbing to the four of us to witness the effects still emanating from an intercultural and interfaith marriage and from the death of a son and husband in war.

Within days, I received another call from Bishop Gosnell in San Antonio. "Bob."

"Yes, sir?"

"Scott Field Bailey (the Bishop Coadjutor) and I will be in Sewanee for the Trustees meeting in April. I want to go ahead and ordain you to the priesthood while we're there. It'll save time and money when you graduate, so you can go on to your next assignment as a fully qualified Air Force chaplain."

"Yes, sir. I'll get it arranged." *Holy God, Holy and Mighty, Holy Immortal One, Have mercy on me.* I quickly dialed the phone, "Terry, we've got to talk." The Dean gave me an immediate appointment and I drove the four miles to his office with a huge knot in the pit of my stomach. What would the faculty say about this?

In our conversation, Dean Holmes assured me that he understood the bishop's reasoning, and would support me with the faculty. I insisted that I didn't care to have another fight about where the liturgy would take place. I had done two years of fieldwork, including a year as a deacon, in the parish in South Pittsburg, and strongly believed it should take place there. He seemed to slump lower in his chair, but agreed with me.

Chapter 9

I didn't seek to create any kind of problems for others at Sewanee, but I seemed to have a lot of trouble avoiding it. As I set about selecting participants in this very important day in my life, I included both faculty and other students. Everyone was invited to attend; and the parishioners began preparing for the service and the reception following.

As Easter Day approached on April 18, the clouds around me began to darken even more. While I prepared for ordination to the priesthood, Dean Holmes and I began to confer with each other about a problem growing toward scandal in the School of Theology. As President of the Student Body, I was often taken into his confidence. Robbie, as President of the Seminary Spouses Association, had come to me with a story, circulating among the wives, of spouse swapping among the students, including at least one faculty member.

Both Terry and I were now slumping deeply into our seats. The Dean said he would rather deal with a dozen cases of alcoholism than to face this crisis. I couldn't have agreed more. At the end of a very long hour, we had agreed to approach the people whose names had been connected with this conduct and to warn them to cease and desist immediately. Though we made our calls, I was never sure that anything changed other than the noticeable cooling of once friendly relationships and the fracturing of trust.

I was beginning to learn that moral outrage and damage control would be a part of church life just as it was in business, government, and the military. The very people who were set apart as examples to others were perhaps even more subject to the seductions of power, money, and sex than other segments of the population.

While my parents had taught me to "hate the sin but love the sinner," I found it very difficult to separate the people from the actions. I believed that leaders are called to a higher standard, and that failure to achieve that higher goal necessarily robbed the person of leadership. I hoped the dean would find a way to safeguard the Church as well as the seminary's reputation.

Lent was upon us once again, providing the full range of liturgies and observances of those holy days in the life of the Christian community and in the life of the seminary. While not nearly as austere as my Lent in Hanoi, this one was no less filled with darkness. I tried to take as much time as I could to reflect on God's work in my life as He moved me toward ordination.

In the midst of the social and moral concern in the School of Theology, the Board of Trustees convened, and the date arrived for me to kneel before the bishops to commit myself to the vows of a priest. Family members and old friends drove and flew in to proclaim their support for the new ministry. Robbie made vestments. Father Jack and Bettie Wilson were beaming with joyful anticipation. Many students and faculty members were excited and helpful in preparing for the day.

For a few days around the Feast of St. Mark, I was in the company of people who believed in God and in his call of me to the office of priest. It was a calm in the midst of the storm that was brewing on the Mountain.

At the appointed hour on Wednesday, April 28, to the tones of ancient hymnody, the quaint language of the ordinal, and the joy of all of us gathered together, I took the vows of a priest as set forth in the Book of Common Prayer. As Bishop Gosnell intoned the words of the *Veni, Creator Spiritus*, I knelt before them. The bishops and priests gathered around me and laid the full weight of their hands upon my head as Bishop Gosnell continued, "Therefore, O Father, through Jesus Christ your Son, give your Holy Spirit to Robert; fill him with grace and power, and make him a priest in your Church. May he exalt you, O Lord, in the midst of your people; offer spiritual sacrifices acceptable to you, boldly proclaim the gospel of salvation; and rightly administer the sacraments of the New Covenant. Make him a faithful pastor, a patient teacher, and a wise councilor. Grant that in all things he may serve without reproach, so that your people may be strengthened and your Name glorified in all the world.

All this we ask through Jesus Christ our Lord, who with you and the Holy Spirit lives and reigns, one God, for ever and ever." And the people responded in a loud voice, "Amen."

The weight of those hands upon my head seemed most burdensome and I trembled under them. When they were removed following the prayer of ordination, I felt as light as a feather. I had fought against this moment for ten years before surrendering and then struggling through another four as I strove to be able to answer the questions of the examination of the Ordinal.

Now I was dressed in the vestments crafted for me by my beloved Robbie, and holding our first blessing as parents in my arms as pictures were taken to record the day. My Methodist parents, Robbie's Baptist parents, and my old Catholic friend and former crew commander, Mel Polek were there to add their blessing as truly ecumenical witnesses to the hope for God's Kingdom on earth.

Thursday was the normal day for the seminary Eucharist in St. Luke's Chapel. My classmates, eager to acknowledge my ordination, pressed me to be the celebrant the next morning.

Ordination to the priesthood

At first I protested that some in our community might be offended, but relented because ordination was of God, and much of God's confrontation with the world was thought to be offensive. As I celebrated my first Eucharist as a priest, I was filled with the awe of suddenly finding myself at home, much like I had felt when I stumbled into the Church of Our Saviour in 1965. I knew in my heart that I was where God had placed me.

In May, I received orders to report to the chaplain's office at Andrews Air Force Base in Camp Springs, Maryland. I had asked to be assigned to combat forces, but instead I was going to start my ministry at the home of Air Force One. I thought the personnel people at the Chief of Chaplains office were ignoring me; Robbie thought I was being placed in such a prominent place as a sign of the Chief's and God's favor. It would be years before I ever began to understand her spiritual insight in this matter.

We flew to Maryland to locate housing and to arrange for the shipment of our household goods. Base housing was limited, so we bought a town home in a suburb of Upper Marlboro, a few miles from the back gate of Andrews.

That last month at the School of Theology was very hectic. Robbie continued to suffer from morning sickness and was homesick to be with her parents. I sent her home for a two-week visit while I oversaw the packing and shipment of our household goods. As I drove off the mountain I stopped at the stone pillars marking the extent of the Domain of the University of the South.

The limit of the Domain was one where departing students would touch the roof of their cars to grasp their guardian angel for their time away from this holy place; and where returning students would touch the roof to release her to fly free in the haven that was Sewanee. I stopped that day to pray for the indwelling of the Holy Spirit, and to touch the roof of my car one last time.

Chapter 9

Theological reflection, born out of prayer and seeking to find God's hand at work in all events of human experience and life, was just a thread, not yet woven into the tapestry of my life, as I made the trek up the east coast toward Maryland and a reunion with my wife and son. Later I would give thanks to God for not letting that thread break. But on that day, I made the trip slowly to my first assignment as a priest and a chaplain, never expecting to return to Sewanee, Tennessee. Unbeknownst to me, my Guardian Angel would be working overtime to break through the sealed door of unredeemable events, behind which I now placed the pains and heartaches of the School of Theology.

Chapter 10

A New Chaplain

Within a few days, we were moving into our three-level townhouse home in Upper Marlboro, Maryland. Built into the side of a hill, the center floor and the lower floor were at ground level. The center floor contained the living room, dining room and kitchen. The family room was below, and the bedrooms above.

The room that would be Stephen's had been used by the former owner as an office, and was painted with a red ceiling and shutters. The first few nights, the baby was very restless, screaming out whenever we tried to put him in his crib. To me, the room seemed oppressive with its dark ceiling; so my first chore  was to paint it and the shutters white. That also solved the problem with Stephen, and marked an interesting relationship that he and I would share for many years, the parallel emotional response to life events.

The Senior Staff Chaplain, Colonel A. C. (Ace) Holler, had been a navigator like myself, wearing both the wings and the cross above his left breast pocket. I thought it would be a real blessing to work under such a man, and alongside what I deemed to be a good crew of young chaplains – Methodist, Catholic, Baptist, Congregational and Jewish.

The military chaplaincy is one place where ecumenical action and cooperation has the opportunity to lead the religious community. Chaplains are assigned to care for all the military members and their dependants, and must function as pastors to everyone who seeks them out. A large base like Andrews would have a Jewish rabbi, several Roman Catholic priests, and a number of Protestant clergy, including an African-American and someone from a liturgical church, and maybe an Orthodox priest. Each chaplain is assigned to care for the members of two or more squadrons, to minister to them as a counselor and advocate, to participate in and pray over their various ceremonies, and to be available to them for spiritual counsel and guidance. Worship services are designed for the entire base community, and the congregants are not necessarily associated with any of the units to which the presiding chaplain is assigned. A smaller base might have only two or three chaplains, usually Catholic and Protestant, the numbers of available chaplains being the limiting factor.

Coming from the crew force, my vision of the way in which we would work together was similar to that of a B-52 crew. Each chaplain was a specialist in his own faith or denominational group, and brought that expertise to the team to accomplish the overall mission of the chaplaincy to provide for the free exercise of religion on military installations around the world and to care for the souls of the men and women committed to our care. There was no place for denomination competition in the military as we cared alike for all the people. Each chaplain had at least three constituencies: the assigned units, drop-in counselees, and the worship group. The field was ripe for cooperation and mutual support among the various chaplains.

I learned that I had replaced a Lutheran chaplain, and would be responsible for the liturgical service at Chapel Two, the former Camp Springs Methodist Church. The old building reminded me of Christ Church, South Pittsburg – white clapboard siding, steeple, stained glass windows, and an altar. Surrounding it was a cemetery dating back before the American Civil War. On my first Sunday, Robbie and I were both surprised to find that the congregation was largely African-American. My limited experience of liturgical Protestant churches was that they were mostly Caucasian, and I looked forward to a new experience with a mixed congregation.

The second week, only a handful of retired personnel and their spouses came to services. I was dumbfounded. When I spoke to Chaplain Holler about it on Monday, I asked him if he hadn't put me in the "Gospel service" by mistake. He assured me that I was to continue to offer liturgical worship at that hour on Sunday, but I had a gnawing sense that it was a mistake.

My office was in a brand-new chapel located in the base exchange complex and near the enlisted housing area. Armed with a new degree and just enough training in "proper" church architecture to be highly opinionated, I declared the place to be both ugly and unworkable. The building didn't look like a church, the color scheme was not to my taste, the cork bulletin boards in the offices smelled of smoke, the roof leaked, and the sidewalks had not yet been completed. Perhaps the worst thing of all was that the entrance to the building faced away from the housing area and all the sidewalks approached from the base exchange parking lot. My training told me that the message of the building was that it was not the place for the airmen who lived in the dormitories behind it.

Andrews had about 6,000 enlisted personnel assigned to duty. Single members were housed in dormitories; but most of the married men and women were ineligible for on-base housing because of their junior grade.

The cost of living on the economy of suburban Maryland placed a significant hardship on these young married couples. As a result, family economic stress was prevalent, and marital difficulties abounded.

It seemed to me that the chaplains had a great responsibility to the enlisted men and women to provide them with a spiritual haven in the midst of their troubling living conditions. However, the worship services were geared more to retirees than to active duty personnel, and more to officers than to enlisted personnel.

Even so, worship services were sparsely attended. The total Sunday attendance at six Protestant services rarely exceeded 800, with a similar total at seven Catholic masses. Retirees and their families accounted for about half of that number. The main chapel would seat all the active duty communicants at one time. But the worship program was geared toward wide variety in the name of providing for the widest number of traditions: liturgical (Episcopal and Lutheran, etc.), Gospel (largely African-American), contemporary, traditional, and conservative.

I began to lobby the chaplains to consider changing our emphasis by holding only one Protestant and one Catholic service on Sunday morning and to provide other services at shift-change and other hours throughout the week that would accommodate enlisted workers on the base. That idea found no root among the chaplains.

My transition from seminary into the chaplaincy did not go well. I had an idea of parish ministry from seminary fieldwork; and I had a hope for the meaningfulness of chaplains in the lives of military members and their families. But neither of those vague concepts had prepared me for conducting a "ministry of presence" in the units assigned to me. I felt confident and competent with counseling, marriage preparation, liturgies and preaching. But I felt exceptionally awkward making visits to work areas on the flightline, maintenance shops, and mission planning rooms, the very places I had known so intimately a few years earlier. It never occurred to me that my discomfort came from approaching danger – that of opening the sealed door of my memory.

The units I was assigned to cover as a chaplain included the crews of Air Force One, the Presidential aircraft, and of the National Emergency Airborne Command Post (NEACP, pronounced "knee-cap"), the so-called "Doomsday" airplane, as well as the various support and maintenance squadrons that made their missions possible. While I enjoyed visiting in their areas, and even flying in the front of the NEACP aircraft on one occasion, I never did feel like much more than an odd appendage to them. Only on rare occasion was I asked to counsel with the assigned personnel; and none of them ever attended the worship service I led.

During the first few months, I searched for things to do in the office, welcoming counseling appointments, projects, and paper work as a diversion from the frustration that grew from seeing great need and no solutions. Perhaps I was just too far out of step with the institutional chaplain service to adapt easily. Rather than opening the door of my experience to find God's hand at work, I opened it only to shove more "unredeemable" experiences in.

With a second child on the way, I set about building a new bunk bed for Stephen as he outgrew the crib. Robbie and I had found plans for a "fire truck" bed in a *Good Housekeeping Magazine*, enlarged it to accommodate twin mattresses, and set out to build it for our son. As I had discovered in the ceramic shop on Guam, working with my hands freed my mind to ponder the things that led to spiritual turmoil.

I set up shop on the lower level of our townhouse and purchased the necessary materials – wood, hardware, paint, and tools. In good weather I was able to do the sawing in the back yard, then bring the pieces into the basement family room to assemble.

In mid-August the project was beginning to take shape. From the raw materials, an antique fire truck began to emerge. It had plywood tires with white sidewalls, running boards, bumpers and an engine compartment that doubled as a toy box. Windows were cut into the sides to open up the bottom bunk, and yellow "ladders" served as bed rails for the upper one.

As I started to assemble the project for painting, Robbie called down the stairs saying she thought she was in labor and appealing to me to come up to time her contractions. Since the baby wasn't due until mid-October, I thought she was imagining things. So, I had her bring the stopwatch downstairs where I could continue working while timing her contractions. After four or five such events eight minutes apart, it became apparent that things were not as they should be.

Finally, I put the tools away and helped Robbie back upstairs to the car and a quick trip to Andrews and Malcolm-Grow USAF Medical Center. The doctor was no more pleased than we were about this development, and gave her medication to stop the contractions and told her to stay in bed as much as possible. He wanted her to carry the baby at least another six weeks.

Finishing the bed took on a new urgency when we returned home. If the baby made her appearance earlier than mid-October we would need a place to put Stephen and enough time to get him out of the crib. Two weeks later, we once again made a trip to the hospital to stop the contractions, and again two weeks after that.

Working evenings, I finally finished the bed. I was really proud of it and Stephen was excited about having such a neat structure for a bed and play area. Once the paint was dry, I disassembled it and carried each piece up the two flights of stairs to his bedroom. The largest piece was the base, containing the running boards and "wheels" and being longer than the others by the length of the engine compartment. As I took it down the hallway and began to make the turn into his room, a big problem became apparent.

The base was too long, wide and deep to maneuver into the room! The "boat in the basement" cliché reared its ugly head! I returned the main section to the basement for modification. I decided that if I cut the running boards off (which were connected to the wheels), everything would fit through the bedroom door and I could patch it back together in the room. Fortunately, it worked.

The bed filled the room, making it difficult to maneuver around it for bed-making and other tasks. But Stephen loved his new toy and enjoyed climbing on it and pretending to race down the road on his way to a fire. Getting him to actually sleep in it was another matter.

One of the benefits of living in Maryland was that we were close to family and friends. My sister and her family lived in Baltimore, as did Mel Polek and his. Visits with each of them provided welcome times of fellowship and joy in the midst of my growing frustration with the chaplaincy.

Chapter 10

That fall, though, was marked by the sadness of my grandmother Gertrude Certain's death at age ninety-three. When I was a boy growing up in Garden City, Georgia, she lived in a small mobile home on our property and was my favorite Scrabble partner. When I was having difficulty learning to tie my shoes, she offered me a dime if I got it right – problem solved! But after we moved to Maryland in 1963, she had elected to move in with her youngest son, Lyle, on St. Simon's Island rather than moving with us. During the intervening thirteen years I had seldom visited with her, and our letters and phone calls were sporadic. Still, her death felt like an awful passage.

My father and mother were on a trip to England at the time, scheduled to return to the States in about a week. Dad had left instructions with his brother that, should Grandmother die, he was to go ahead with the funeral without waiting for them to return, since the difficulty and cost of changing tickets was too great. However, since their return was only three days beyond the funeral, I pleaded with my uncle to postpone it until Dad could be present. Actually, I was overbearing in my insistence, acting like the know-it-all recent seminary graduate that I was. I was also feeling guilty about things left unsaid to my Grandmother; and about my inability to get away from military duty and my obligations to my family to attend the funeral myself.

On October 20, we made our last trip to the hospital. The baby was full term, so the labor pains were allowed to continue. Because of the false alarms, her primary physician was slow coming to the delivery room, arriving just in time to see the birth of Mary Foster, our healthy baby girl. After two months of trying to prevent her birth, we were both overjoyed to have her in the family.

In mid-November, Robbie brought the children to our little chapel service, where we used the Episcopal service of "Thanksgiving for the Birth of a Child" to celebrate her arrival.

The following week, Chaplain Holler called me into his office to tell me that I should not have baptized my daughter at the base chapel. I was both puzzled and aggravated. I explained to him that I had not done that yet, but that I intended to do so in January. He felt it was unwise to do so because some people who came from traditions that did not baptize babies would be offended and it would be best to take her to a civilian church off base.

I reminded him that all liturgical churches baptized infants and that there should be no objection from any of the regular participants in that service, with the one possible exception of the organist, who was an employee, not a congregant. I fully intended to conduct that service for the benefit of the worshipers and the convenience of my family, and if the organist objected, I would give her the day off when we baptized Mary.

I left his office wondering how long I would last as an Air Force chaplain. While crewmembers of different grades were free to confront each other as equals and professionals, the look on Chaplain Holler's face told me that the same was not true among the chaplains. This situation seemed very similar to the controversy that had surrounded Robbie's confirmation service at Sewanee, and conjured up many of the same feelings within me.

By the time 1977 began, I thought I was getting the hang of being an Air Force chaplain. As the project officer for the base prayer breakfast, I had invited Dean Terry Holmes to be the guest speaker, and we enjoyed a sell-out crowd. Chaplains Hiram (Doc) Jones (United Methodist), LaVerne Schuller (Roman Catholic) and I held an interdenominational Communion service that also went well. Since we couldn't really share in the receiving of the elements of bread and wine, we said the prayer of consecration over separate elements and communicated our people at different stations in the chapel. It was a step in the direction of understanding for Catholics, Protestants, and Episcopalians that would not have been possible a few years earlier.

The Certain family at Mary's Baptism

The Sunday liturgical service had settled into a good routine, with a handful of faithful congregants, mostly retired, and my little family. On the Feast of the Baptism of Our Lord in January 1977, with my parents and other friends joining in the worship, we baptized Mary, marking her as Christ's own forever.

One Sunday, as I was facing the altar saying the consecration prayer over the bread and wine, I heard some giggling among the people. As I glanced over my shoulder to see what was happening, there was Stephen standing behind me with his arms raised like mine. It was all I could do to keep from laughing out loud; and it was a moment of great pride for me.

One of the duties the chaplains shared was weddings. Each of us was assigned a particular weekend and was responsible for preparing the couple and officiating their service, regardless of denomination. Of course, Catholic and Protestant weddings were handled separately. One week I was given an appointment with a couple who sought to be married in the summer and wanted to start the process of scheduling the chapel.

When I met with them, I determined that they were legally barred from using our chapels. The bride, while the daughter of a retired Air Force sergeant, was over twenty-three and no longer eligible to use government facilities; the groom was a civilian with no military connections. Neither of them were part of any religious group, though the woman claimed to be a Congregationalist by background. Rather than turn them down completely, I referred them to John Smelzer, the hospital chaplain, a Congregationalist pastor and a major, for further determination. He, too, turned them down on the grounds of ineligibility. I thought that was the end of the situation; but it would return several months later.

About the same time, a Navy enlisted man and his fiancée approached me about their wedding. This one, too, struck me as a problem. Since he was divorced, I told him that I couldn't officiate without a lot of difficulty, and referred them to the Navy chaplain at Andrews instead. Over the next several weeks the Navy chaplain also became concerned, in part because the prospective groom never brought in his divorce decree as requested. Then, on the day of the rehearsal, the chaplain discovered that the groom was not divorced and may have had two wives already. He denied that suggestion at the rehearsal, but failed to show for the wedding. When he reported for duty the following Monday, he was arrested and charged with bigamy.

In the meantime, I was finally scheduled to attend the Chaplains' Orientation Course at Maxwell AFB in Montgomery, Alabama. After groping my way trying to be a new priest and a new chaplain, I hoped the six weeks in school would help me understand how to adapt to both roles. While I learned a few things about how the chaplaincy was organized and how to keep up with various reporting requirements, the course was really designed for people who had just entered the service but who had at least five years of ministry under their belts. My situation was reversed from that.

Chapter 10

Being separated from my wife and children was not the most pleasant time, either. I missed the little ones, and Robbie began to suffer from weakness and numbness. At first the doctors tested her for multiple sclerosis, but that proved negative. The real cause would remain elusive for years to come. I felt as frustrated and helpless as she must have felt when I was in prison, wanting to be with her but constrained by military necessity. Fortunately, my sister and her husband lived in Baltimore, and were able to care for my family in my absence.

When I returned from the Chaplains' School, Doc Jones came into my office to tell me that Chaplain Holler had gotten a call from the Chief of Chaplains office in Washington wanting to know why a member of the chapel community had been refused a wedding at Andrews. As he told the story, it sounded like it might be the same couple that Chaplain Smelzer and I had turned down a few months earlier. Chaplain Jones confirmed that it was indeed the same couple. I made an appointment with Chaplain Holler to explain to him the circumstances of the rejected wedding. He seemed to understand our reasons.

A couple of weeks later, the staff was discussing the various difficulties we were having with scheduling, especially with weddings, because of the number of personnel from other area military installations that came to us for services. I reminded the group of the rejected wedding that had resulted in a call from the Chief of Chaplains office. Chaplain Holler stated that he was going to do that wedding, though it had "nothing to do with a call from the Secretary's office." I was amazed. We needed the Senior Staff Chaplain to support us in our efforts to focus our ministry for the Andrews community, and his decision undercut our efforts.

Chaplain Holler insisted that it was important to officiate at weddings of dependants of retired military members because those retirees were an important lobby with the Congress.

The Secretary of the Air Force had instructed the bases to cater to them, and he intended to do just that. I insisted that the Chaplains Service could not do so without violating our ecclesiastical responsibilities to represent and not to compete with our denominations, and that such an order was unlawful.

This situation seemed to confirm all my worst fears about the importance of most chaplains to the troops. The people who needed us were the young men and women of the active duty force. Our civilian counterparts were much better equipped to take care of senior officers, retirees, and former dependents. This controversy reminded me of the senior micromanagement of the Vietnam War and Linebacker II that resulted in untold unnecessary suffering.

A few days later, my old mentor from South Pittsburg, Father Jack Wilson, called to tell me he was being considered for the rector's position at St. Barnabas-on-the-Desert parish in Scottsdale, Arizona. He was pretty sure he would get the call and, if he did, wanted to know if I could leave the Air Force to become his assistant. That temptation was all I needed; and I made up my mind hard and fast. The only problem was, Jack didn't receive the call to St. Barnabas.

I called Bishop Gosnell in San Antonio to see if he had any openings and if he would be willing to take me off active duty. I dreaded asking him and felt that I was letting him down by even considering leaving active duty. In his usual gracious manner he put me in touch with the Rev. Marvin ("Red") Bond at St. Peter's parish in Kerrville, who was looking for an assistant. The pay was only about half of what I was making in the Air Force, but I figured we could live with that because of the difference in costs between the Texas hill country and the Washington suburbs.

I made an appointment with the Chief of Chaplains, Lt. Gen. Hank Meade, and went to discuss my future with him. I explained to him that I was discouraged and disillusioned with my place in the chaplaincy. I was as confident as ever about my call to the priesthood, but I no longer had that same confidence about military ministry. The biggest problem was the obligation I had accepted when the Air Force sent me to seminary. The pay-back time was calculated at three months for each month of school, which in my case meant another eight years.

At the end of the hour, he said, "Bob, the first thing you have to be is a priest; the second is a chaplain. If you can't become a good priest on active duty, I'll release you, providing you retain a reserve commission to continue your educational commitment. Then, if you decide to come back any time before you make major, you can do it. But if you'll stay, I'll send you anywhere in the world you want to go." He offered to send me to Europe if I would stay in, agreeing that Andrews was a difficult place to work. I felt that Robbie would be unhappy that far away from her parents and sister. I elected to leave active duty, and submitted my resignation effective September 1, 1977, with leave to start in August. My reserve commission started the following day.

Robbie was none too pleased with my decision and tried to assure me that we could adjust to the chaplaincy. I was so blinded by arrogance, stubbornness, and rage that I simply couldn't hear her point. The economic loss would be hard to bear, but I didn't care and knew that God would help us adjust to that peripheral concern if I was faithful to his call.

When I was putting the "for sale" sign in front of the house, a man driving by spotted it, stopped to ask the price, and agreed to buy it right there on the spot. That seemed like enough of a sign from God for me to be convinced that my decision was the right one.

Within the month, we were packed up and ready to leave. As we departed Maryland I knew that God had been at work in our family life, in Stephen's growth and Mary's birth, and in the times we had shared with family and friends in that place. Robbie's continued health problems were worrisome, but her spirit and her faith were strong. Placing my active duty chaplaincy in the "unredeemable" collection I was amassing would cloud my vision for all the good that was ours as we moved west.

Chapter 11

A Retreat from the USAF

Way of the Cross, Station 1

Christ speaks: In Pilate's hands, My other self, I see My Father's will. Though Pilate is unjust, he is the lawful governor and he has power over Me. And so the Son of God obeys a son of man. If I can bow to Pilate's rule because this is My Father's will, can you refuse obedience to those whom I place over you?

Man replies: My Jesus, Lord, obedience cost You Your Life. For me it costs an act of will – no more – and yet how hard it is for me to bend. Remove the blinders from my eyes that I may see that it is You whom I obey in all who govern me. Lord, it is You.[1]

When we arrived in Kerrville, Texas several days later, I discovered that the moving company had placed our household goods in storage for a few days before starting them on the way across country. Spending a week in a motel with two small children was difficult, but not terribly unpleasant.

Finally we were notified to meet the truck at our rental house to receive our goods. It seemed like the movers were unloading all day, and as the last boxes were removed from the truck, I realized

---

[1] Clarence Enzler, *Everyman's Way of the Cross.* Notre Dame, Ave Maria Press; 1970.

177

that some critical items were missing. "Where are the beds?" I asked.

"Oh, they're in the truck that's coming tomorrow." We were tired and looking forward to sleeping in those beds, but it could wait another day.

That rental house was the smallest structure we had lived in since we were married. None of the furniture seemed to fit. The fire truck bed had to be placed diagonally in Stephen's room. In order to open a dresser drawer in our bedroom, we had to move to the side because of the clearance between it and the bed. The living/dining room was so small that, whenever we had guests, we couldn't get into the kitchen without going outside and around to the back door. In spite of the cramped nature of life in that house, the yard was large and life was very pleasant in the Texas hill country.

St. Peter's Episcopal Church, Kerrville, Texas

St. Peter's parish was a growing congregation of 500 or so congregants plus a parochial preschool. After over a decade as the only priest, the rector, "Red" Bond, decided to call an associate.

The timing of his need with my desire to leave active duty seemed to be another sign of God's favor; and we began our working relationship on a good footing. My office was newly outfitted and quite comfortable and accessible. Red assigned me to lead the junior high youth group and to participate on equal footing in pastoral and liturgical ministries.

In the fall of 1977, Bobby Thomas' remains, along with Don Rissi's and Walter Ferguson's were returned to U.S. control and turned over to the surviving family members for burial. Dick Johnson called me to ask if I planned to attend Don's memorial. I declined because I was not sure that the family would welcome my presence. My last conversation with Joan had left me with the impression that my confirmation of his death had been a source of substantial hurt for her and her sons. I couldn't bring myself to seek out the arrangements for the other two men.

The occasion of their repatriation was an opportunity missed to open the door to so much in my life that I had placed beyond the reach of divine action. On one level, I wanted to go, to pay respects to my fallen friends, and to open the lines of communications with their families. But on a stronger level, I feared the confrontation, both with the families and with the memories of so much evil and tragedy. I could not see that I was living my life out in compartments: one for church, one for the family, and one for pain and suffering.

The people of the parish welcomed us into their hearts and homes, and we quickly adapted to civilian life and parish ministry. Many of the parishioners would remain friends and correspondents for decades. I was thrilled to have a full range of parish ministries: counseling, visiting hospitals and nursing homes, teaching, preaching, celebrating the Eucharist, taking communion to the people in the retirement home at Hilltop Village. Even the junior high group was a blessing, though I often felt like a fish out of water when I was with them.

Chapter 11

Participation in the life of the Diocese of West Texas was also a blessing. The clergy conference in the fall of 1977 gave me the opportunity to meet the men who led congregations throughout the south-central part of the state and to enjoy the sense of common purpose and mutual respect that characterized the group. The diocesan convention that winter introduced me to the entire family of church leadership.

Preaching was one of the things I enjoyed the most, and the response of the congregation was very encouraging. My routine was to read the lessons early in the week, think about them for a few days, prepare an outline by the end of the week, and go to the office at 5:00 on Sunday morning to type out my manuscript. The rector encouraged me to preach from the outline, but I was not comfortable with the idea.

One Sunday morning, I was forced to change. Having slept through the alarm clock, I woke with a start forty-five minutes before the first service of the day. Hastily showering and dressing, I arrived at St. Peter's about fifteen minutes before the service, with nothing done but the outline. Red was visibly concerned with my late arrival, but the sermon went well. In fact, the congregants said it was one of my better efforts. I was relieved and gave the credit to the Holy Spirit for rescuing me from myself. Unfortunately, I missed a bigger insight: if I would allow the Holy Spirit to work in the place of my darkest fears, I would find the hand of God working with great power for my salvation.

Robbie searched for part-time work in the community so she would be able to spend time at home with the children, but not so much that she lost the social interaction with adults that she valued. She worked at the parish day school, and a couple of days a week a few blocks away at a gift store owned by one of our parish members.

Her cousin, Jack Phillips of San Antonio, was a frequent visitor. He and I went hunting for deer and turkey a few times.

Red and I also hunted together, and I brought home both a turkey and a buck during the season. Unfortunately, the family didn't think much of either animal. Stephen, incredulous that I had shot a deer asked, "Dad, do deer have eyes?" Maybe he thought they had to be blind for me to get one. The turkey, which my mother helped us clean and cook, was as tough as jerky and tasted awful.

Stephen's question came back to memory a number of times during moments of prayer and reflection as well as in the amusing stories of family life. Had I stopped to ask why, I might have understood that even the "dead" past could be the window to new vision and insight if I could just unlock the door to the place I kept so much that I considered spiritually sterile or even evil.

By the early spring, Robbie and I were so happy in Kerrville that we asked permission to buy our own house. Red and the Vestry quickly agreed, and they loaned us the money to make a down payment. We found a house that had rooms large enough to hold our furniture and with a large family room that had been converted from a garage. Some work was needed to bring it into order – paint and other minor repairs. Members of the parish volunteered to assist with their time to help keep the costs down.

Our Kerrville home

The house was located on a hill below street level, with a steep drive down to the carport. The large yards held over two dozen live oak trees and lots of open area for the children to play. An odd thing about the house was that a door from the family room to the front yard had been sealed shut. I couldn't see any reason for that, so I removed the caulking to make access to the front easier. Within a few days, we found the problem. A rainstorm caused water to flow in a torrent down the drive and against the front of the house. It quickly came through the door, soaking the new carpet and ruining the pad below. Before we had the carpet re-laid, I had to have a wall built across the front of the old garage to channel the water around the side of the house. That solved our water problem.

My first assignment with the Air Force Reserves was in a non-paid position with a C-130 unit based at Kelly AFB in San Antonio. While it was only about seventy-five miles away, the monthly trips for duty seemed to cross light years of comfort and meaning. All of the most uncomfortable feelings from Andrews would descend upon me as I approached the base. The lack of pay didn't help those feelings, and made it more difficult for me to justify continuing to participate, especially on Sundays. When another chaplain left the unit, I was able to train for pay, a big plus in light of our tight financial condition. My physical health continued to be monitored by the Air Force and I drove to San Antonio to Brooks AFB, a few miles east of Kelly, for my annual physical. By now they were pretty routine.

Robbie's health, however, continued to be something of a problem. The numbness and weakness she had experienced in Washington still defied diagnosis. Even a trip to Massachusetts General Hospital produced no results. Whenever she was feeling low, members of the parish were quick to respond to her as pastors and caregivers.

In the summer, a tremendous rainstorm struck the hill country. Water was several inches deep in the roads as I drove to the office that day; and I found that experienced residents had decided to stay home. The next day was clear; and as I sat in my office making phone calls, one of the ladies from the parish thrift shop came in to tell me there was a large water hole in the driveway. That didn't seem very odd to me, but she informed me they couldn't see the bottom of it. While I figured the puddle was simply filled with muddy water, I walked across the street to have a look.

The "puddle" I had imagined turned out to be an old cistern, about 15 feet deep and located in the middle of the driveway. The parish van was in the garage, but couldn't be moved because of the hole. It looked like the cistern had been designed to catch rainwater from the roof of the old rectory-turned-thrift-shop, capped with cedar timbers and covered with about a foot of dirt. The cedar had finally rotted away and the heavy rains had caused it to collapse. We laid a couple of folding tables from the parish hall across the opening until the hole could be filled.

A few miles south at Camp Capers, the storm had been much more serious. The rising Guadalupe River had covered the road and threatened the cabins filled with junior high school campers. The counselors had strung a rope to a nearby hill to serve as a handhold and led the campers to safety. When the road cleared, the camp was evacuated and the cleanup began. Much of the camp had been flooded, massive trees bent over, and many small animals drowned. Before children could return, all that had to be cleaned up and the septic fields dried out again.

A few days into the cleanup, Bishop Bailey called St. Peter's and asked me to go to the camp to assist with supervision of the repairs. A couple of college students on the staff had been slightly injured because they had been standing downwind from a large pile of debris when contaminated gasoline had been thrown on to burn it.

The fumes had collected on the lee side of the pile, and when a torch was thrown in the resulting fireball had singed the students' hair and caused some slight burns. The Bishop thought I would be a vigilant and safety-conscious influence, and I really appreciated his confidence.

As the end of August approached, I asked Father Bond for an appointment to discuss my ministry assignments and our working relationship. It seemed to Robbie and me that since the time we had bought our house, Red had been showing some irritability with me, even to the point of preaching what seemed like "rebuttal" sermons to mine. I wanted to clear the air, and to try to change my youth assignment from junior to senior high school. Even after a year, I still felt completely at sea in providing them with a good program.

I began the conversation by saying that since people were beginning to trust me, they were starting to come to me with complaints about him, but that I never entertained such conversations and always referred the person to him for resolution. Red agreed that that was the appropriate thing to do. When I said that I would appreciate it if he would reciprocate by similar referrals, he declined, saying he would deal with me if anyone in the parish had a problem with me. His statement caught me by surprise and I couldn't think of a way to discuss the matter further.

I felt very anxious when I put forth my request about trading junior and senior high youth groups. His response was made with a sharp edge, "You'll do what I assign you to do." While I didn't really expect him to give up the high school group, I was unprepared for the sharpness in his voice and the anger in his face. I made a quick decision that surprised even me.

"I don't suppose you would mind if I look for another place, do you?"

"Be my guest."

It had been barely a year since I had resigned my commission and moved my family halfway across the country to central Texas. We had just gotten settled into our new house, and selling it could be a big problem. I dreaded telling Robbie about the meeting and that we would be moving again as soon as I could find another parish.

I called Bishop Bailey and told him I wanted to move and he assured me he would put the word out in the diocese. I also notified the national church deployment office and called some of my seminary classmates for assistance.

Within the next six weeks I was interviewed for a number of positions. The first was to come on the staff of St. Luke's, a large parish in San Antonio; but that one didn't seem to fit. Next, I was interviewed for the chaplaincy at the University of Mississippi; but that, too, didn't seem like a match. Bishop Bailey put my name in for the parish in Brady, Texas, but its distance from a major medical center seemed unwise with Robbie's continuing health problems. John MacNaughton, rector of Christ Church, San Antonio, offered me a position there. While I was pleased and would have loved to work with him, I explained that I didn't seem to be doing too well as a staff member, having resigned two such positions in as many years. He seemed to understand, but I felt sad to have said no.

In the meantime, two parishes closer to our families' homes included me in their searches for rectors, and each issued a "call" at about the same time. One, in Tollville, Arkansas was in a rice-growing area east of Little Rock; and the other, in Yazoo City, Mississippi, was in a cotton and soybean area in the Mississippi delta. Both were appealing, so I called Bishop Bailey for an appointment.

When I told Father Bond that I was going to San Antonio to talk about the calls with the bishop, he nodded and seemed pleased. On the drive down, I wondered what I would say to the Bishop. I felt pretty torn by all the decisions I had to make and wanted to fulfill any obligations I had to West Texas. Brady, Christ Church, Tollville, and Yazoo City were all open options as I arrived at the church center later in the day.

When I walked into the reception area, I was told that the canons were in with the bishop, and he would be with me soon. In a few minutes, Canons Jennings and Veal came out, exchanged pleasantries with me, and I went in to talk with the bishop. I told him about the difficulty I was having making a decision and that I would choose one of the options within the diocese if he wanted me to stay. His response left me puzzled, "The Lord will use you wherever you go." It sounded like an invitation to leave. I told him I would use the clergy conference scheduled for the following week as a retreat to decide.

I was still conflicted when we met at Camp Capers the next week for our annual clergy meeting. The first evening, I joined the other clergy at Bruno's Curve, a local beer hall, for a drink. Canons Jennings and Veal invited me to sit with them to talk. They reminded me of their meeting with the bishop the week before. They confirmed that Fr. Bond had urged the bishop to move me on quickly. I couldn't believe that my ministry had been so fatal in Kerrville. Jennings and Veal assured me that I was OK, but that rectors frequently had difficulty keeping associates in growing parishes.

While that helped somewhat, I found the decision a lot easier to make. There was no way I would stay in West Texas now. Tollville, while an intriguing parish, was too remote for Robbie or me. That left Yazoo City. I called the Senior Warden and accepted their call; and I called Bishop Gray in Jackson to thank him for submitting my name to Trinity parish.

In the meantime, Robbie had additional health problems in mid-September, this time requiring surgery. She was just getting back on her feet when it was time to begin packing for the move.

We put our house up for sale or lease, hoping that we would have the same experience as we had when we left Upper Marlboro. But by the time we left, we had no offers to buy and only one to lease. So, we signed a lease and hoped the tenant would decide to buy it once he moved in.

After our experience moving from Maryland, I decided that we should do it ourselves this time, saving Trinity parish some money and insuring that our things would arrive when we did. Robbie thought I had grossly misjudged how much a U-Haul truck would carry; but I was confident she was wrong. She wasn't.

One of our parishioners was a professional mover and offered to help us pack and load. I went to the U-Haul distributor, told him how many rooms we had in our house, and signed for the truck indicated by their moving chart. We spent a couple of days packing books, dishes, and clothes into boxes, then picked up the truck. By the time the truck was half full, we still hadn't moved more than a quarter of our material possessions out of the house. Under Robbie's "I told you so" look, we unloaded the truck and exchanged it for their largest one. She still wasn't impressed.

After several more hours of loading, it was once again clear that the truck was too small for our stuff. So off we went to rent their largest trailer to tow behind the truck. Robbie still wasn't impressed. As we packed the last possible item into the trailer, there was still enough in the house to fill our Volkswagen and a pickup truck – none of which Robbie wanted to leave behind.

My brother Neal came to my rescue, volunteering to take leave, drive from Barksdale AFB in Shreveport, Louisiana with his pickup truck, get the rest of our boxes, and tow our laden VW to Mississippi.

Chapter 12

Learning the Ropes

Philippians 1:3-11

Every time I think of you, I thank my God. And
whenever I mention you in my prayers, it makes me happy.
This is because you have taken part with me in spreading
the good news from the first day you heard about it. God is
the one who began this good work in you, and I am certain
that he won't stop before it is complete on the day that
Christ Jesus returns.

You have a special place in my heart. So it is only
natural for me to feel the way I do. All of you have helped
in the work that God has given me, as I defend the good
news and tell about it here in jail. God himself knows how
much I want to see you. He knows that I care for you in the
same way that Christ Jesus does.

I pray that your love will keep on growing and that
you will fully know and understand how to make the right
choices. Then you will still be pure and innocent when
Christ returns. And until that day, Jesus Christ will keep
you busy doing good deeds that bring glory and praise to
God.[1]

---

[1]*The Contemporary English Bible*, (Nashville: Thomas Nelson) 1997, ©1995 by
the American Bible Society.

The rectory of Trinity Parish was enormous compared to our Texas homes. Rooms were about twice the size as those in our house in Kerrville, leaving plenty of room for the children to play. The fire truck bed finally had a space that did it justice. The entry led into a formal living room. To one side was a large sunroom, which we used as a family room; to the other was a formal dining room. Adjacent to the formal dining room was a family dining room, the kitchen, and the laundry beyond. A central hall opened from the living room and led to the bedrooms. The eight-foot width made it useful as another indoor play area. The children's bedrooms shared a bath, and the master suite had its own. Unusual for homes in the Mississippi delta, there was a small basement, though it was prone to flooding.

The Rectory on a rare snowy day

Within a few days, Robbie's father, Robert Wade came down from Arkansas, declared our furniture too small for this new house, and returned within a month with new, larger pieces from his store. For the first time since seminary, we were in a home that felt large.

The parish offices were located in Jones Hall, a large frame building that had been a funeral parlor some years earlier. In addition to an office and library for the rector, we also had a large open area set up as a chapel and several other rooms for Sunday School, a nursery, and other uses.

Shortly after my arrival, Mary Ann Cortright, who was serving as the Christian education director, asked me about purchasing or renting some filmstrips or movies for program use. I asked if they were available from the diocesan audio-visual center, and she replied there was no such thing. The Diocese of West Texas had had an extensive library of such aids for the congregations to borrow and I was surprised that Mississippi did not. I suggested that she talk to the bishop about starting one, which we could house in one of our unused rooms. Within the next few years, we had built a large collection of educational materials for the Diocese.

Life and ministry in Yazoo City became exceptionally full in a very short time. While I had been told that the people would give me enough rope to hang myself, I experienced it quite differently. The "rope" was more of a safety tether. They were willing to follow my lead, to support my activities outside the parish, and to keep me from going too far afield. These people would teach me the difference between the ropes.

During the nearly seven years I served as rector of Trinity Parish, I was always engaged in at least one board on the diocesan level and one in the community. My work in the diocese included family life, youth, chemical dependence, church structure and governance, stewardship and renewal. I was on the alumni council of the School of Theology and the board of trustees of the University of the South, a delegate to provincial synod and a deputy to General Convention of the Episcopal Church.

I seemed to have an insatiable hunger to be of service at all levels of the church as well as in the community.

Chapter 12

The Bishop and Vestry were supportive, Robbie was tolerant, and I threw myself into whatever I undertook. After the constrictions of movement and acceptance I had experienced for the previous five years, I was finding creative freedom as well as respect from friends and colleagues around the church.

In the interim before my arrival, several members of the parish had attended a Cursillo (Christian renewal) weekend. One of the rules of the organization was that the parish rector had to agree to their continued involvement. So, in early 1979 Robbie and I attended a Cursillo to clear the way for others. During the course of some conversation, I asked if the Diocese of Mississippi had the high school version, called Happening, which I had heard about in Kerrville. They didn't. A few weeks later, I got a phone call from Bishop Gray.

"Bob, I understand you're interested in bringing Happening to the Diocese."

"Sir? I asked a question about it at Cursillo. West Texas has it and I was just curious."

"Well, I'd like for you to get it started here. Just tell me what you need and I'll provide it."

"Well, first, I need to go to one. Then we'll need to bring a team from West Texas to put on the first one here."

Duncan Gray was a true gift from God. He always exuded confidence in me and whenever he gave me a job to do, he let me find my way to success. Thus began a long love affair with Happening and work with teenagers. Father Joe Rowland and I flew to Corpus Christi later in the year to attend, then contracted with the team to come to Jackson a few months later. Several adult members of Trinity parish became leaders in the movement, and most of our teens eventually attended one of the twice-a-year events held in parish halls around the state. Even my children got involved making gifts and nametags for the participants.

As the diocesan spiritual director for Happening for the next five years, I found a lot of insight and growth for myself as the teens helped me reflect on my own youth. As a very shy and introverted young man, my social skills were weak in high school. When our family moved to Maryland in the summer of 1963, it meant a move from a 5,000 person town to a 5,000 person apartment complex, and from a small high school to an enormous one. Even though I managed to become the drum major of the band, I was never socially at ease.

Even when I went to college, I had difficulty with acceptance, and was not asked to join a fraternity until the middle of my sophomore year. It was there that I finally began to feel OK about my own acceptability to others; but that feeling was severely challenged in the aftermath of the war in Vietnam. Among the teens of Mississippi I was accepted as a mentor and friend, a priest and confidant. In their care, I began to accept my own youth as an important and grace-filled part of the journey in Christ I was traveling.

Before moving to Mississippi, I had checked with the Air Reserve Personnel Center (ARPC) about changing my reserve assignment to something more convenient than San Antonio. I was told that there were no paid positions for chaplains in nearby bases, but I could work for retirement points wherever I chose. Yazoo City was about 250 miles from several bases: Columbus and Keesler AFBs in Mississippi, Barksdale AFB in Louisiana, Little Rock and Blytheville AFBs in Arkansas. When I checked the map, it appeared that Keesler in Biloxi would be the easiest. But first, I wanted to get settled into parish life. By the beginning of the summer, I was ready to get started, but decided to wait until the new fiscal year began in October.

On my first trip to Biloxi that fall, I was excited to get back into uniform, even though I didn't know what the duty would be like at the tech training base. Because of the distance, I planned to drive down on Sunday afternoon, spend Monday and Tuesday on duty, and then return to Yazoo City.

Chapter 12

In preparation, I got a haircut to put me into compliance with Air Force grooming standards and made sure my uniform and shoes were properly prepared. On Monday morning, I reported to the Center Staff Chaplain's office. Waiting for the Colonel to arrive, I was thumbing through the base newspaper, spotted the new pay scale and quickly realized that I was still making about half of what I would be earning if I were on active duty.

I was feeling really bad about that when I heard footsteps in the tiled hall, punctuated with the unmistakable sound of metal taps. When the senior chaplain walked through the door, I was taken aback by his taps and by the Army-style military creases in his blouse. He went to his office and had me wait another five minutes before summoning me. He greeted me to the base, then told me I needed to get a haircut, because "this is a training base."

My bad feeling about the pay was quickly replaced by my disdain for this too-military chaplain. I told him I had just gotten a haircut, would be here for only two days, and if anyone challenged me, I would explain that I was on my way to the barber. This assignment was not going to work out.

During the next year I planned and cancelled several trips, actually getting down to Biloxi about half the time I intended to go. It seemed that each time I scheduled a trip someone in the parish would get very ill or die, and I would stay home to take care of the pastoral crisis. Since the Air Force wasn't paying me, I had little incentive to leave the people without a priest in times of their need. After the fiscal year ended the next fall, I decided to go inactive with the reserves and spend all my time on more rewarding work in the church.

One of my greatest comforts was an evening ritual of reading to the children. I was amazed when they would sit for an hour or more listening to me read *The Hobbit* and the *Lord of the Rings* trilogy and the entire seven volumes of the *Chronicles of Narnia*.

I became quite adept at making, and remembering, the voices for each of the characters in the books. I also discovered new insights as I listened to those voices speak to the deeper meaning behind the words. With the children snuggled close and lost in the visions of their imaginations, we slowly completed the eleven books and my spiritual life deepened with each volume. I often prayed that these same words would form into a foundation of spiritual insight for Stephen and for Mary.

Life at home was filled with people coming and going. The yard was a great place for children to play, and the fire truck bed was fun for inside. Neighborhood children were around all the time, as were parish teenagers who came by both to visit and to keep the children when Robbie and I went out.

As the children grew to school age, Robbie returned to her career of administration in the local Head Start program, and evaluated teachers for certification on a tri-state circuit. But she continued to be plagued with a variety of health problems, some of which required surgery. My frantic pace distracted me from my familial responsibilities, causing a good deal of stress for her as the burden of raising the children fell mostly on her shoulders.

Our closest friends in the parish were a local doctor and his wife, Harry and Laurie Dowdy. Harry had grown up in Missouri near Robbie's hometown, knew her parents through the furniture store, and had served in the Navy. We began hunting and fishing together, and gradually spent more and more time as social friends and in various ministries in the church. They enjoyed our children, and I was able to introduce them to a priest and attorney who arranged private adoptions. Within a few years, they were able to adopt two sons.

In my prayer time each morning, I struggled with all the conflicting demands on my time and sought God's guidance. Even though I was frequently discomforted by my choices, I found too much personal gratification from being seen as a church and community leader to accept any warning signals about the health of my own family.

In 1980 I was asked to sit on the board of the Warren-Yazoo County Mental Health Association. In the year I served, I gained new insight into the difficulties of mental health services in the two counties, but found the drives to Vicksburg to be distracting from my work in the parish. So after a little more than a year, I resigned.

About three months later, while I was meeting with Bishop Gray in his office in Jackson, his secretary knocked on the door to announce that a sheriff was looking for me. I was stunned! When she showed him in, he handed me a subpoena naming me as a member of the Mental Health board in a lawsuit. Fortunately, my name was misspelled and when I pointed that out to the deputy and told him of my resignation, he took the document back and left.

I was embarrassed as I explained to Bishop Gray that the nurses at the hospital were suing the Director and the Board for the Director's alleged sexual harassment of the nursing staff. While I had no direct connection to him or the hospital, I decided then that it was unwise to serve on civic boards in a litigious society.

That spring, several of us from Trinity attended a conference on ministry to inactive members. It was an extensive course in pastoral care and listening skills that we found to be important for ministries to active, inactive, prospective, and new members of the parish. As with so many ministries in which we became involved, a couple of us became trainers and offered the course multiple times in a number of parishes over the next five years.

Trinity Episcopal Church, Yazoo City, Mississippi

For me personally, a one-hour block on "anniversary stories" began to open the locked door into which I crammed all the traumas of life. Dr. Savage, the author of the program, pointed out that people frequently have very sad periods near the anniversaries of personal losses – the death of a spouse, parent, or child, the loss of a career, etc. The point of the block of instruction was that people needed extra pastoral care on these anniversaries, and that we should develop a system to remind ourselves of such events in their lives. I remember my mother telling me years before that her mother had died in the spring of the year and that her father always "took to bed" near that anniversary and eventually died within a few days of the date of his wife's death. A light was beginning to dawn for me.

As I listened, I realized that my personal stress from Christmas to Easter each year might be caused by more than the liturgical cycle. Having been shot down a week before Christmas and released a week before Holy Week, I was probably experiencing some kind of anniversary reaction at the same time that the Church's liturgies and programs were at their most intense.

197

Chapter 12

When I discussed this new idea with Robbie, she agreed that it made sense. I was most intense, demanding, controlling, and volatile during those months. It seemed that rage was just below the surface at the very time that the Church was experiencing its most joyful seasons.

Words spoken by Oswald Chambers on New Year's Eve 1916, to a gathering of British soldiers in Cairo, Egypt whose lives had been turned upside down by World War I gave added insight to my own spiritual depths. Chambers said, "At the end of the year we turn with eagerness to all that God has for the future, and yet anxiety is apt to arise from remembering the yesterdays. Our present enjoyment of God's grace is apt to be checked by the memory of yesterday's sins and blunders. But God is the God of our yesterdays, and He allows the memory of them in order to turn the past into a ministry of spiritual culture for the future. God reminds us of the past lest we get into a shallow security in the present. Let the past sleep, but let it sleep on the bosom of Christ. Leave the irreparable past in His hands, and step out into the irresistible future with Him."[2]

I thought that knowledge was power, and that in knowing about anniversary stories I could better understand my own emotions and develop coping skills to be more even-keeled. My prayers became more focused during the seasons of Advent to Easter for relief from stress and anger; but knowing what was happening was not enough to open the door completely. It would be a long time before I could let those memories sleep in the bosom of Christ. Without divine guidance, my knowledge was merely impotent information.

That fall, John Walker of the Vietnam Veterans Leadership Program in Washington called to invite me to participate in their discussions and writing projects. It was quite an experience to be involved with professional writers who were trying to start telling the story of the soldiers who had gone to Southeast Asia as young men and returned as exiles in their own country.

---

[2] Chambers, Oswald, *My Utmost for His Highest*, (United Kingdom: Marshall Morgan & Scott) 1927. Selection for December 31.

John had recently published an article in the *Anglican Theological Review* and asked me to do a reflection piece on his and others in the same issue.

The series of articles dealt with the sense of exclusion from the community felt by returning veterans and proposed societal rituals that would facilitate reincorporation. Previous wars had victory parades and laudatory editorials that were conspicuously absent from Vietnam.

I was flattered to be asked to write the article and proud to have it published. But it would be more years before I would really feel that all of me was home again. The Leadership Program took me to the Nation's capitol for the next several years, enabling me to watch the progress of construction on the Vietnam Veterans' Memorial on the Mall.

In October 1980, my brother Neal, still on active duty with the Air Force, called. He was stationed at Barksdale AFB in Louisiana and was assigned to receive and secure the Presidential aircraft, Air Force One, when the President was traveling. President Carter was on a last-minute campaign swing and would be stopping into Jackson for a speech. Neal suggested that I meet him at the airport for a visit while the President was in town.

Robbie, the children, a couple of teens from the parish, and I drove down to visit with Neal at the Jackson airport. I recognized some of the crew from Air Force One from my days as their chaplain and had a small reunion with them. When President Carter returned, he was standing at the bottom of the airstairs waving to the cameras when he spotted us about thirty yards away. He walked over, introduced himself, and knelt down to speak to Stephen. As he stood again, he saw my camera and asked if I would like to take a picture. I was dumbfounded, but readily accepted.

A few days later, Mr. Carter lost his re-election bid to Ronald Reagan. When Iran waited until after the inauguration to release our hostages, I wrote the former President to express my sadness that he had not been in office to welcome them home after over a year in captivity. I knew what joy President Nixon had found in welcoming the POWs home after Vietnam, and knew this President had agonized over the Embassy workers who had been held under the Ayatollah's regime. I enclosed the photograph I had taken with him and my family, which he signed and returned.

In July 1981 the Certains gathered for a reunion in Columbus, Georgia. Dad asked me to plan to preach at St. Luke United Methodist Church. All of my siblings, their spouses and children gathered at my parents' home and Mother busied herself preparing the meals. My brothers and their families, staying at a hotel nearby, began partying early on the Saturday afternoon, and I became increasingly inebriated. At dinner, the food ran out before everyone was served. Unknown to me, my oldest nephew was asked to take my van and go get burgers for him and his cousins to save Mother the embarrassment of knowing she had under planned.

By then, I was hungry, tipsy, and fearful that I would do a poor job the next morning. When I left to drive back to the hotel and found the van missing, I went ballistic. My overreaction that night had little to do with the events of the day, but the wake left behind triggered a crisis in the family that would last for years. Insight into the caldera that was eating my soul and separating me from my family, from God and his people would not come until much later.

I had slowly developed a routine of erupting, slamming the door shut again, spiraling into remorse and guilt, and trying to make up to those around me as best I could without really addressing the internal issues or even naming them. As I went to God in prayer, I could feel his hand pulling at my head to turn me in the direction of opening the door of my grief; but I resisted like a drowning man fighting off his rescuer. Consequently, neither the family nor I would heal quickly from that awful night; and my ability to avoid another blast was nil.

Even lesser flares of temper were beginning to separate me from the people I loved in family and parish. Throughout my life I had been prone to popping off when upset or angry. Once it was over, it was over for me and I rarely thought about it again. That was not necessarily so for other people, and many of them came to fear my quick ire and me.

In 1982, I joined the Little Theater group for a local production of "Man of La Mancha," the story of Don Quixote. Though I was typecast as the priest in the play, I learned some very important things for the future. One was a line spoken by Don Quixote when he was accused of being a madman, "The greatest madness of all is to see the world as it is, and not as it ought to be." For Don Quixote that meant seeing windmills as dragons to be slain and seeing the harlot Aldonza as the pure maiden Dulcinea.

Chapter 12

For me, it reminded me of my college fraternity. When the national fraternity was ready to revoke our charter in 1967, we determined to grow and to improve. The next fall we pledged all the "losers" we could find, young men who had been blackballed by other fraternities on the campus. In the spring of 1969, our chapter was named the best in the nation as well as on the campus. We had looked at people who made poor first impressions and seen something of worth in each of them, perhaps because our evaluators had looked at us and seen a glimmer of hope in spite of our awful record and appearance.

From there it was an easy step to understand Paul's comment in First Corinthians that "not many were powerful, not many were wise" when they were called into Christ, and to understand the Church as the place where we should see the world as God sees it – as it ought to be. In my prayers, I petitioned God to make me as I ought to be, but without taking me into the darkness first.

Juxtaposed beside this important line, when Don Quixote died, my character sang Psalm 130 in Latin. When I read it in English at a funeral soon after, it struck me as an expression of my soul's longing and desire. But I was not confident that there was any real hope that "he shall redeem [me] from all [my] sins."

Out of the depths have I called to you, O LORD,
LORD, hear my voice;
    let your ears consider well the voice of my supplication.
If you, LORD, were to note what is done amiss,
    O LORD, who could stand?
For there is forgiveness with you;
    therefore you shall be feared.
I wait for the LORD; my soul waits for him;
    in his word is my hope.
My soul waits for the LORD,
More than watchmen for the morning,
    more than watchmen for the morning.

O Israel, wait for the LORD,
    for with the LORD there is mercy;
With him there is plenteous redemption,
    and he shall redeem Israel from all their sins.

In 1982, the meeting of the Vietnam Veterans Leadership Program was on November 8-10, putting us there for the dedication of the Vietnam Veterans' Memorial on Veterans' Day. Because my duties in the parish necessitated my early return, I made my trek to the wall on the tenth. There were many veterans and their families already gathered at the wall in reverent awe. I pushed myself toward the center, knowing that the earliest KIA/MIAs were on Panel 1E and the last were on Panel 1W. There, on rows ninety-four and ninety-five were the names of the men of Charcoal One and the others who gave their lives in December 1972 to bring the war to an end and to free the POWs. Before I thought, I found tears streaming down my face and my hands reaching out to touch their names.

As I flew back to Mississippi that afternoon, I wondered what the weekend would hold. On the Sunday after Veterans' Day, the adult Sunday School was the scene for a most unusual hour for such a small parish. Seven Trinity members had been involved on one side or the other of the war issues, and sat as a panel to discuss their points of view. I flew heavy bombers and was a POW. One man worked as a civilian in Southeast Asia; another was in the Air Force on ground duty in South Vietnam; a third was a Navy scientist working on chemical weapons; one was an Army officer who inducted draftees in New York City and notified families of battlefield deaths; his wife had participated in anti-war protests; and the final member had done alternative service as a conscientious objector. The purpose of the panel was to demonstrate how Christians could respond faithfully and differently to the same set of critical circumstances, and to promote the healing of divisions that might have been caused by the different actions. The hour we had allotted to the panel was barely enough for the panelists to tell their stories. The surprising thing was that few in the parish, including the panelists, really knew how each of them had been affected by the war. Unfortunately, we left further conversation and understanding up to the individuals.

As a result of my participation with the Vietnam Veterans Leadership Program, Chief Judge Weinstein of the federal court in New York that heard the Agent Orange case asked me to join a panel of Vietnam veteran advisors to devise a plan to distribute the $180,000,000 settlement fund. He called twenty-six of us to Washington to hear various proposals put forth by the plaintiffs' attorneys, the judge's attorney, and others. After several months of digesting thousands of pages of documents and deliberating over a half-dozen plans, we finally settled on our own. We concluded that awards should be limited to 100% disabled and indigent veterans, and to the children of veterans born with physical or mental defects. Even so, awards would be small.

It struck me that after twenty years, the veterans were just as idealistic and altruistic as they had been when they went to Vietnam in the 1960s and early 1970s. Everyone on the panel wanted to help those who could not help themselves and those who, through no fault of their own, had disabilities that hampered their full enjoyment of the benefits of freedom.

In the parish, the leadership was also concerned about the helpless and the hopeless. When Firestone Tire and Rubber Company closed their retail store next to the church in 1979, we wanted to buy it for additional parish programs. The price was well above our ability at the time, but by 1983 it had dropped by half. At that point the Vestry decided to purchase it for the building and the parking, and to prevent another business from opening up next to the church.

Trinity parish, in cooperation with several other community churches, had begun a free lunch kitchen in our parish hall in late 1982. The old Firestone building became the new home for the ministry now named "Manna House."

On March 8, 1983 we received a devastating phone call that Robbie's mother had died. Margaret Wade had been ill with emphysema for some years and tethered to an oxygen tank for the last several. An elegant lady, she had been a bastion of strength and calm for Robbie during my imprisonment, and always made us feel at home in her presence.

Robbie, of course, was heart-broken. Losing a parent at such a young age was difficult, and we all had left a lot unsaid. When we gathered in the family home, our daughter Mary, just learning to play the piano, sat down and played "When the Saints go Marching In." We were all in tears, both in grief and in pride at her sensitive choice.

Chapter 12

A couple of months later, I received a letter from the Air Reserve Personnel Center. As I looked at the envelope, I assumed it was the "get active or get out" letter notifying me that I could no longer complete twenty years of service within thirty years after my commissioning. When I opened the letter, I found to my surprise I had been promoted to major in the USAF Reserves.

I went to the phone and called the Center in Denver. "How could I be promoted to major? I haven't done anything in three years and haven't had a good year since I left active duty. I thought I was out of time to complete a career."

"You were promoted in the 'fully qualified' category rather than 'best qualified.' So it didn't matter that you are in the inactive reserves. You still have a couple of years before you'll lose your ability to get in twenty years; but if you're going to do that you need to get active now."

"Can I get paid?"

"Of course."

"What's different? Last year I was told there were still no paid positions open."

"You were a captain then. Now that you're a major, there are plenty of places."

"Oh. Can I go back to Blytheville?"

"I don't see why not. I'll clear it with the base chaplain, Lt. Col. Darryl Highsmith."

"I know him. He was the senior Protestant chaplain at Andrews when I was there."

Returning to Blytheville AFB was a good move. I knew the mission and the stresses on the crews and other personnel. Robbie's Dad was there and it would give me a reason to go up regularly, and Robbie and the children would be able to enjoy going with me for my annual two-week tour of duty.

I also found that I was a "returning hero" in the minds of the young crews who now populated the base along with the senior commanders who had been on crews when I had been a decade earlier. That gave me immediate rapport with them as a chaplain, and also gave me encouragement to fly in a Stratofortress again for the first time since I ejected over Hanoi.

Before I could fly, I had to overcome an old demon. A number of sights sent me back to the winter of 1972-73. French architecture, with ornate wrought iron and tall double doors, as in the New Orleans French Quarter put me back into the ride through Hanoi on 19 December 1972. For many years, whenever we visited Robbie's parents in Blytheville, Arkansas, I would go to the base. The main entrance led directly to the flight line. If a B-52 was parked at the end of the drive, I would have to turn aside no later than two blocks from the end of the boulevard. The closer I got, the more dangerous it felt to be near my once familiar and beloved BUFF.

Now I couldn't avoid facing my old fear. But the Strategic Air Command didn't make it easy. First, the Wing Commander had to get clearance from SAC headquarters to make an exception to allow me, as a reserve chaplain, to fly along as a passenger on a training mission. Second, I had to schedule a trip to Little Rock AFB to get a currency "ride" in the altitude chamber. Third, I had to have a current flight physical. Finally, I would have to fly during an annual active duty tour. The process took several years with each step separated by months.

In the meantime, my training in history came to good use. As I was reviewing some photographs and scraps of documents from the parish archives in 1982, I realized that the Episcopal Church had had a presence in Yazoo County since 1834. In preparation for the upcoming 150th anniversary, I determined to write a history of the church. I completed it in 1984 in time to have it printed, complete with historic photographs, for the celebration.

My secretary, who helped to type and proof-read the manuscript, urged me to send a copy to the School of Theology to determine if they would give me some credit toward a doctor of ministry degree. I explained to her that since I was not enrolled in the program, and since the project was already complete, it would not be acceptable.

Chapter 12

Under her repeated insistence, I finally sent a copy to the Dean of the Doctoral program, Professor Don Armentrout.

His reply was beyond my wildest expectations. He said that the book would qualify as the doctoral project, and that an endowment at the School was sufficient to pay the tuition and fees if I chose to enroll. I no longer had any excuse to avoid the advanced degree, and planned to begin classes in the summer of 1985. When I told Bishop Gray about the decision, he offered to let us use his house on Rattlesnake Bend Road in Sewanee for the summer session.

In the fall of 1984 I got a notion to build a kit car, a replica of a 1928 Mercedes SSK, on a Volkswagen body. I found a used VW beetle and ordered the kit. When the truck pulled up with the kit, it was in a box 8 feet long, four feet wide and four feet high. Some of the men of the parish helped me remove the body from the VW chassis; and I spent part of each day for the next six months building the little roadster. Working with my hands on a project completely outside my normal duties as a priest gave me a peaceful respite, and a great deal of pride when I was able to drive it around the block for the first time.

The following year, I bought a smaller project, a dollhouse kit to make for Mary. Again, I felt great pride as I built the house and much of the furniture, and even more joy as I watched her excitement as I built it and when she was able to play with it.

Beneath the surface of these "projects" there was a significant spiritual struggle with vocation, place, ministry, and direction. Previous projects – the ceramics shop on Guam, the O'Connor den in the summer of 1973, the fire truck bed in Maryland, the remodeling of the house in Kerrville – had all presaged a change in direction in my life. Perhaps unfortunately, the struggle occurred below my consciousness, and certainly outside my articulation. To observers, each project seemed to be a retreat from the pressures of life rather than a time when God was forming me for the next stage of ministry.

1929 Mercedes SSK replica

The Doll House decked out for Christmas

Chapter 12

Parish life in Yazoo City was similar to any small congregation in the country. We celebrated the passages of life with baptisms, weddings and funerals. We struggled with finances, attendance, and ministries. We worked hard and we laughed a lot. We also lived through the deaths of infants and teenagers, broken marriages, failed crops and businesses. Passion for the Lord's work ran high and it occasionally showed itself in conflict over the direction we should take.

Through it all, we grew in spiritual depth as well as in the work of discipleship. Adult education and spiritual renewal drew members and non-members alike. With time, we had to renovate and reopen the second floor of Martin Hall, enclose a chapel in Jones Hall, and add the old Firestone store as Scott Hall for ministries. With Robbie's leadership the parish opened an early childhood development program for children aged two to four, which we dubbed "Trinity's Tutored Tots." Friendships were made, lives were changed for the better, and the Lord was glorified in our praises.

We also had our strife. I continued to have dark moods from Advent through Easter. I often struggled with the organist or choirmaster in the selection and performance of music. On one occasion, the treasurer got so frustrated with me she literally threw the books at me. But the good things about Trinity Parish were that there was not another Episcopal Church in the county, and we thought of ourselves as family. So no matter how we might argue, we settled our disagreements quickly and moved on.

As the parish prospered, so I grew in confidence and maturity. The challenges of life in rural Mississippi were the kind that helped me to find my foundation as a priest and my confidence as a disciple so that I believed I could handle more. From time to time, I would put my name into various parishes looking for a new rector from inside the diocese to as far away as Georgetown, DC. Each time I would be passed over, usually coming in second, and would feel the old sense of rejection and lack of self-worth return.

Sometimes I would try several more places, other times I would accept that Trinity Parish was where I belonged.

Unlike the Catholic or Methodist Churches, bishops in the Episcopal Church cannot assign clergy as rectors of parishes. Instead, the parish vestry elects its own rector, or senior priest, and issues a "call" to fill the position. The bishop does have to approve the election and, in the case of a priest moving from one diocese to another, the losing bishop has to issue a "letter dimissory," which must then be accepted by the gaining bishop. Once the rector takes charge of the parish, he gains tenure and cannot be easily removed unless guilty of serious violations of church or civil code. As a result, once elected, a rector has the option to remain in one place until mandatory retirement at age seventy-two. In my mid-thirties I had a career goal of moving to bigger parishes, bigger cities, and greater responsibilities. The prayer of St. Augustine, "My soul is restless, O Lord, until it rests in thee," was not yet an insight into my own spirituality.

Learning the ropes of ministry in Yazoo City was truly invaluable: the small but dedicated staff, the volunteers working on Happening, Tutored Tots, Manna House, and the audio-visual center, the deep commitment that such a strong group of folk had there under my priesthood. It was a vibrant and exciting part of my spiritual journey. With time, I would grow not only older, but wiser, realizing I have fewer answers than any of us thought we did at the time. We were transforming the world, ready or not. I rejoice and give thanks for the time in Yazoo City. For the passion and commitment and determination not to accept things as they are, but to seek vibrant life in Christ, to new and deeper commitments, to move toward what ought to be. We made some mistakes, but not the deadly one of not trying, of not giving our best, of not seeking to grow.

211

Chapter 12

In the spring of 1985, the Church of the Holy Apostles in suburban Memphis, Tennessee approached me to consider becoming their rector. I was very discouraged about getting a move to a larger parish within the Diocese of Mississippi, and wanted this to be a good one. Robbie and I both felt ill at ease during the interview process, but figured we could make it work just as we had in Yazoo City. Our discomfort centered on the way in which various people on the search committee and vestry seemed to have different intentions and agendas. While we didn't like it, that characteristic was not foreign to our experience with groups. So when the call was extended, I accepted and made plans to move the family in time for school to start in August.

Chapter 13

Stress Upon Stress

Psalm 88
O Lord, my God, my Savior,
  by day and night I cry to you.
Let my prayer enter into your presence:
  incline your ear to my lamentation.
For I am full of trouble;
  my life is at the brink of the grave.
I am counted among those who go down to the Pit;
  I have become like one who has no strength
Lost among the dead,
  like the slain who lie in the grave
Whom you remember no more,
  for they are cut off from your hand.
You have laid me in the depths of the Pit,
  in dark places, and in the abyss.

It was nearly midnight when we finally arrived in Memphis in August 1985. We all quickly fell into bed, exhausted from the day of loading our belongings. It seemed like only minutes had passed when the alarm went off. We drug ourselves over to the rectory to meet the truck.

Woven in and out of the tapestry of life in Memphis was a cacophony of circumstances and events that seemed to be set into little cubbyholes unrelated to one another, but which affected and colored all the events that would occur in the next four and a quarter years. These circumstances included physical things like housing and automobiles; family events of illness, death, education, and growing children; parish life events centered on becoming both unified and mission oriented as well as funding, decision-making, and construction; and personal involvement in civic work in the community and the nation, Air Force reserves and veterans affairs.

Shifting gears on the converted Volkswagen was one thing; shifting them in the rest of life was another thing altogether. As adept as I thought I was at keeping all the things I enjoyed doing working well, almost everything would crash to the floor while we lived in southwest Tennessee.

One of the problems with moving from a 4,000 square foot rectory into one half that size is that things don't fit very well. My father-in-law had always visited shortly after a move and replaced our furniture with items that fit the space, and we came to Memphis with large pieces that fit the Yazoo City home. We had left the fire truck bed in Mississippi for use by friends, and had tried to rid ourselves of other items we didn't think would work, but we still had oversized furniture for the dining and living rooms. It wouldn't be long before Robbie's dad visited again.

The most difficult item was a sofa bed that I wanted to place in a fourth bedroom I would be using as a study. Try as they would, the movers could not make it turn the corner and go through the door. It was even worse than trying to fit the fire truck bed into Stephen's room in Maryland since the sofa bed couldn't be disassembled. We finally had to remove the window, slide it through the opening, and replace the window. I didn't want to even think about what would happen when we no longer wanted it.

During a break in the afternoon, we drove by the church to show it to the children. The grass in the field was waist high, and the whole facility appeared to be unkempt. From the back seat Stephen said, "This place could use Dad's touch." He knew that I was a stickler for maintenance and landscaping as signs of hospitality and devotion. Holy Apostles Church did not exhibit those visual cues.

The following day, we drove back down to Winona to pick up the car. The battery had been dead when it quit a couple of nights before, and now it was fully charged but no other problem was found. By the time we drove into Memphis, the battery was depleted again. One of our parishioners was a VW mechanic, so I took the car to him to help me identify the problem. As he looked at the engine, he picked out one wire and said, "What's this?" I identified it as a ground wire, and he moved it to another location. No more problems.

I dismissed these incidents as moving problems, not as signs of God's hand at work. Coupled with our discomfort at the financial package negotiations, the former rector's evasive endorsement of the parish, and our abdominal tension, those things should have given me some idea of how life would play itself out in Memphis. Like the struggle with the sofa bed, I had a very difficult time leading the congregation, not for the lack of trying on anyone's part, but because my motives in coming there were very personal. I had taken the reins out of the hands of the Holy Spirit.

While the parish understood itself as very friendly, it quickly became apparent that they were comfortable mostly with themselves. Even Robbie was not readily welcomed or incorporated into the fellowship in the Sunday coffee hour. Neither Vestry nor Search Committee members offered to take her by the hand and introduce her to the people. After three weeks she took matters into her own hands and stood with me in the line after church to greet people on their way out. As something of an introvert myself, I wasn't really sure how to help the people become more welcoming of strangers and newcomers, but my extroverted wife would be a major asset in making that transition.

Then there was the misplaced wire. If the ground wire is connected incorrectly, the alternator won't charge and the battery is quickly spent. Rather than trusting the Holy Spirit, I had begun to trust my gifts as if they were something that I had developed on my own. My "ground wire" was in the wrong place; but my eyes were not open to see it. John Baker had spotted the physical one in about thirty seconds. It would take a much longer time to identify and correct the problem with my soul.

Unfortunately, these were not insights when I made the decision to accept the parish's call to become their rector. It would be some years before I ever applied the discipline of theological reflection to them. The concerns did point to challenges we would have to face together as a family and as a parish, but challenges my pride told me I could handle.

As the relationship began, life was pretty good. Our first Sunday, Wanda Goodrich, head of the Altar Guild and a member of the search committee, asked Stephen and Mary to be oblationers. When they arrived at the Altar with the bread and wine for the Eucharist, Stephen pointed into the carafe and whispered, "Dad, there's a fly in there." Flies in the south are always present, and the aroma of the port wine had attracted one of them. As the anthem ended, I didn't know what else to do but to ask Wanda to replace the wine while the organist continued to play. That story has held fond memories for us ever since and serves as a reminder of God's sense of humor.

In a few weeks, senior warden Brian Pecon celebrated his fortieth birthday with a parish picnic at his estate in Germantown. In Yazoo City dinners on the ground were opportunities for people to share their favorite recipes in a glorious feast and to visit with their friends and neighbors. We were very surprised to enter their back yard to the sight of families clustered together on blankets eating only the food they had brought. The scarcity of sharing of both food and fellowship pointed to another challenge we would face.

In the Air Force, I was continuing to travel to Blytheville for reserve duty, now on a monthly basis. For the past couple of years in Yazoo City, I had jumped through the hoops of USAF requirements to requalify in the altitude chamber and to petition for Strategic Air Command approval to fly on a training mission in a B-52. The final requirement was to be on an active duty tour as opposed to a monthly training day, which I arranged in November.

Blythe Spirit - November 22, 1985 7

After almost 13 years

Chaplain remembers old times

by Amn. Heather Schroeder
public affairs division

Chaplain (Maj.) Robert G. Certain adjusts his helmet in preparation for the flight.

Imagine yourself as a B-52 navigator during the Vietnam War. While flying a mission over Hanoi your plane is shot down and you are forced to eject.

Maj. Robert G. Certain did just that. He ejected from a B-52 at 32,000 feet and was captured by the enemy Dec. 18, 1972 after landing at a farm northwest of Hanoi.

"The enemy observed us coming down and we were surrounded post haste," said Major Certain. "We were captured within 15 minutes of hitting the ground."

Major Certain was held prisoner for three and one-half months before being released March 29, 1973. He was one of three crew members that survived the attack. Three others perished

when they went down with the plane.

"For a long time I was real squeamish just looking at the planes sitting out there on the flight line. I guess it was just the healing of memories that kept me from getting into another B-52 after that," he said. "Two years ago, after being reassigned to Blytheville Air Force Base, I decided to get back on board."

"You don't get to fly on a B-52 just because you want to," said Major Certain. In order to fly on a B-52 you have to meet a lot of requirements. For one thing you have to be on active duty status and you have to be current on your flight physical and altitude chamber. Then you have to be

approved through numerous channels.

And so, after almost 13 years, he boarded a 97th Bombardment Wing B-52. With the help of Lt. Col. William H. Campbell, the former 340th Bomb Squadron commander, and Capt. Harry G. Edwards, project officer, he was able to get approval to be a passenger on the nine-hour mission.

"It was like old times," he said. "However, we were a little slow getting started. We had to abort the first take-off because of a mechanical problem and we had some pressure problems. We lost the first 45 minutes of the mission."

Major Certain now serves as a reserve chaplain for the 97th Bomb Wing.

The crew members synchronize their watches before the flight.

Chapter 13

Twelve years and eleven months after my shoot-down over Hanoi, I climbed into the Stratofortress for a routine training mission. The mission conjured up even more of the last flight. The crew were children – about the same age I had been on Guam. I was now the same age as Dick Johnson when we flew our last flight together. Time certainly has a way of changing one's perspective.

I decided to watch the take-off from the upper deck vantage point of the instructor pilot's seat. As we reached the first decision speed, the co-pilot hit the water injection switch, but two engines didn't receive the proper flow of water. The pilot aborted, and for the next 45 minutes we sat on the end of the runway, burning enough fuel to make the takeoff without need of water.

Memories of the waterless take off from Guam in 1972 flooded back. As we sat on the ground, I must have looked pretty pale, because the young pilot asked if I wanted to get off. But I chose to stay.

I took a trip downstairs to look over the Offense Team's cockpit, recognizing little from a decade earlier other than the oxygen panel. In the previous thirteen years the navigation and bombing equipment had been so modified and upgraded I recognized little of what the offense team was doing. I felt like I had been in hibernation, waking to find the world vastly changed.

Finally, we took off on the mission, rendezvoused with the tanker for refueling, flew a high level navigation leg, and a low level simulated bomb run with missile launches. In spite of my unfamiliarity with the navigation and bombing stations, the mission was very much like many I had flown from the same base.

I was just an observer, but one undergoing a major change – the conquering of old fear. I was grateful for the opportunity and proud of my courage to face the "ghost of Christmas past." Nevertheless, I was happy and relieved to have it behind me. The fear was gone, and so was the intrigue. My love affair with the BUFF had returned, as had my longing to fly.

In the parish, the first challenge to face us was the sluggish conclusion of a capital campaign that had been conducted in-house during the interim before I arrived. The goal had been $600,000 but had fallen short by half. As we discussed our next step, the Vestry determined to sell three of the parish's nine acres for an office park to raise the rest of the money needed to build a new worship building. We were united in the decision and thought it to be in the best interest of the parish.

When Holy Apostles had been established, it was a parochial mission of the Church of the Holy Communion in "East Memphis." That large parish had bought the land and built the first building, mostly multi-purpose space. The large room used for worship quickly became single-use worship space. In the minds of the parishioners it was inappropriate for dinners, dances, or other fellowship gatherings. As the church grew to over 300 members, it really needed classrooms, a "proper" nave, and the recovery of the large room for a parish hall.

In order to sell the land, we first had to survey the neighborhood to gain their support for the proposal. The church was located on a corner of a busy intersection, with the undeveloped section to the side. The back half of the property was in woods, the front contained the church and the field. Much to our surprise, we discovered an Episcopalian family living directly behind the church that had no idea they could have walked fifty yards to worship rather than driving ten miles into Memphis.

The only indications of a church we had were an "Episcopal Church Welcomes You" sign at the drive, obscured by boughs of a pine tree, and a church sign in brown and tan, parallel with the street and easily visible only from the window of the barbeque restaurant across the street. Even our twenty-foot cross of brown steel blended with the board and batten building behind it. With the generally unkempt appearance of the facility and the timid nature of the people when greeting strangers, we clearly had our work cut out for us if we were to grow into a substantial congregation. Each passing day brought more excitement to the congregation as we identified new solutions and directions to old problems.

Two difficult practices in the financial operation of the parish were the size and authority of the finance committee, and the secrecy of pledges. The finance committee had fourteen members, most of whom did not attend worship on a regular basis, or had been members for less than a year. There was a rule that the Vestry could not authorize expenditures of more than a hundred dollars without the prior approval of that committee. The rule was clearly out of conformity with the Canons of the Episcopal Church. Finance committees are advisory only; Vestries are the legal entity charged with making all business decisions.

Church of the Holy Apostles, Memphis, Tennessee

In December, I dissolved the finance committee and appointed an executive committee of the Vestry as the new one. The Vestry and the committee understood the problem by then. A finance committee was simply an inappropriate group for new or marginal members. We needed advisors who were dedicated to the vision of the parish, who were significant contributors to its budget, and who were willing to step out in faith to make both the vision and the money work.

The problem of pledge secrecy was that the Rector was not allowed to have access to them. Not only did that handicap me in my pastoral and leadership responsibilities, it also meant that there was no mechanism to judge candidates for parish leadership, including the Vestry, against the norms of church membership: to be "faithful in work, worship, giving and praying for the spread of the Kingdom of God." That practice wasn't resolved until 1987, and then only by the direct instruction of the bishop.

Some help began to come from unexpected sources. Tony Hill, a vocational deacon in the Diocese of West Tennessee, called to offer his services to me. We had met briefly during an earlier search process, and I was at first reluctant to discuss his transfer to Holy Apostles with him. When he first called, I could feel anger building in my chest because he had been on a search committee from St. Elisabeth's that called someone else. At first I welcomed a face-to-face meeting as an opportunity to tell him how badly that committee had handled both the interviews and the letter of rejection. But within a few minutes of getting reacquainted, I accepted his offer and joined him in petitioning the Bishop for the move. Our two families went on to become close friends.

Again, I failed to see the fullness of God's hand in Tony's approach. As long as I held any grudge about events of the past, I could never really accept new graces as they came along.

Chapter 13

The discipline of theological reflection was still an ill-developed part of my prayer life. I never even looked at pleasant events and interchanges as opportunities for Divine leadership of life, much less at the stressful ones. I was grateful that the distance between Tony and me evaporated in moments, but I accounted for it as my own generosity and his pleasing personality, not as the gift of the Holy Spirit.

Within weeks of reviewing our Sunday morning routines, the people of the parish grasped the need to present the parish in a better light to the neighborhood, and to provide hospitality to anyone entering our doors. The coffee was moved from the kitchen to the reception area, members greeted new people and invited them into conversation, the grounds were cleaned up, and maintenance and housekeeping were improved. Pine boughs were trimmed away from the driveway sign, and plans were made to build a better one when the new facility was constructed the next year.

My first year as pastor and priest seemed to be turning out well as 1985 ended and as we celebrated our first Christmas together. Goals were clarified, plans for construction were set, and more funds were beginning to appear. The land sale was the one item that gave some people pause. The property was not large enough to build a school, and the maintenance of it was expensive if we really did it properly. However, we would have to end our annual barbeque cooking contest, a very big event in the parish's life, though not one that added either members or money to the mission and ministry of the congregation. After weighing all the considerations as best we could, the Vestry and I presented the sale to the congregation and to the Diocese for approval. Everyone agreed, giving us confidence to move ahead.

As the annual parish meeting approached in January, another small but worrisome practice came to light. Diocesan canons provided for the Vestry to elect both wardens from its own number.

While Mississippi had had the same canon, I had always been able to be the sole nominator for the position of Senior, or Rector's, Warden. Here, I was told that my predecessor had tried that once, only to have the Vestry elect someone else, a person who did not get along with him. While I again felt the warning tension in my abdomen, it seemed to me that the best plan was to go along for the first year, and to work to have the canon changed to allow rectors to appoint the Senior Warden. It came as another surprise to discover that the rectors were divided about the canon, insuring defeat of any change in convention. However, the Vestry elected a man I truly liked, Rock Janda, as the new Senior Warden for 1986. We would work well together for the coming year.

The Bishop and Convention were gracious to welcome me into the circle of leadership. Bishop Alex Dickson appointed me chair of the St. Columba Conference Center Board and the Convention elected me as a diocesan trustee of the University of the South, where I served on the alumni council of the School of Theology. In addition, I consulted with various parishes on stewardship canvasses, and taught the Lay Education and Development course as I had in Mississippi.

The Vestry proceeded with our plans to sell property to fund the construction. By the spring of 1986, a contract was signed to sell three acres to a development corporation for the construction of a planned unit development office park. That summer, as the family prepared to go Sewanee for my first six weeks of study toward my doctor of ministry degree, we broke ground.

When the big trucks arrived a few days later to establish the pad for the new nave, one of them sank to its axles. Samples indicated very wet subsurface soil, necessitating considerable excavation and installation of a compacted clay foundation. As the cranes tore into the earth, they pulled up stumps, boards, chains, and other debris. It was apparent that a streambed had been badly filled in to level the ground and to construct the original buildings.

It never occurred to me that we might be building over more than a simple physical swampy bog. Parish life seemed much improved and we were having a decent time together as priest and people in spite of the little glitches. Technology would solve the problem with the soil; but the interior of our personal and corporate lives were much more difficult to identify and to work on. In my early morning devotions I offered up prayers of petition for guidance and resolution, but I didn't listen for answers, instead forging ahead in accord with human judgment.

That summer, we lived in Bishop Gray's home at Sewanee. Overlooking a bluff on a secluded gravel road outside the Domain, it was perfect for study, reflection, and relaxation. Stephen and Mary spent time in the summer camp in Monteagle, and Robbie and I enjoyed quiet time and renewal of old friendships among the faculty and doctor of ministry students of the University. Rock Janda kept me posted on the progress of construction, but I wasn't required to spend much time thinking about that project. We returned to begin our second year at Holy Apostles with renewed energy and confidence that this was indeed a good call.

Robbie had finished two years of her Education For Ministry course in Yazoo City, and sought a way to complete it in Memphis. Because of the time involved, I had let my license drop and no one at Holy Apostles was involved with the four-year course of study. She located and joined a group at the Church of the Holy Communion, the sponsoring parish for St. Mary's School. That choice turned out to be more of a blessing than either of us imagined at the time, serving as her only consistent support during the years of turmoil and trouble that lay ahead. It also led to her employment as a kindergarten teacher at St. Mary's School beginning in September.

I continued to be involved in ministries outside the parish and the church, including ongoing service on the advisory panel to Judge Weinstein of New York for the distribution of the Agent Orange settlement funds.

Military life was changing dramatically in the decade following the end of the War in Vietnam. Downsizing and base closures were hot items in the Congress, with representatives and senators wanting to close bases everywhere except in their own states and districts. That year, Blytheville AFB was renamed for General Ira Eaker, commander of the Eighth Air Force in Europe during WWII. Soon after, one of the Stratofortresses on the base received a copy of the nose art from the B-17 known as the "Memphis Belle," now restored and on display on Mud Island in Memphis. Dubbed the "Memphis Belle III," the original belle for whom she was named was present to break a bottle of champagne on her nose. Perhaps no more than a political maneuver to keep the base open, it was nevertheless a moving experience for this cold and hot warrior.

Because of my proximity to Blytheville, I could drive the 90 miles on Friday morning, spend the day at the chapel, have lunch or dinner with Robbie's dad, and return home, all on a day I was not scheduled in the office. Because I was rarely at the base on Sundays, my duties focused on counseling, special project planning and other events in support of the chapel program.

I continued to find the first two weeks of November as a good time to do my annual tour of active duty. In the parish's life, the Every Member Canvass was being conducted, but it was on a kind of autopilot by then, with everyone knowing their duties and executing the plan.

In the fall of the year, my parents called to announce that one of my brothers was an alcoholic and had just entered into the twelve-step program of Alcoholics Anonymous. I was startled by that announcement for several reasons, but mostly because I had started to be concerned about my own daily highballs. For the next few months I determined in the morning that I would not drink that night; but the first thing I did as I came home from work was to pour a large scotch and water, and on particularly stressful days, two.

Chapter 13

One afternoon near Thanksgiving, as I sipped the drink and pondered my growing inability to follow through on a simple decision, my ten-year-old daughter asked, "Daddy, why do you drink one of those every evening?"

I didn't have an answer and mumbled, "It helps me relax," knowing that it sounded like a huge lie in my own ears. In reality, the guilt I felt and my failure to keep promises to myself added to the sense of irritation at daily events, rather than smoothing their rough edges. That day I decided to stop on my thirty-ninth birthday, December 4, 1986. I failed.

On December 9, I called my brother. When he asked how things were going, I replied, "Pretty well. I do need to take some steps to improve, though."

The conversation moved ahead for about thirty more seconds before he suddenly stopped and asked, "What did you say?"

I was hoping that he would hear the "steps" code word, and simultaneously hoping he wouldn't. I was relieved when he didn't, and even more relieved when he did. "I've been bit, too."

"What do you mean?"

"I think I'm an alcoholic,"

"Wow! Why do you think so?"

"Well, I've always seen you as a normal drinker. When you joined AA, I had to face my own drinking habit."

"I'll give you a choice. You can come here for an evaluation, or I'll come to Memphis. Come to think about it, I've got a frequent flyer ticket. Why don't I send it to you, and you can fly up here to go to a meeting and talk with some people who have helped me?" I chose to fly there.

Robbie had gotten so used to my annual winter ill humor by then, that she was surprised and annoyed that I considered myself to have a drinking problem, much less alcoholism. That day marked a new phase in my understanding of freedom; but it also marked the preface to the darkest year of our lives and to my personal "dark night of the soul."

First, we had a glorious bright spot. After many delays, we finally moved into the new worship space, celebrating our first Eucharist on Christmas Eve 1986. We had designed the building so that entering worshipers would face the Baptismal font as a symbol of our salvation. Seating faced the lectern/pulpit, where the Word of God was proclaimed for our edification, and the Altar, where we received the life-giving body and blood of Our Savior. Behind the altar were large windows overlooking an azalea garden and the woods beyond. Hangings behind the font and altar were made by parishioners and reflected our joy and our commitment to share in Christ's eternal priesthood. That day was a sign of the Lord's favor in the midst of troubled times.

Unfortunately Robbie had a bad bout of strep, brought about by a weakened immune system. Between services on Christmas Eve, the choir, in a loving gesture to her and to me, went to our home to serenade her with carols. This parish was really becoming home to us and our circle of friends grew ever wider.

The Baptismal Font, Easter Day

227

Beginning in 1987 I also served as president of the College of Clergy. That position, too, would challenge my diplomacy and leadership. While we were a small diocese, with fewer than forty congregations and fifty clergy, we were also somewhat divided. There were large parishes and small, city and country, liberal and conservative, growing and shrinking. It was the kind of diversity the Church had always seen as an asset. In West Tennessee, it seemed to be a liability, with friction and distrust between many of the pairings.

The General Convention's decision in 1976 to authorize the ordination of women to the priesthood had not met with universal acceptance. The new Book of Common Prayer authorized on first reading the same year was also a continuing issue in the Church a decade later. Both of them, especially women's ordination, were very sore issues with the Anglo-Catholics among us.

Through the grace of God, the fellowship of AA, over 300 meetings in 1987, the support of the family and those friends in whom I confided, the desire to drink vaporized like dew on a sunny day. All the feelings I had tried to numb now demanded attention. The insecurities that plagued me in my youth, the horrors of war and imprisonment, the struggles with conflict in the church, and a sense of inadequacy as a representative of God came flooding out.

Over the years, the people who sought sobriety in AA would teach me that the experiences of life could be sources of strength and hope rather than pain and despair. Whenever I feel uncertainty, a meeting will be a haven for understanding and confidence. Whenever I feel strong, I know there is someone in the meeting who needs to hear from me. By working the steps of the program, I began to find a freedom I hadn't felt since the day I climbed aboard the Hanoi Taxi. But just as I had not yet come truly home from prison, I knew I would have to stay close to my new friends to find freedom from the fears that had beckoned me to drink.

My attitude improved at first, along with my energy level. I began to feel intoxicated with life and joy in Memphis and at Holy Apostles, and my routine praying of the Morning Office returned to its former depth. I was slowly learning just how powerless I was without the firm guidance of the Holy Spirit, and how much I needed to return to the days when I had trusted so completely.

Storm clouds were beginning to gather overhead, turning our sense of well-being in the direction of foreboding. During the Christmas holidays, Robbie's sister called and scolded her for not being present when she was ill and during the final illness of their mother a few years before. It was the first time in her life that Robbie had experienced any harshness from her sister. A very tight familial relationship had suddenly turned very sour.

In spite of that unexpected turn, good things began to happen and I blindly believed that I had moved out of the secret dysfunction in my soul. I was asked to serve on the team of a Cursillo weekend, sharing priestly duties with the Rev. Ann Carierre. A day school located at a nearby church was being forced out, so they came to us and asked to move their operation to our facility, giving us another draw for young families in the neighborhood. The Convention elected me as a Deputy to the General Convention to be held in Detroit the following year, which also meant that I would once again serve as a delegate to the Provincial Synod to be held at Kanuga, North Carolina.

The Vestry decided to sell the rectory and to give me a housing allowance to purchase my own home. It was presented as a reward and an opportunity for us to build equity. While I liked the idea, I also knew it would be very tempting to use the proceeds to finish paying off the new building, and once that money was gone, the parish would have a hard time coming up with the housing allowance. I insisted that any proceeds be put into a reserve account and restricted to supplement the housing allowance. I was discomforted by the assurances of the vestry.

While my gut, the place the Holy Spirit nudges me first, told me not to do it, my head agreed to the sale. By the time the family moved into our new home, controversy over the sale and our purchase of a house some deemed inappropriately large had swelled to a tropical storm.

One odd event during the move was that the sofa bed was easily removed through the door of my study. The second was that I slipped and sprained my ankle while taking items to the car, putting me on the sideline of getting settled for several days. Were they omens, signals from God to pay attention, or mere circumstance? Whatever they were, these events did not enter under the scrutiny of theological reflection.

Family life took a major dive in the early summer. Robbie's sister, Mary O'Connor, whom she always simply called "Sister," was brought to Memphis for hospitalization for mental problems, Stephen had begun skipping school and showing signs of depression, I was beginning a downward spiral into darkness, and all the needy people in the family tore Robbie's emotions to shreds. Sister's diagnosis was finally determined to be Huntington's Disease. That explained the phone call of the year before and the strained relationship since. When I read the diagnosis, I stepped off the cliff into the abyss of terror, depression and spiritual collapse. The experience with the patient at the San Antonio State Hospital a dozen years earlier sent deep and inconsolable fear into my heart. Did Robbie have the same gene? If so, did Stephen? Did Mary? *God, have you doomed my family?!*

On my next trip to Blytheville for reserve duty, I caught myself looking for unprotected bridge abutments. I could "skid" off the road and crash into one of them, ending my darkness once and for all. I was in very deep trouble. Back safely in Memphis, I called Dr. Jim Pang, Sister's psychiatrist, to make an appointment for therapy. He had now talked with Sister, Robbie, and me.

He diagnosed me with Post-Traumatic Stress Disorder, and put me on anti-depressants. My fear was not just a fear of a genetic disorder, it was a reliving of the awful experience of being in a situation that was completely beyond my control and over which I could exercise no influence. However, I kept the focus in the therapeutic sessions on my fear of Huntington's, brushing away the doctor's suggestion that my short time in Hanoi could have any really detrimental effects on me. I knew I was wrong, but did not want to open that Pandora's Box with the terror of genetic disease already out.

Just as my downward spiral began, the neighboring Episcopal Parish of All Saints called a new "traditionalist" rector. The Bishop, who instructed the parishioners to follow his oversight and that of the priest without complaint, installed Carl Cannon as their rector. About fifty charismatic, neo-Pentecostal parishioners moved their membership to Holy Apostles because we had become very welcoming of a wide variety of people from various spiritual persuasions.

Because of their divisive history at All Saints, I called the leaders of the transferring members into my office to tell them that if they were coming as a church in exile, they could keep going; if they were coming to join this parish, they should plan to disperse into the congregation. I also tried to convince the continuing membership that these folks didn't pose a threat to us. The parish was on a tightrope before, now it was on a razor's edge, and I was very shaky in my mental and spiritual health. The leaders of the incoming group agreed verbally and assured me of their devout intent. The next year was one of relaxed concern as they seemed to bend over backwards to merge themselves into the ongoing life of Holy Apostles.

I observed my fortieth birthday alone and in the dark, no longer able to open the Prayer Book at home, much less pray the Daily Office.

Chapter 13

I had hoped for a traditional "Holy Apostles fortieth birthday," complete with a surprise party and gag gifts; but people were afraid to bother me in my dark dungeon. All my signals were convoluted and unreadable. I wanted outside contact and expressions of love, concern, and support – ministry from the Christian community that I served as pastor; but I stayed inside the house with the drapes drawn, the lights off, and refused to answer the phone. I felt so separated and alone, I might as well have been in my cell in the Heartbreak Hotel.

Afterwards, Robbie told me that Brian and Peg Pecon had offered to throw the party, but she had put them off. That resulted in a terrible argument; but there was no way that even my wife could have read through all the defenses I was putting up to keep away the very things I wanted the most.

Christmas was very difficult. I felt like the walking dead, but also found the liturgy of Our Lord's Nativity to be a time of warmth and peace, lifting me high enough to see the light of Christ. I was beginning to feel like a drowning man bobbing to the surface for air, and sinking quickly into the depths soon after. The altar and pulpit were the only two places I felt really alive; and many people commented that the sermons I preached during those months were especially meaningful and spiritual.

By January 1988, I had rallied, at least for the moment, as we prepared to host the convention of the Diocese of West Tennessee in our new and remodeled facilities. Everyone pulled together to make the event both efficient and gracious. We had come a long way in less than three years and were known across the Diocese as a friendly and welcoming community, diverse in our membership, and kindly disposed toward other parishes of whatever style and vision. Our membership had grown by twenty percent in the same period, and the leadership was determined to make the parish work spiritually and financially.

This year, Bishop Dickson asked me to take responsibility in West Tennessee for the Bishop's Happening Movement as I had done for so many years in Mississippi. I agreed, mostly because I loved to work with teens, and because my favorite teen, my son Stephen, was at the age to attend. I thought we might be able to connect on a spiritual level, rather than on the strained surface level of father and teenaged son.

I also served on the Standing Committee, the Family Life Commission, the AIDS Task Force, as well as attending the Synod and General Convention. As in Mississippi, I believed these to be part of the fulfillment of my ordination vows, and I relished in being part of something larger and less stressful than the parish. Unfortunately, I still had not learned to count the cost to my soul or to my family.

In spite of improved confidence in my work outside the parish, I still tended to react to every little controversy within as though it were an unscalable cliff. In the midst of a confrontation over the release of pledge cards at a spring vestry meeting, I offered my resignation and walked out. Fortunately for me, the wardens realized how low I had gone and called Bishop Dickson. He immediately intervened personally as a pastor and friend to my entire family, rallied the Vestry, and helped the congregation to support us in our time of trial.

He also instructed the Vestry to turn over all pledge records to me immediately. I was so upset by this time, I checked the Vestry records first, discovering that half of them, including the newly elected Senior Warden, did not pledge anything to the financial well being and mission of the parish. The downward spiral into the abyss was not yet complete.

The Vestry, at the bidding of the Bishop, agreed to give me a three-month rest from parish administration, and my associates Noland Pipes and Senter Taylor, along with deacon Tony Hill, took care of day-to-day operations. I continued to make Sunday appearances, rotating the duties of Celebrant and Preacher with the others.

I could see support and concern in the eyes of the congregants, but my heart was cold. Those hours gave me a bright spot in the week, but drained me of all energy by Sunday noon.

My observation of Robbie was that my beloved wife of sixteen years was at her wits end in coping with the multiple tragedies and controversies of the year, but I felt a wall between us and couldn't help. The son that I loved so deeply was in his own dark night, like some kind of parallel universe to my own, and I was helpless to assist or even to speak words of love and encouragement to him. That spring, while I was attending an Air Force Chaplain's course, Stephen's counselor diagnosed him with school phobia. His fears were aggravated by the frequent school changes he had experienced both from our move and from the progression from elementary to middle school. Our daughter Mary seemed to roll with the punches, providing a calm in the eye of the hurricane that swirled around her. But Robbie and I both worried that she was more deeply affected than we could see.

I felt as if I were living in the Pit described in Psalm 88. Rather than prayers of thanksgiving and petition, I was more and more speaking lamentations to God, "You have laid me in the depths of the Pit, in dark places, and in the abyss." I felt as though a great stone rested on my chest and I was truly powerless to remove it. I was deaf to words of encouragement or support. Life was dimming to deeper shades of gray and my soul seemed to be shriveling within me.

The cycle of darkness that had always plagued me from Christmas to Easter was truly the worst in 1987-1988, worse even than the prison experience itself. There the days were predictable, the friends close, the enemy easily identified, and the hopes of peace and repatriation fresh. Here I never knew what to expect each morning, joy or despair, excitement or strain, encouragement or confrontation.

In May, thanks to the therapy from Dr. Pang, the medications he had prescribed, the fellowship of AA, and a returning sense of support from key members of the parish, I was beginning to feel the burdens of life lighten and the sky clear. I foolishly decided that I was feeling so well that I could stop the therapy and wean myself from the anti-depressants.

We left for another summer at Sewanee where I continued my studies in spirituality in pursuit of a doctorate in ministry. We had purchased a "fix-up" house the previous summer out in the country at the very end of Rattlesnake Bend Road, not far from the summer home of Bishop Gray of Mississippi in which we had lived the year before.

Robbie thought I was mad to buy the little house in the woods, which was surprising. She could normally make a silk purse from a sow's ear, but she could see no redeeming value in this little wreck. The price was right, and the contractor who was doing the repairs and upgrades was inexpensive. We arrived to a transformed dwelling, and the family found it and the surrounding wooded acres to be a pleasant retreat.

As the summer ended I realized that I would still need three hours of credit after the 1989 summer to be able to earn my Doctor of Ministry degree. The School of Theology was offering that amount of credit for a "Practicum in Spiritual Direction." The candidate was required to conduct a hundred hours of supervised spiritual direction in order to complete the course. Professor Bob Hughes explained that I could gain the time through group, rather than individual direction. He agreed with me that I could write a course in spiritual growth and direction, teach it to a group of parishioners, come to Sewanee every other month for his supervision, and earn the necessary three hours. By the time we returned to Memphis in August, I was feeling refreshed and the family closer after six weeks in our mountain retreat at the end of Rattlesnake Bend Road.

I had been struck by how closely the twelve steps of AA were aligned with the Anglican spirituality as set forth by the Book of Common Prayer. It would be possible for me to develop a fourteen-week course in spiritual living (introduction, twelve steps, conclusion) and teach it during the spring. I had spent most of my time at Sewanee studying Anglican spirituality, prayer, and hymnody, and was eager to share the insights I was finally gaining with the people of Holy Apostles.

I called the course "The Spiritual Quest: Christian Spiritual Direction in Twelve Simple Steps." My purpose was to respond to the growing hunger in the parish for a deeper spirituality and in the AA group for a link back into the Christian faith and church. AA and the Church together had managed, in spite of their respective flaws, to work during my dark night and to bring me light and peace. The course seemed like an answer to both sets of friends, as well as to me. I could develop the course in the fall and teach it during Epiphany and Lent of 1988. By exercising the discipline of theological reflection in this one cubbyhole of my life, perhaps I could eventually trust my entire anxiety closet to the care of God.

Within thirty days of our return from Sewanee, life changed again. Robbie's Uncle Lucian called from Blytheville to say that Robbie's father had collapsed in the doctor's office, was in cardiac care, and not expected to live. A week earlier, he had called St. Mary's School, gotten Robbie out of class and asked if it would be alright if he spent part of her inheritance to buy a new Cadillac.

We both thought it was funny that he would call to ask permission, but never dreamed the inheritance would come so soon or so tragically.

While my strength was rising, Robbie's collapsed. I picked Stephen up from school, drove to St. Mary's to get Robbie and Mary, and sped up I-55 to northeast Arkansas, hoping and praying that we would get there before he died. That was not to be. By the time we drove into the hospital parking lot, Robert Wade had died and his body had been removed to the mortician's. It would be the next day before we could see his body and say prayers of commendation over it. Our moods swung between steely determination and copious tears.

Robert Wade had been heart-broken over Sister's disease and his will to continue in business had evaporated. He was at the end of a going-out-of-business sale and had sold the store to another company. His death was officially listed as heart failure. Unofficially, it was clear to us that it was better stated as a "broken heart." He had named Robbie as the executrix of the estate, which was split between her and her nephew, Robert O'Connor. Robbie's dad had taken Sister out of his will when she was confined to the nursing home. Had she inherited any money, her medical benefits would have been suspended until the inheritance was depleted. This way, her son would be able to benefit from his grandfather's estate and Sister's medical care would not be compromised.

As a result of this tragic climax to an awful year, Robbie entered her own dark night. I was sure it would be over one day, but I was too close to my own to be of much help. She turned to my female assistant priest, Senter Taylor, for her spiritual nurture. Stephen and our daughter Mary were groping their ways through puberty and the teens without much positive help from either of us, regardless of how much we tried.

The good news was that my daily praying of Morning Prayer was finding meaning and direction again; and the development of Spiritual Quest was bringing me into a more coherent expression of my love of God and confidence in his guiding hand.

The bad news was that we decided to keep the new Cadillac. It was too big and brown to suit Robbie's taste, but she couldn't bring herself to sell it, and Robert O'Connor was too young to drive. I sold one of our cars and started driving the Cadillac for my own.

When the every member canvass was completed, the pledges for 1989 were down twenty percent from 1988. The toll of the year, and possibly the presence of that car, had now affected the financial stability of the parish, always barely balanced even in a good year. As I feared when we sold the rectory, salaries had to be adjusted downward to balance the budget.

That fall, Robbie and I also began enjoying the company of Carl and Linda Cannon. Carl was the rector of All Saints, the parish that had split upon his arrival. Carl told me that when his father died, he had inherited a Cadillac, too, followed by the same downturn in pledges.

At this point in their lives, the Cannons owned an airplane and invited Robbie and me to fly with them to Sikeston, Missouri for dinner one evening. As a result, I was hooked again on flying. Within a few weeks, I had my medical form updated and took refresher flight lessons to be able to act once again as pilot in command of a single-engine aircraft. Like building the fire truck bed, the doll house, and the car, flying offered me a diversion from the ordinary in my life and gave me times of withdrawal and refreshment, freeing my mind to be open enough to hear God's voice. Exercising a skill known to so very few provided a boost not only to my strained ego, but also to my prayer life. Soaring above the countryside I could gain the perspective to return to the duties and tasks below.

The more I flew, the deeper my spirituality and the more creative my efforts became.

Carl Cannon was one of the Anglo-Catholics; and I was one of the priest's employing a female priest, and very "broad church" in my liturgical preference. One lunch at a monthly clergy meeting, I came out of the cafeteria line, noticed Carl, and sat at the table with him. The other priests at the table, all dressed in black clergy shirts and suits, fell silent. Their dress set them apart as Anglo-Catholics, while other clergy were dressed in mufti or in blue or gray clericals. One asked me, "Are you sure you want to sit here?"

"Of course, why not?"

"Look around."

As I glanced around the room, all the other clergy were seated at tables, but with one row of tables separating them from this group in the corner. I was stunned. In spite of our differences over churchmanship and the ordination of women, I could see no reason to cordon off the Anglo-Catholics like they had the plague, or for any other division or rancor within the small family of clergy in West Tennessee.

When I was first ordained, we valued high, broad, and low church worship, the presence of liberals and conservatives, activists and contemplatives. We saw our mix as our strength and a sign of the majesty and variety of God, not as a weakness to be overcome by ridding ourselves of those who disagreed with us. The controversies of the 1960s and 1970s that plagued the nation, the war in Vietnam, the Civil Rights movement, the women's movement, and that plagued the church, Prayer Book revision, ordination of women, were still causing division among us. Some issues could be seen; others were doing their damage below the surface.

Had I had any insight, I would have grasped the importance of that luncheon not only for the way the Church was becoming dysfunctional, but also for the impact of those events on my own soul's health. So much of my personal history in the 1960s and 1970s was stuffed into my anxiety closet that I had forgotten it even existed.

Chapter 13

Could the "presenting" issues causing friction in the fellowship of the clergy be false ones, masking the greater hurts of a decade and more in the past? While I knew intellectually that such was true in the conflicts of the Holy Land and Northern Ireland, I couldn't draw similar conclusions in the diocese, the parish, or me.

At Thanksgiving, my parents and my sister-in-law, Genie, came for a visit. I took advantage of the opportunity to plan a surprise fortieth birthday party for Robbie in the cafeteria at St. Mary's School. Since Robbie was in the market for a new car of her own, Genie and I went car shopping with her. As the afternoon waned, I suggested that we try again another day and show Genie the school while we still had some sunlight.

As we drove into the driveway to St. Mary's, Stephen and another young boy darted from behind a berm and ran behind the building. Fortunately, Robbie didn't recognize our son, and stopped at the front door and called to the gardener to be on the lookout for the vandals she had seen. We entered the majestic front doors and Robbie proceeded to show Genie every room on both floors in the old mansion. Finally we entered the enclosed walkway to the annex that housed more classrooms and the cafeteria.

As we passed the cafeteria doors, Robbie noticed some figures silhouetted against the outside windows beyond. "Robert, somebody's in there."

Genie and I still maintained our composure. "Maybe we better check it out."

"Be careful."

I opened the door, leading Robbie by the hand. The lights came on to reveal over fifty people – the Bishop, our family, friends from the parish, the school, her Education For Ministry group, and from other places and times – gathered there to celebrate this big birthday. She was offered a rocking chair, with a walker placed nearby as a joke, and presents were brought to her to open and to enjoy. It was a wonderful surprise, done up in the "Holy Apostles" way.

As planned, I began teaching Spiritual Quest on January 11, 1989. As a result, the central steps of examination, repentance, confession, and absolution would come up in the midst of Lent, a most appropriate time in the cycle of the liturgical year. Nearly twenty people from the parish, including Robbie, and my AA group joined the course. By opening my soul just a little to them in lecture, they were able to share their souls with a friend during the second hour of the evening. Surely the presence of God was in that place and in the people gathered.

In preparation for teaching the middle steps, I made a journey to Sewanee for supervision and to make a comprehensive auricular confession to Father Hughes. I had made my last confession in 1976 to John Westerhoff during an Ash Wednesday Quiet Day at St. Mary's Convent; but I knew I had left out some things from my youth and college years that still bothered my conscience, things I had not spoken even in my Fifth Step with my AA sponsor. Without confession, absolution and amendment for those youthful indiscretions and the brokenness of the previous eleven years, I would not be able to teach others about the grace of these steps. Even so, I continued to keep large blocks of my life history locked away from God's healing touch.

The spring of 1989 was much brighter than the darkness of the previous two years, but there were still enormous challenges to be faced, including a growing level of criticism from the people who had moved over from All Saints two years earlier. My patience with them was waning and my defensiveness growing as I was second-guessed about nearly every decision I made. I felt like everybody knew how to do my job except me.

Afraid of another cycle of bitterness, and burdened by the deep disappointments of the last two years, I called Bishop John MacNaughton in San Antonio to see if he would bring me home to West Texas.

Chapter 13

By the time the family headed to our mountain retreat for my last summer of work on my doctorate, I was beginning to hear from some parishes seeking a new rector.

The search committee from St. Alban's Episcopal Church in Harlingen, Texas started interviewing me for the position of rector as the summer ended. Following a visit from the committee to Memphis, Robbie and I visited the Rio Grande Valley to continue exploring the possibility of a call, which was issued and accepted in early October. I agreed to start on the first Sunday in Advent, the same Sunday I had begun my ministry in Yazoo City in 1978.

Had I really been paying attention to my AA program and to Spiritual Quest, I might have realized that this move just might fit the definition of "geographical cure." The thought even crossed my mind, but I determined that the troubles that plagued Robbie, Stephen, and me in Memphis needed to be left far behind. Our fear of Huntington's Disease seemed suppressed for the moment, Stephen had adapted well to a new school, and Robbie was coping with her father's death and her sister's confinement. Without nagging doubts in the pit of my stomach, I was confident that the Spirit was in this move.

During the summer, I had bought a little book by William Madow entitled *Transitions*. He described the process of moving from one place to another, pointing out that you could not arrive at the new place without saying good-bye to the place you were leaving. As he explained, in between leaving and arriving, people experienced a kind of void, a no-man's-land of regrets and uncertainty, anticipation and hope. The parallel of his work with the story of the Exodus from Egypt was obvious. It also paralleled the leave-taking my family and the parish would soon experience.

After discussing the book with my secretary and confidant, Wanda Goodrich, I decided to teach a short course to the parish to prepare them for their next interim experience.

Conducted over parish dinners during late October and early November, I felt that the large group of participants could better understand the difficult five years we had shared, look forward to the future, and cope with the interim with more strength than they had before I came. The tenure was ending well, in spite of the personal trauma in the family and the challenges of a growing but awkward parish. I was finally learning to weave the thread of theological reflection into the tapestry of my life in Christ.

In the question and answer time during the final session, I was asked what they might expect from the Bishop for interim leadership. One parishioner, a faithful member of the choir and normally a quiet supporter, challenged a suggestion that a female priest might be appointed, threatening trouble if it happened. Having had a successful relationship with my female assistant, Senter Taylor, and having sponsored another woman, Susan Crawford, to seminary, I lost my composure and snapped back that they would be in serious trouble if they took that attitude. With another statement, which I received as baiting, I slammed my book and dismissed the parish with angry parting words, just the opposite of my intentions and hopes.

Robbie was so upset that she left the church and started walking home alone. Some shocked parishioners went looking for her and gave her a ride the rest of the way. I fell into dark guilt and a renewed fury over the occasional confrontations that had punctuated my tenure in that place and had spoiled my attempts to make things even a little bit better. Later, when word came that the parishioner had deliberately staged the confrontation to provoke an angered response from me, I felt betrayed and humiliated, not only by my own reaction, but by his treachery. I couldn't wait to shake the dust of that place off my feet.

Chapter 13

My brother Neal retired from the Air Force that fall. As he was preparing for a civilian position, I introduced him to a parishioner who was a senior pilot with Federal Express, who in turn introduced him to the personnel chief. Once that door was opened, his own skills took over and he was quickly hired as a pilot. He stayed in our guest room during his initial training, and when I accepted the call to Harlingen, he offered to buy our house.

Since St. Alban's did not own a rectory, Robbie wanted to build a new house for us. Again, Neal was appearing on the scene of our lives as a gift from God. Since his wife and daughters would not be ready to move from California until the end of the school year, we could leave our household goods in place until our new home was ready. In the meantime, we could live in a furnished apartment.

Chapter 14

Challenges and Disappointments

Isaiah 40:29-31
He gives vigor to the weary, new strength to the exhausted.
Young men may grow weary and faint, even in their prime
they may stumble and fall; but those who look to the Lord
will win new strength, they will grow wings like eagles; they
will run and not be weary, they will march on and never
grow faint.

Stephen and I drove to Harlingen the week after Thanksgiving
with a full car and an overloaded pick-up truck towing a boat and
trailer. He was only fifteen, but did well on the four-day drive. Had
we had Granny Clampett in her rocking chair, our caravan could
easily have been taken as a scene from the *Beverly Hillbillies.*

The first day's journey took us only as far as Yazoo City, where
we spent the night. Our second stop was at my sister's house in
Louisiana. Day three took us along the Gulf Coast into Victoria,
Texas. Finally, on the fourth day of travel we arrived at the southern
tip of Texas.

We unloaded our boxes into the apartment and the office, and
proceeded to enroll Stephen in school. Robbie and Mary were
finishing up the semester at St. Mary's School in Memphis, where
Robbie taught and Mary was a student, and would join us in the
middle of December.

Chapter 14

When the family drove into Harlingen a few days before Christmas, the temperature had plummeted to eighteen degrees. The citrus crop in the Rio Grande Valley was devastated, as unpicked fruit froze and tree trunks split with the cold. The weather warmed to the thirties in a few days.

One of our first challenges was to complete our house plans and find a contractor. By the middle of February we had the design and lot we liked and awarded the contract to build it. The contractor took just over seventy days, and we looked forward to being able to move in. Neal's family was ready to leave California in May and to join him in our old house in Memphis. So, as he needed to ship our household goods to us, we were ready to receive them and move into our home. We completed the unloading of the truck on a Friday, arranged the house on Saturday, and on Sunday afternoon came home from lunch to continue the settling-in process.

Immediately, Robbie began to complain of an upset stomach, and then severe pain in the middle of her back. I called a doctor in the parish, and he came over to see her. He diagnosed gallstones, and had her admitted to the hospital right away for surgery. As I waited in prayer for her to come out of this latest physical trial, I wondered why every joy in our life was counterbalanced with troubles, especially for my wife. It would be many years before I could hear the gentle voice of God telling me that the good things were sent to balance the trials, not the other way around.

Once again, I felt like a juggler trying to keep church, family, and Air Force all moving smoothly. Each of them continued to have a profound effect on my relationship with my Lord, but after years of separating them, I would not experience temporal or spiritual life as truly integrated. The lessons from Memphis were out of reach.

Living on the southern tip of Texas meant that I would have to change reserve assignments for the first time since I had reactivated eight years earlier. The closest Air Force Base with a need for mobilization reserve chaplains was Lackland, the basic training site for new recruits. Located in San Antonio, it meant a 250-mile drive.

I could still manage to train one Friday a month, but would have to make the trip on a Thursday evening after work and return on Saturday.

However, I found a more pleasant way to go. I decided to continue flying. At the local airport, I found a plane for sale at a reasonable price. In March 1990, I bought the 1972 Comanche 250, and proceeded to gain my instrument rating. Having the plane meant that I could make the trip to Lackland in an hour and a half, land at adjacent Kelly AFB and catch a base taxi across to the basic training center.

While the Comanche flew well, it had been neglected for several years as it sat mostly idle in a hanger, making maintenance more expensive than I had been led to believe. When I took it in for an annual inspection in the spring of 1991, I discovered that the propeller blades had to be replaced. I loved to fly, but I was upset by the hidden costs.

I frequently used the plane to fly to various meetings in the Diocese of West Texas in Corpus Christi, San Antonio, and the Hill Country. Because piloting was so very different from my daily routine, and because so few people had the skills of instrument flight, I found both pride and comfort in my abilities as an aviator. One rainy day, when I was asked to fly the bishop from McAllen to San Antonio, we entered the clouds a few minutes after take-off and did not descend out of them until we were on final approach at San Antonio International over two hours later. He was amazed that I could find my way across south Texas without reference to the ground and be lined up with the runway at the end. Flying replaced building things as my "mantra" for times when I needed to work through difficult issues.

Chapter 14

On the church front, two big challenges were presented within the first few months. First, the headmistress of the school was serving in an interim appointment and would be retiring in the fall of 1990. The vestry had decided to wait until I arrived before beginning a search for a new one, so that needed to get underway. We placed advertisements in the newsletter of the National Association of Episcopal Schools as well as in several trade magazines. Applications trickled in from around the country, but most were either inappropriate candidates or people who commanded much larger salaries than we were prepared to pay. One parishioner had applied, but was lacking experience and credentials. The vestry asked if Robbie would be interested in the position.

Because of her candidacy, I excused myself from the interviews, asking the committee to make their selection for presentation to the Vestry. Their decision was unanimous, as Robbie was the only candidate with both credentials and experience to lead our 350-student school. The Vestry and I, along with Robbie, were concerned about the wisdom of the husband-wife team; but decided that it was the best thing for both parts of the institution.

The second challenge came from the rectors in Brownsville and McAllen. Soon after the first of the year, they called on me to inform me that the Diocese of West Texas was planning a capital funds drive for an adult conference center and other projects and suggested that I should get the parish ready by preparing a joint campaign to do any capital work we needed.

I met with the Vestry and discovered they were already thinking about several ideas to expand the ministry, especially with the school. Over the next few months, we planned to replace some old temporary buildings on the campus with an addition to the school, to rework the play yards, and to make some improvements to parish offices, parking lots, and other facilities.

But before all that could get under way, we were faced with roof leaks in one of our older classroom buildings.

The junior warden proposed replacing the flat roof with a pitched one as a permanent solution to a nagging problem. The roofer he hired had a decent reputation and began work by stripping off the old roof. I questioned why he would do that, but he insisted that he could be done quickly, and would have the new roof constructed and watertight within a week. Unfortunately, before the week was out, a front moved in with heavy rains. The roofer was nowhere to be found as water poured through the roofs and finally collapsed the ceilings in six classrooms.

The Vestry was outraged when they discovered the roofer had not bought a bond. We fired him and hired the contractor from my house to come over on an emergency basis and repair the damages and get the roof completed. During the next two weeks, we held classes in every nook and cranny of the church for the children displaced by the reconstruction.

In November 1990, I received a call from a parishioner requesting an appointment. I had no idea who he was, nor did my secretary. Since he declined to state the reason for his visit, I assumed he was upset about something. As the hour approached, I kept watch on the parking lot to see if I recognized him. When he got out of his car, I knew that he and his wife were regular attendants at the early Sunday Eucharist, but they always left without going through the line at the back door. My curiosity was now piqued.

As we talked, Bill told me that he and his wife had been listening to my hopes for the parish, and knew that I wanted some renovations done to the offices and that we needed an additional priest on the staff. He asked which I would prefer. Since we were beginning to develop plans for a capital campaign, I said I would prefer the second priest now and that we could handle the renovations as part of the campaign.

Bill said he would like to fund the priest for two years. I was stunned! "How do you want me to handle that? Do you want to be part of a selection process? Do you want to wait until we have someone in place and pay monthly?"

He smiled and said, "How about this?" and handed me a handwritten check for $100,000. "Sue and I have been really blessed in the past year, and we want to share this with the church."

That was one of the most exciting days in my ministry. I called the wardens to tell them about it, then the bishop to ask for his nominations. None of us had any idea of being able to bring on a second priest during the foreseeable future.

Bishop MacNaughton recommended an old friend of his who was leaving a parish in another diocese. The priest had been recently divorced, and felt that a change in parish was necessary for a fresh start. All indications were that the divorce was a result of growing estrangement and not any misconduct, so the bishop believed it would be a good move. He came down for an interview and we agreed that we would make a good team. He wanted to focus on pastoral ministries, and I needed to focus on administration and fund-raising.

Within a few months, I had the opportunity to add a recent college graduate to the staff to serve as our youth minister. This young man was exceptionally personable and evinced a deep commitment to Christ. The timing of these staff additions in the midst of an international crisis seemed especially providential.

When Iraq invaded Kuwait in the fall of 1990, I was concerned that there might be a recall of reserves at some point in the impending conflict. During Desert Shield, I checked with the personnel center and was assured that any recall would involve chaplains more junior than me. I had been promoted to Lt. Colonel, making me less deployable than I had been a year or two earlier. However, I did offer to use my training days in any way necessary to meet the needs of the active duty chaplaincy. I was told that most of the reserve chaplains had called in with a similar offer.

However, when President Bush ordered the beginning of Desert Storm to force the Iraqi invaders out of Kuwait, the odds of a recall became a good bit higher, particularly if the war resulted in many casualties over a long period as was being predicted at the time. Within a few days of the beginning of US military operations, I received a recall notice to report to Lackland AFB to replace a senior chaplain who was being sent to Saudi Arabia.

I asked the vestry to hold my place open until I returned in three to six months. We quickly made our plans for the separation, and the parish held a reception to wish me well. However, the reception turned into a victory party when the war ended on a Thursday before I was to report on Monday. While I was home packing, the personnel officer called to cancel my orders.

We then began planning for a capital funds campaign to meet our goals and to support those of the Diocese. The campaign went well, topping our original goal by a comfortable margin. The campaign chairman had done a very good job of leading the parish effort.

In July 1991, Robbie and I flew to Phoenix in the Comanche to attend General Convention as exhibitors. I had printed "Spiritual Quest" for use as an adult education curriculum and wanted to introduce it to the larger church as it gathered for its triennial convention. We had some modest success with sales, made a lot of networking contacts, and renewed old friendships from around the church.

Halfway through the convention, Robbie returned to Harlingen and the youth minister flew out to replace her as my assistant in the booth. He brought the bad news that Robbie's car had been totaled a few days earlier by one of Stephen's friends, but fortunately no one had been hurt. Robbie was already en route, and was told by Stephen when she arrived home. She was furious that the car had been borrowed by a teenager without her permission and was very angry with the youth minister for allowing it while he was supervising our children in our absence. The strain in relationships among Stephen, his friends, my staff members and us were the worst results of the accident.

When it was time to return to south Texas, there was a minor problem with one of the instruments in the plane necessitating its replacement, but the part was unavailable. My frustration finally peaked and I offered to sell it to the dealer in Scottsdale. I didn't like his price very much, but I accepted it and flew home on a commercial airline. Six months later, I bought a newer plane, a 1984 Mooney 201.

In those few months, the storms of events had left me with a nagging sense of warning in the depths of my soul. The Air Force, my family, and the parish all had shown fissures that I tried to keep in

separate compartments. I feared that together they would overwhelm me; but keeping them separate meant that I could not address them as a cohesive whole. Eventually, the stress of one area would spill over into the next, like seawater through the compartments of the Titanic. God's hand would pry at the seams to bring me to unity within myself, but I struggled against his gentle touch.

As things began to settle down after Desert Storm, the leadership at the Air Reserve Personnel Center did some reorganization to better respond to any future contingencies.

A big change was to place a senior Catholic and Protestant reserve chaplain at each major air command headquarters. I was selected for the Strategic Air Command based at Offutt AFB in Omaha, Nebraska. I was thrilled at the appointment and saw it as an opportunity to put to rest my old disappointment at not being welcomed home from Vietnam by the Command twenty years earlier.

Getting to Omaha by commercial airline was a bit of a challenge; but I was able to get permission to fly my Mooney into Offutt and make the trip with some ease. However, I was not to make very many trips to SAC headquarters. A couple of months after I was attached there for training, the President announced a major reorganization of the Air Force in which the Strategic Air Command would be closed, with its assets merged with those of the Tactical Air Command into a new Air Combat Command. That change would occur in June 1992.

In October 1991, General Lee Butler, the Commander-in-Chief of SAC (CINCSAC), called me to his office. He told me he had heard that I was unhappy with the command's response during Operation Homecoming in 1973. I related that the then-CINC, General John Meyer, had failed to welcome the former POWs home, and seemed to have held us responsible for our own shoot-downs. He asked what I thought could be done to correct that situation.

"Well, sir, you could just let it ride. It was a long time ago, and we've all pretty much moved on with our lives. But if you want, there are a couple of things that come to mind. First, you could write a letter to all of us, saying a review of SAC history had revealed this oversight, and you wanted to give a belated welcome home and to commend us for our bravery and sacrifice. Second, you could invite us all to attend the stand-down of the Command."

"Chaplain, would you draft the letter for me? Then locate all of the B-52 crewmembers who were POWs in Vietnam and let's invite them up."

"Yes, sir." Ten B-52s had gone down over Hanoi that Christmas, with sixty-one men on board. Thirty-two had been captured and eventually returned to the U.S. in March 1973. Over the next three months I was able to locate all but one of the thirty-two for the CINC's letter and invitation. Eighteen of us accepted and planned to attend the final act of the Strategic Air Command as its banner was furled.

For thirty-five years the B-52 served as the centerpiece of the nuclear triad (ground launched missiles, sea launched missiles, and recallable aircraft) that kept the chaos of World War III at bay. "Peace is Our Profession" was not only the motto of SAC, but aptly describes what all branches of the American military strove for during that time.

I became very focused on the organization of the reunion as a way to bring some healing of old wounds for me and for the other former POWs from the final campaign of the Vietnam War. Perhaps the peace we had fought for would finally become personal. As a navigator, I had prided myself on "situational awareness," knowing how each part of the total mission fit together, where the dangers were, and what the escape routes or alternatives would be. It very slowly occurred to me to apply the same skill to the mission of being a whole person in Christ.

At the same time that I was planning the SAC reunion, my old friend Jack Wilson called to invite me to involve St. Alban's in an exchange with a Russian Orthodox parish near Moscow. He was trying to set up several such relationships to assist Russian parishes to learn how to operate in freedom, now that the Soviet Union was no more. Robbie and I planned to accompany him and other church leaders to Moscow, St. Petersburg and several other communities in May 1992.

The timing of the trip was such that Robbie and I would celebrate our twentieth wedding anniversary in Moscow just days before the scheduled the stand-down of SAC, a juxtaposition of events that made my head reel!

During my early years as a B-52 crewmember, I had been part of the force that trained to destroy military targets near each of those cities. To travel there in peace, then to return to the headquarters of the command that had been the strongest credible threat to the Soviet nuclear forces was a lot to digest.

When Robbie and I reached New York from Russia, she returned to Harlingen to attend Stephen's graduation from high school. I offered to cancel my attendance at the reunion, but he encouraged me to go. Though it felt like a wrong choice, I elected to attend the reunion with my old cellmates and to witness the historical passing of the Strategic Air Command.

SAC Ex-POWs at Command Closure

Chapter 14

Following the closure of SAC, I was reattached as the senior Protestant reserve chaplain at headquarters, Air Mobility Command at Scott AFB, Illinois. It had been nineteen years since I last visited Scott to receive my clean bill of health following ninety days of investigation for cancer.

The summer included a niece's wedding in Atlanta, to which we flew as a family, and a week at Camp Capers in the Hill Country. In August, Stephen entered college in San Antonio as the rest of us got busy with school and church in Harlingen. The fall proved to be difficult for all of us as life continued to be filled with personal challenges and disappointments. My greatest disappointment was my growing estrangement from my son. As I watched him struggle with his growing maturity, I felt helpless to guide him through the pitfalls of his teens. So much of our emotional lives seemed to be on parallel tracks, but my aversion to the strongly emotional events of the last twenty years kept me locked away from him at the time of his need. Even when we seemed to understand each other, we still missed connection. It seemed we were locked in a dance whose steps neither of us knew.

Robbie and I both had some personnel problems at church and school that were difficult to resolve. I was concerned about my assistant rector's performance and Robbie was dealing with some faculty issues. At the same time, our dearest friends from Yazoo City were experiencing marital strife. I flew over to Mississippi to visit with them as friend and priest, then invited them to spend a few days on South Padre Island to talk through their misunderstandings. By Thanksgiving it appeared that none of the fall's problems would be resolved amicably, and I was beginning to question my abilities as a leader, and to feel estranged from my Lord.

On Friday, December 18, 1992, I was home on my weekly day off when the Bishop called. At first, I thought he was calling because it was the twentieth anniversary of my shoot down and capture during the Vietnam War. Instead, he was calling to tell me that he had called my assistant to San Antonio and expected to suspend him within sixty days from the ministry because of misconduct in his previous parish. I felt as bad that day as I had twenty years earlier. The Bishop and I both had hoped it would turn out differently and we both felt betrayed by the deceptions that were becoming so apparent.

My struggle was made even worse by the memory of the Sewanee scandal of 1976. Once again, I was reminded that moral outrage and damage control are as much a part of church life just as it is in business, government, and the military. The very people who are set apart as examples to others are perhaps even more subject to the seductions of power, money, and sex than other segments of the population. The results of those seductions affect the lives of everyone connected to the community and challenge the faith of even the strongest believers.

A short poem I had referred to many times came to mind. It spoke of the sadness of broken vows, the confusion of society, change, and the longing to remain in relationship.

> I feel like I'm caught
>
> In mid stream changing horses,
>
> Acknowledging priests' weddings,
>
> And ministers' divorces.[1]

At a time when I needed divine guidance more than ever, my prayer life was becoming more perfunctory. In January, I had planned to make a two-week trip for the Air Force Reserves, but decided to cancel it after the assistant's suspension.

---

[1] Cecily Crossman, "Signs of the Seventies," in New Day (Melborne, FL: Crossman Publishing Co., 1978), p. 15.

Robbie did an exceptionally good job leading the school, and she found it immensely rewarding. Construction on new classrooms and the play yards had gone well and she brought high quality to the educational program. By the spring of 1993, we were beginning to get some grumbling in the parish about having a couple running the entire institution. We discussed the possibility of her finding another job after five years of leadership, which would have been in the summer of 1995, if the growing controversy didn't settle down. Following the other serious issues as it did, I suspected that the real object of concern was my leadership, not hers.

In May, 1993 I attended the Air Force Senior Chaplain School at Maxwell AFB in Montgomery, Alabama. The Chaplain School offered periodic professional courses for each career state, as well as special courses for specific ministry skills. I found each one to be valuable for both parts of my ministry. They also gave me the opportunity to renew friendships among the chaplains and to visit my parents in nearby Columbus, Georgia.

Two weeks after my return, we held a large fund-raising event for the school, the "Rhinestone Roundup," at the senior warden's ranch north of town. In real Texas fashion, there was food galore, and the show was opened by comedian Andy Anderson and starred Kenny Rogers. It was the highlight of the Rio Grande Valley social season, and raised about $50,000 for our school.

On Friday, June 11, the senior warden came in to talk about the state of the school. He was upset that the reserve funds had been depleted over the last couple of years, and wanted to dismiss Robbie as headmistress as the person responsible. I explained to him that the decision to use the funds had been made by the Board of Trustees before Robbie had been hired and their reason had been to enhance teacher stability and recruitment in the aftermath of the economic problems that followed the 1989 freeze.

Those intentions had been met and the funds were now being replaced as the economy improved.

Kenny Rogers and the Certains at the Rhinestone Roundup

He didn't accept my explanation and insisted that Robbie should have prevented it. I told him that she was not the responsible party and that the matter was finished. I went on to say that his responsibility as senior warden did not extend into the school, and that he was to stop lobbying to make changes without my agreement. Our conversation spiraled into a fierce argument about leadership in the church and ended with his resignation as senior warden.

Two days later, I left on an Air Force trip, filled with remorse and guilt about the argument, and hoping for some kind of resolution when I returned. Unfortunately, that would not occur even though I apologized for losing my temper as soon as I got back to town. The disappointment I had in myself for my poor response to a situation I thought I could handle weighed heavily on me for the next several months. I was entering the darkest spiritual crisis I had experienced since 1988, though by comparison this one was pretty mild.

Chapter 14

As school ended in 1993, I planned to make a tour of the Air Mobility Command bases east of the Mississippi River. The two-week trip took me to Air Force bases in Little Rock, Charleston, Washington, Wrightstown, Plattsburg, Peru, and finally the Command HQ in Belleville before my return to south Texas the end of June. This was a reprise of the trip I had cancelled the previous year when my assistant was dismissed. For the most part, the trip was very beneficial to the Mobility Command reserve chaplain program; and I was able to use the many hours of flying time to settle down from my upset with the senior warden.

A week after my return, Robbie and I planned a big flying vacation. First, we flew to Colorado Springs, Colorado to attend the twentieth anniversary reunion of Vietnam POWs. The second leg took us across the plains to Omaha, Nebraska so she could see the Strategic Air Command Museum. After a brief stop there, we climbed aboard to fly northeast toward Madison, Wisconsin to visit my brother, Phillip, and his wife.

A weather front had been stalled along the Mississippi River for some time, and as we flew toward Madison we could see the heavy clouds to our east. About forty miles from our destination, the weather report called for Level Two rain showers in the vicinity – not a huge challenge for an instrument pilot with a well-equipped aircraft. By the time we were twenty miles out, the showers had blossomed into Level Five thunderstorms, exceptionally dangerous for continued flight. By then we were between the two thunderstorms and had to proceed through heavy rain and moderate turbulence to the next community for a safe landing. Robbie was very upset and I was relieved that God had been with us through the peril of the storm. In hindsight, we should have landed well west of Madison rather than risk flying near those storms.

A few days later, we climbed into our Mooney again to fly to Little Rock, Arkansas to visit Robbie's sister, Mary; then on to New Orleans for a visit with my sister before returning to Harlingen.

I found the trip to be exhilarating; Robbie found it to be nerve-wracking.

The youth minister left for seminary in the late summer of 1993. Within a few months, though, he left school and broke off communication with me. My confidence in myself as a mentor and rector really suffered with this additional disappointment. My daily routine of praying the morning office of the Prayer Book virtually ceased as a spiritual numbness settled into my soul. I felt like I was back between the storms of Wisconsin, with no option but to forge ahead by force of will.

Within weeks, the season of Advent began, and I knew that the events of the past year would add more stress on the recurring anniversary story of imprisonment. Through the late summer and fall I had the good sense to seek counsel from another priest and from a psychologist, but the old anxiety closet was pretty much bursting at the seams. The day after Christmas, Robbie, Mary and I boarded the Mooney for a week-long trip to New Orleans, Memphis, Little Rock and Yazoo City to visit family and friends. Flying became an exercise in escape from the burdens of life as well as moments of spiritual refreshment. When I was at the controls of the plane, I felt confidence, competence, and peace.

The new year began with a new sense of determination. We could not afford to replace the staff members we had lost in 1993 because the money was going into the capital campaign payments. Robbie was fully engaged with the school, Mary was a junior in high school, and Stephen was in college in San Antonio. I stayed busy with the parish, diocesan work, and the Air Force.

On March 21, on my way to Scott AFB, I flew into Barksdale AFB in Shreveport, Louisiana to visit the Eighth AF Commander, Lt. Gen. Steve Croker, who had been the Wing Commander at Blytheville when I was a reserve chaplain there. Bill Buckley, the Commander for Logistics at Barksdale in 1994, saw my name on the VIP schedule. He remembered that I had wanted to go to the seminary, but did not know I was a reserve chaplain.

Chapter 14

He went to the flight line at the scheduled arrival time, but no plane appeared. Not knowing the General had planned a big welcome at base operations I had parked my private Mooney in the transient area.

Bill checked with Base Operations. No one knew anything; but one of the airmen said that he saw a Colonel with the Commander in the VIP Lounge. Bill walked over and opened the door. We both stood up and Bill's and my eyes fixed on each other. "Bob, is that you? It's me, Bill, Bill Buckley." This was the first time we had seen each other since the briefing room on Guam, 18 December 1972; and his insistent calls over Laos for fuel status rang in my ears when he said his name. Neither one of us was prepared for this meeting. It was truly a shock. The anger that I felt when I saw Howard Rose on the tarmac at Blytheville AFB in April 1973 began to rise within me. This was not the right time or place to react that way. Besides, I couldn't understand why I would feel such intense anger. Suddenly, I was back in Hanoi. *Don't show negative emotion. Stuff it. Control yourself. Be polite but cautious. What is he doing wearing eagles?* Bill's face showed excitement and joy at this reunion. We shook hands, embraced, talked briefly and then he departed while General Croker and I continued our visit.

As I continued my trip, I wondered about my reaction to Bill. Like Howard Rose, he had become another lightning rod for a decade of unresolved frustrations and fears. Both men were only tangentially related to the things that happened to me in Hanoi. Perhaps God was trying to open my heart to let his healing touch take away the pain of those days; but, if so, I wouldn't understand it that way for quite some time.

Two weeks later, I was off again to fly to a couple of reserve chaplain workshops at Langley and Griffiss Air Force Bases before dropping in to Washington to attend the Episcopal East Coast Chaplains' Conference sponsored by the Suffragan Bishop for the Armed Forces and held at the National Cathedral's College of Preachers. I returned to Harlingen on May 28, expecting to leave again in two weeks.

Within the week, a call came from the Air Reserve Personnel Center to alert me that I was now the last alternate available to fill the AF reserve seat in the Air War College class beginning in August. The personnel officer asked if I was still interested, to which I responded affirmatively. This late in the summer, I doubted that the seat would open up, but I called the senior warden to discuss the matter with him. I told him that I really felt a need for a sabbatical, and that this opportunity, which we all thought was dead, might open up. If so, I would ask the Vestry for an extended leave of absence in exchange for a commitment from me to return for another five years.

I had been taking the Air War College course by correspondence for over a year, and had one paper left to write, "The Shape of USTRANSCOM in 2010" – not exactly a paper in my field of expertise. I had approached the readiness chaplain at the Chief of Chaplains office about resurrecting the survey from my senior year at seminary and writing a paper on the moral and ethical issues facing Air Force combat officers and chaplains in the planning and conduct of war. I thought we were far enough removed from Vietnam to moderate the tensions noted a decade earlier. He told me that the Air War College paper should focus on "operational concerns" and not on the chaplaincy. Once again I was discouraged by the official response of the chaplains, but chose not to press the issue further.

In an attempt to gain some insight, as well as some creditable quotes about the Transportation Command, I made an appointment to meet with General Ron Fogelman, commander of both Air Mobility Command and the U.S. Transportation Command, for an interview. He granted me fifteen minutes on one of the days I was to be at Scott.

During the course of the conversation, the General asked me what I thought of the utilization of reserve chaplains during Desert Shield/Desert Storm. Caught a bit off-guard, but not without a clear and strong opinion on the matter, I told him I thought we had not been used to the best benefit of the service. I explained to him that the rules governing active duty (AD) and inactive duty (IDT) training days meant that we could not be, or were not, called to fill positions opened by deployments of active duty chaplains to the theater of operations. While I knew chaplains, including myself, who were ready and willing to go to any base at any time to minister in that time of national crisis, very few of us were ever called upon to use our AD and IDT days anywhere other than our normal base of assignment.

General Fogelman said, "I think I'll have one of my Air Command and Staff College or Air War College students write a paper on that this year." I told him that there was an outside chance that I would be filling a reserve seat, and he said that if I did, he would ask me to write it. I left the office with my quotes, and a good deal to think about.

The next day, I received another call from the personnel center to inform me that another primary reservist had backed out of the War College, and asked if I still wanted to go. If so, I needed to report the following Tuesday, June 21, for a three-day orientation course for Reservists and Guardsmen. I was really excited, but things had to happen quickly in the next few days.

I called the senior warden at St. Alban's and told him that I was going to be able to go to the War College after all, and asked him to call a meeting of the vestry to discuss the sabbatical proposal. I sent him a fax with what I thought would be an equitable financial arrangement. Since the Air Force would be paying my salary, I asked only that they continue my pension payments and our medical insurance. The remainder of my compensation could be used to hire an interim priest to take charge while I was away. Robbie would stay to lead the school, and I would return in the summer of 1995 with a commitment to stay for another five years.

Although a year of active duty would add to my eventual military pension as well as Social Security, I did not want to have a hole in my Church Pension Fund account. The Episcopal Church retirement system was calculated on both income earned and total years of active service. I was pretty sure my best eight years of income were still ahead of me; but losing a year might have significant results down the line.

We flew to Montgomery, Alabama to attend the orientation course. While we were there, I located an apartment and bought basic furniture for it. On Friday, we returned to Harlingen on a commercial flight, leaving the Mooney at Maxwell.

When I met with the Vestry the first of the following week, it quickly became apparent that there was division about granting my request for a ten-month leave of absence. After going over my thoughts and plan, I left the room for them to deliberate in my absence. When I returned, the senior warden told me that they didn't think it would be a good idea for them to grant my request.

I was exceptionally disappointed. I told them that I was caught in a very difficult position. If I backed out of the College at this point, the Reserves would not be able to send a replacement and would still have to pay for the seat. That could result in the loss of the seat altogether, and would certainly hinder another chaplain from having the opportunity. If I didn't go, I would probably feel so let down that I would start searching for a move. And, of course, if I left, the parish would be faced with trying to find a new rector and a new head of school at the same time. The vestry seemed unmoved by my appeal, leaving me to feel like they wanted me to leave. So, with a knot in my stomach, I told them I would resign in order to attend the College.

The next morning I called Bishop MacNaughton to tell him about my opportunity and decision and to ask him to try to find me a place when I returned the next summer. He assured me of his support and his desire to have me return to the diocese, and that he was pretty sure there would be some openings for me at that time.

Chapter 14

Robbie and I decided to get our house ready to sell and to put it on the market immediately. Some houses in our neighborhood had been on the market for over a year, and we were concerned that we sell it before the end of the next summer.

Though these events occurred in close proximity to one another in time, it seemed to me they were widely separated. Like the actions between the SAM hit and my ejection in the winter of 1972, the timing of many events eluded me because of the walls of separation I had built around each portion of my life and ministry.

Chapter 15

A Time of Refreshment

O God of peace, you have taught us that in returning and
rest we shall be saved, in quietness and in confidence shall
be our strength: By the might of your Spirit lift us, we pray,
to your presence, where we may be still and know that you
are God; through Jesus Christ our Lord.
Book of Common Prayer, 1979, p. 832

Resigning from St. Alban's for a ten-month fixed tour of duty in
the Air Force was a very chancy thing to do. Bishop MacNaughton
could make no guarantees about my return, but both of us believed
that there would be such an opportunity. Robbie stayed behind in
Harlingen to lead the school for one last year; Stephen had left
college to work on South Padre Island, and Mary was a senior in
high school.

As Mary and I drove around the Gulf coast toward Alabama in
early August, I felt a great deal of excitement about having such a
promising sabbatical from parish leadership. My only regret was
being separated from the family; but having an airplane meant that I
would be able to fly back to Harlingen on a monthly basis at the very
least. It was good to be able to spend an uninterrupted few days with
Mary. Once I got settled in Montgomery, I put her on a plane back
to Texas for her final year of high school.

Chapter 15

Two weeks after I left for Montgomery, we received a bona fide offer to buy our house. The full-asking offer was too good to turn down, so we agreed to vacate within the next two weeks. Robbie and Mary found an apartment to rent, and I called the Air Force Transportation Office to arrange for our household goods to be picked up and put into storage until we relocated the next summer. The quick sale, while it put a lot of pressure on Robbie to move without me during the school term, was a sign of God's favor to us. It was clear that whatever move we faced next would be without the burden of finding a buyer for our home.

Stephen was having considerable difficulty adjusting to adulthood and to college. In early October, we decided it would be best for him to stand out a semester, to move in with me in Alabama and find a job near the apartment. Even though he continued to struggle, it was good for us to live together. In the three months he was in Alabama, I got to know him as an adult, to sit with him in church, and to appreciate his individuality. By February 1995 he was ready to return to Texas. I regretted that and felt that we were just beginning to have an open adult relationship.

The apartment was located about a mile from the Episcopal Church of the Ascension. I decided to remain anonymous, so wore a coat and tie when I went on Sunday, and slipped out without staying for coffee hour. I told the rector that I was a student at the War College, but nothing more. However, one of my classmates, Navy Lieutenant Commander Frank Borik, had joined the church choir. When he spotted me in the congregation, he blew the whistle on me. The rector invited me to assist and preach on Sundays, but I declined until after the first of the year, citing my need for a real sabbatical as the reason. Besides, I wanted to sit with Stephen in the pew and to kneel in prayer beside him.

The class was made up of several hundred senior officers: mostly Air Force lieutenant colonels, but with some colonels and several officers each of the Army, Navy, Marines, Coast Guard, National Guard, and Reserves. There were also forty-nine officers from other nations around the world, and a few government service civilians. Getting to know them, I came to believe that the future of our armed forces was in very good hands.

Because I had a few hours a week to spare from studies, I was able to do a good bit of flying, gaining my commercial license and my certified flight instructor certificate. On a planned trip to Texas in October, I was due in Corpus Christi for the wedding of a former acolyte. As I flew over southern Mississippi I noted that the oil pressure seemed to be about a needle-width lower than normal. All other indications seemed fine, but I kept a close watch on the needle for about a half hour. Sure enough, the oil pressure was dropping very gradually. As I approached Lake Charles, Louisiana, I radioed air traffic control that I wanted to land. When they asked why, I stated that it was precautionary to check my oil pressure. The engine was running well, the temperatures were OK, and I thought I might have a gauge problem. As I began to let down through the clouds for the approach, I heard another aircraft call the tower for permission to land. He was told to hold west of the airport because of an emergency on the field. *"Oh, great,"* I thought. "Tower, 5808 Papa, do you want me to go around?"

"Negative, 08P, continue."

That was odd. Why would they make someone else hold and let me land during an emergency? As I descended below the clouds on final approach, I saw the reason. The fire trucks were lined up on either side of the approach end of the runway. I was the emergency!

The landing was smooth and the rollout normal. I taxied up to the fixed base operator's hanger to a waiting crew of mechanics. After shutting down and climbing out, I walked up to the cowling. One of the men pulled the propeller through a half arc, heard some clicking sounds, and said, "I think you've lost a cylinder." When he put the compression tester on the engine, it turned out that I had lost compression on two of the four cylinders.

First I called the airlines to see if I could get to south Texas that day and back to Montgomery on Monday. From Lake Charles, that simply was not possible. Next I called Robbie to tell her I wouldn't be home that weekend, and would be heading back to Montgomery as soon as I could figure out how. The airplane needed to be left for a couple of weeks to have the cylinders replaced. The call to the groom was deeply apologetic. I had been looking forward to the wedding of a young man I had watched grow to adulthood.

Finally, I called the Maxwell Aero Club to get one of the instructors to fly to Birmingham to pick me up. I felt really bad about having to stop the flight and miss the wedding; but I felt very good about my airmanship and ability to handle an inflight problem that could have easily developed into a real emergency had I continued. Maybe I had learned from Wisconsin to quit early at signs of trouble.

As classes began, I started to think about papers that I would like to write. At first I thought I would write the paper for General Fogelman as we had discussed a few weeks earlier. But then I heard that a great number of newly declassified documents dealing with the Linebacker II campaign had been delivered to the Air University library. I had made up my mind to delve into them to bring some closure to my POW experience when the General announced a visit.

Even though I was technically a member of the Air Reserve Personnel Center rather than Air Mobility Command, I was invited to attend a reception for AMC officers with the Commander.

As I stood in the corner of the room chatting with some other officers, I saw General and Mrs. Fogelman enter the room. I told myself that he wouldn't remember me, so I stayed off to the side. However, I was wrong. He came up, introduced me to his wife, and said, "Dear, this is the chaplain who is going to write that paper for me."

The Linebacker II paper evaporated, and the original paper proposal came back to the fore. The next day, we were told that the President of the United States had just appointed Ron Fogelman as the next Chief of Staff of the USAF. Now, I was really committed to the paper. I could never refuse the wish of someone in that position.

While I saw the possibility that a paper about the utilization of reserve chaplains in times of national emergency as a positive element in the Total Force matrix, I had a sense that the Chief of Chaplains and his staff would not be very open to my point of view. Consequently, I determined to base the paper on USAF regulations and procedures and on the written record of staff meetings of the Chief of Chaplains in Washington and of the Command Chaplain of the Air Reserve Personnel Center in Denver. All those documents were available in the Air University library. I found a number of inconsistencies in the Chief of Chaplains staff's comments and decisions that seemed to be a determined effort to keep individual mobilization chaplains from assisting with the emergency. While I tried to frame the final product in a positive way, I knew the Chief of Chaplains would not like what he read.

In part I said, "In times of high military stress (war, emergency response, frequent deployment), the chaplain really earns his position on the commander's staff. ... When men and women in uniform are in harm's way, there is no substitute for a 'Godly person' in uniform and present with both combatants and their families, ... as the chaplain becomes the calm 'eye of the storm' raging around him or her."

Chapter 15

Unfortunately, the operational plans for Desert Shield and Desert Storm did not include the recall of reserve chaplains along with their units; and when active duty chaplains deployed to the forward operating areas, the families left behind were left without chaplain support. The experience of the desert war demonstrated the difficulty, without reservists, of maintaining adequate ministry in both the area of operations and in the Stateside bases. It also demonstrated that reserve utilization was poorly organized and executed, including the failure to provide documentation for the assignment of chaplains to contingency hospital staffs. I concluded the paper with a series of recommendations for correcting the problems and measuring the effectiveness of the corrective actions.

After the paper was graded, I printed two fresh copies. The first I mailed to the Chief of Chaplains with a cover letter stating that I knew that this was not a definitive work but that I hoped it would serve to open dialog between active duty and reserve chaplains. The other I mailed to the Chief of Staff.

At first, I heard nothing from the Chaplains; but I did receive a nice letter from General Fogelman thanking me for my work, commenting on the recommendations and encouraging me in my studies. He went on to say that he was sending it on to the Chief of Chaplains with the suggestion that he appoint me as the reserve augmentee to his readiness officer when I graduated from the War College.

A few days later, my supervising professor called me aside to tell me he had received a call from the Chaplains office lambasting him for allowing my paper to get off the Maxwell campus. He had explained that the Chief of Staff had requested the paper and that I had sent the Chaplains a prior copy. No one from the office ever contacted me about it one way or the other.

Suddenly, I felt like I was right back in seminary, with people arguing over my work without including me in the argument.

The people at the Chief of Chaplains office had treated me pretty coolly for years, and the temperature just plummeted to sub-zero. At that point I determined to write my second and larger paper on a subject that I had first proposed during my seminary years: the role of the chaplain in time of war.

In February, the members of the class headed off to various destinations around the world to make visits to areas of high interest. My group had been studying the air operations over southwestern Europe and Iraq. Our stops included Germany, Italy, Croatia, and Turkey to talk to military and political leaders of NATO and the troubled areas of the former Yugoslavia. We were also able to do some sight-seeing, including the Hagia Sophia in Istanbul, the museum that had once been the cathedral of St. John Chrysostom in the early fifth century. It was a real blessing to me to be in a land where Christianity had begun under the evangelizing ministry of the Apostle Paul.

I spent substantial time writing my longest paper of the year, "What, in Hell, is a Chaplain Good For?" The "hell" of the title borrowed from William T. Sherman's definition of "war is hell" and explored the role of the military chaplain as a counselor, advisor, pastor, and fellow pilgrim with combatants in times of armed conflict.

To write the paper, I dusted off the survey I had developed during my senior year at Sewanee, updated it somewhat, and distributed it to the members of my class. While much more limited than I had envisioned in 1975, the study was given a broader base by the variety of combat officers from all of the services.

In the academic setting of the War College, I was finally able to reflect upon some of my own post-war emotions and upon some of the dysfunctional behaviors that formed the cultural caricature of the Vietnam veteran. Was there a spiritual problem that manifested itself in nightmares, domestic violence, withdrawal from society, ritualistic behavior, and even murder and suicide?

273

How was the soldier enabled to leave behind the necessarily violent reactions that preserved his life in battle when he returned to his home and his family? Even in an age when the religious community of the nation was strongly opposed to the violent use of armed force, could that community and its leaders affect redemption and reconciliation to the combatant who had done the nation's bidding? I was really pleased with the paper and believed the conclusions to be important.

In this paper I said, "War by its very nature is uncivilized and lies in the gray boundary at the edge of the western ethical conscience. Theologians and philosophers remind us of the evil we engage in war, and have given us the intellectual tools to plan our methods of making war so that we do not venture too far into the evil. Governments have articulated the purposes of war and set the rules of engagement, usually in conformity with just war theory. They then train their soldiers in acceptable war practice and send them out to destroy the evil threat using admittedly, though restrained, evil force. When the deed is done, the soldier is brought home, thanked for putting himself in harm's way, exonerated of any guilt, and welcomed back into normative society. The chaplain's role in war can serve to keep combat more humane, soldiers more human, and peace more redemptive…

"While the first amendment to the U. S. Constitution separates the State from involvement in the affairs of the Church and prohibits the State from subjecting itself to the rule of the Church, people cannot separate their civic or patriotic lives from their religious or spiritual lives, nor should they try. We have, so to speak, dual citizenship in the City of God and in the City of Man, with responsibilities to each and to both. When we act, in peace or in war, we do so as complete beings, as much from religious conviction as from national interest. The tension between the Establishment Clause and the Free Exercise Clause of the First Amendment suggests that religious faith, ethics, and morals should influence our corporate actions without dictating them.

It also suggests that religious influence is part and parcel of the formation of our society, its ethics, its norms, and its rituals of recognition and purification…

"Thomas Merton once noted that 'where non-violent resistance is impossible, then violent resistance must be used rather than passive acquiescence.'[1] It is the soldier who is charged with the responsibility of committing that violent resistance, and as such, he stands at the edge of human society, the edge that separates the rest of us from the chaos of hell. His conduct in that violence directly reflects on the character of the nation and serves as evidence by which the world judges the nation engaged in war. It is therefore important not just for the well being of the soldier, but also for the well being of the entire society that the soldier be trained and educated to exercise his burdensome duties with integrity, honesty, lawfulness, and moral uprightness. That training and education serve as a 'lifeline' anchored to the society's ethical core; and as long as the bonds are strong, the soldier will not be likely to fall into the morass of evil by committing war crimes or atrocities, and the nation, in turn, will not be condemned. It is also important that some sort of mechanism be in place to 'reel in the lifeline' when the battle is done. Parades and medals provide a secular answer; confession and absolution provide the religious answer…

"Clergy, by definition, stand at the other edge of human society from the soldier, the edge that separates us from the eternal Holy. While that may seem far different from the edge that separates us from the Chaos, the Judeo-Christian scriptures, as well as a host of other religions, tell us that dealing with the Holy is a very frightening proposition, even as frightening as dealing with Evil, for to come face to face with God means instant death. Clergy function as pontiffs (bridges) between God and the community as the soldier serves as the rampart between Evil and the community; and the clergy can serve the soldier by serving as a bridge back from the hell of war.

---

[1] Quoted in James H. Toner, *True Faith and Allegiance: The Burden of Military Ethics*, (Lexington, KY: The University Press of Kentucky, 1995), p. 3-4.

"Walking with the soldier through the fog of fear, but with the confidence that 'nothing in all creation can separate us from the love of God' (Romans 8:39), the Chaplain can serve both his Lord and the soldier by reminding the combatant that he will not face anything (including a horrible death) that Jesus has not already faced and destroyed. He can also hear the soldier's grief at having committed acts of great violence and death, and alleviate his guilt through the assurance of pardon. In that way, the Chaplain speaks for both God and the community...

Over three decades ago, Sir John Hackett told the cadet corps at the USAF Academy, 'The major service of the military institution to the community of men it serves may well lie neither within the political sphere nor the functional. It could easily lie within the moral. The military institution is a mirror of its parent society, reflecting strengths and weaknesses. It can also be a well from which to draw refreshment for a body politic in need of it. ... The highest service of the military to the state may well lie in the moral sphere.'[2] If the military is a reflection and well of the highest values of the nation, then the religious community is a natural ally and should have a keen interest in assisting the armed forces to develop and exhibit the best standards of human civilization...

"The Chaplain Service can and should take some measure of leadership in this matter, first by developing courses for chaplains to educate them as counselors in ethical matters in all kinds of situations. They should develop ways to recruit, train, educate, equip and assign clergy who are particularly knowledgeable to serve in both active duty and reserve billets as an ethical resource to commanders. Participation in Professional Military Education is necessary for chaplains to understand the duties and attendant ethical issues of line or war-fighting personnel, but a supplement for each of the courses would be useful to help chaplains focus on the issues of ethical ambiguity and conflict raised by the military circumstance being studied.

---

[2] Quoted in Toner, *True Faith and Allegiance*, p. 3.

"They should also work with the various service schools (from the Academies and Basic Training bases to technical training and senior service schools) to develop ethical education for both officers and NCOs at their respective levels of responsibility. Chaplains, because of their calling, serve as examples for the people of God for the conduct of a virtuous life. They must teach, as well as live and preach, honorable decision-making. By participating in all phases of military life, the U. S. military chaplaincy can serve as a 'light on the hill' to both friend and foe that religious devotion does not necessarily mean either militant or pacifist extremism. In an era when the future 'clash of civilizations' is touted as likely along religious lines, this may be the most important service the military chaplaincy can perform."

After the reaction of the Chief of Chaplains' office to my earlier work, I decided to bypass his office. Instead I sent it to the Command Chaplain at the Air Reserve Personnel Center for his interest and distribution and to the senior chaplain at the Chaplains School at the Air University in Montgomery.

As the end of the College approached, Bishop MacNaughton placed my name before the search committees of the only two open parishes in the Diocese of West Texas – St. Andrew's, San Antonio and St. Philip's, Uvalde. He was concerned that St. Philip's might be "too small," but I assured him that I just wanted to return to the Diocese and would stay five years wherever I was called. I began to converse with both of them, and to pray that one would work out. Since Robbie's job at St. Alban's ended with the close of the school year and since our house had sold soon after I went to Alabama, it was critical that we find something in a hurry.

I also received a call from Chaplain (Rabbi) Joel Schwartzman at the ARPC, telling me that I was being attached to the Air Force Academy as my next assignment, and asking that I come there immediately upon graduation in order to straighten out a problem they had with some inappropriate (fraudulent) travel vouchers. I was not surprised that I would not be going to the Chief's office as mandated by General Fogelman, but I was not going to fight it, either. Actually I felt like Brer Rabbit being thrown into the briar patch.

Since neither parish in Texas was ready to issue a call when the College ended, Robbie and I flew out to Colorado Springs for a two-week annual tour of duty. The problem with the vouchers had to do with a simple misunderstanding about how to file for rental car reimbursement and was quickly resolved. I discovered that the reserve chaplains at the Academy were asked to do all of their annual time during the summer when the new cadets first arrived and went through basic training. The first three weeks of basic training involved the chaplains in teaching core values, the second three weeks in counseling the basic cadets as they endured the rigors of physical training in the Jack's Valley encampment.

As the tour of duty ended, I received word that St. Andrew's had elected another candidate to be their rector. In conversation with the senior warden of St. Philip's, he expressed his concern that I was "too good" for their little parish and town and would not stay if they called me. All my promises of five years stability fell on deaf ears; and they, too, called another candidate.

At that point, I was feeling pretty foolish. I had no other feelers out, and knew that a "normal" process would take up to a year to complete. In desperation, I called my old mentor and friend, Jack Wilson, now semi-retired in Payson, Arizona, to ask if he knew of anything that I could be appointed to in short order. He said he would check and call back in an hour.

In just a few minutes, Jack called to ask if I could be there on Friday, four days away. I said, "Sure, what's up?"

"Out here, the Bishop screens potential priests before you can talk to a rector or search committee. He's out of town, but will be in his office on Friday if you can make it. Then, if he likes you, he'll send you out to St. Barnabas to talk with Dan Miner about a position he has in pastoral care. Dan has been looking for someone for a year and is anxious to get it settled before he leaves on vacation next week."

It seemed that when I gave up on my own efforts, God stepped in and opened all the right doors. Jack met me at Sky Harbor airport that Friday morning and took me to the bishop's office. After an hour conversation with Bishop Shahan, I was told to be at St. Barnabas in Scottsdale by mid-afternoon. Another conversation with Dan Miner, the rector, went very well, and he asked if I could return on Saturday to meet his associate, John Hall. After that meeting, Dan asked me to return again on Monday to have breakfast with the vestry before I returned to Texas. After breakfast, I was taken back to the church for a private meeting with Father Miner and his senior warden, Todd Langley, and offered the position of Associate for Pastoral Ministries. Naturally, I accepted.

It had been eighteen years since Jack Wilson had asked me to leave the Air Force to join him if he was elected rector of this same parish. Now, through his efforts and the clear grace of God, I was finally being placed in the position first described all those years ago.

From Phoenix, I flew home, then to Montgomery to retrieve my plane, and then returned to Harlingen to pick up Robbie. We flew to Phoenix in the Mooney to look for a house, which we found right away. We made arrangements for the closing, ordered our stored household goods to be released by the Navy, and arranged for movers to pack up our apartment and move our belongings to Scottsdale. Before we returned, Mary assisted Stephen in getting settled into an apartment on South Padre Island.

Chapter 15

Robbie and I dropped the airplane off in San Antonio for scheduled maintenance, then caught a commercial flight to Harlingen to pick up Mary and take her to Fort Worth and enrollment into Texas Christian University. In just two weeks our lives had undergone a major shift. The three-day drive across Texas to Arizona was barely enough for us to begin to comprehend what God was doing with us.

Chapter 16

A Golden Opportunity

Psalm 28:7-11
Blessed is the LORD!
> for he has heard the voice of my prayer.
The LORD is my strength and my shield;
> my heart trusts in him, and I have been helped;
Therefore my heart dances for joy,
> and in my song will I praise him.
The LORD is the strength of his people,
> a safe refuge for his anointed.
Save your people and bless your inheritance;
> shepherd them and carry them for ever.

Robbie and I arrived in Scottsdale on Sunday afternoon, August 20, 1995. Closing on our house was scheduled the next afternoon and we expected to have three or four days to get the place cleaned and ready for the movers. The next day held a couple of surprises. First, the people we bought from didn't expect to be out until Tuesday or Wednesday. Then, just before lunch, the van driver with the household goods from storage called to say he was in town and ready to deliver. Because of the hour he asked to start Tuesday morning.

Chapter 16

We were caught in a bind. If we refused the delivery, it would go into storage and add to our costs. Our real estate agent insisted that the selling family vacate immediately; and with a great effort they were able to do so. They were moving themselves to another house in town, so it was possible.

The next morning the moving company started unloading all the things we had placed in storage when we sold the Harlingen house, enough to furnish a 4,000 square foot home and take care of the lawns. This house was about half that size, and the "lawns" were in desert landscaping gravel. By the middle of the afternoon the garage was full of items for sale and the house was piled high with boxes. The difference between this downsizing and the one in Memphis was that we were now "empty-nesters" and no longer had the Wade Furniture Company to fall back on for replacement furnishings.

When the phone rang, it was the driver of the truck with the furniture from the apartment. He would deliver on Wednesday morning. Though that shipment was much smaller, it did include our second car and a grand piano. When night fell on Wednesday, we were dead tired and could barely move through the house to find a bed to sleep in. The doors had been open for two days in 110° temperatures and the air conditioner simply couldn't cool it off enough to give us a good night's sleep.

Fortunately, I had about another ten days before starting work at St. Barnabas, so we were able to get pretty well settled before then. After eighteen years as a rector of parishes and a year-long sabbatical to reenergize my sense of call, I relished my new role as Associate for Pastoral Ministries. The clergy team at St. Barnabas was outstanding and operated with great coordination and respect. The rector, Dan Miner, was a truly gifted administrator and preacher who surrounded himself with the best staff he could find. I was thrilled to be able to concentrate on the care of people and to let him worry about the administrative headaches that take so much time. God had provided me with a golden opportunity to ease back into parish leadership.

St. Barnabas on the Desert, Scottsdale, Arizona

My sabbatical year had left me with a newfound sense of calm in my vocation, and the assigned ministry in the parish was just what I needed to recover my confidence after the troubling circumstances of the last two parishes. Father Miner gave me responsibility for organizing and supervising all pastoral ministries, ministry development, new member ministries, outreach and counseling services. In addition to Dan and his other associate, John Hall, I also had the assistance of two semi-retired priests and a deacon, as well as a large number of trained lay callers. I was also given an equal load in preaching and worship leadership.

The Pastoral Care team was a real blessing. Not only did we visit several hospitals and nursing homes, follow the care of members confined to their homes, and respond with food and support to families of hospitalized members, we also took care of each other.

The lay staff was equally superb. Christian Education Director Maridean Carrington had a Sunday School with over 500 children; and the organist/choirmaster Curt Sather had an exceptional music program with about sixty adult choir members, two youth choirs and a handbell choir to lead us in singing praises. At 3,000 members, St. Barnabas could offer excellent ministries and attract new people into all of them.

Chapter 16

The sad note to the move was that, with my new reserve attachment, I could no longer use my plane for transportation. The costs were simply prohibitive. So, with great reluctance, I put it up for sale. I did find an aero club at the Scottsdale airport with a Mooney, so I was able to continue flying for recreation.

The clergy conference convened at the Diocesan camp in Prescott in the early fall. When the St. Barnabas clergy arrived, we learned that Bishop Shahan was delayed due to a death in his family. In his absence, the clergy gathering was in turmoil, with many harsh things being said about him to his assistant, a psychologist. I had never witnessed such animosity toward a bishop and sat in stunned silence as I tried to understand what was being said. Even with the bishop's participation the following day, the apparent hostility seemed to be irreconcilable.

As Dan, John and I drove back to Scottsdale after the conference, I began to gain some insight into what had happened. A few days later I called the bishop and offered to share my observations and insights with him. He invited me to meet him and Canon McClain for lunch.

Over lunch, I told the bishop that underneath all the harsh rhetoric of the conference, it seemed to me that the priests of the diocese were asking for a more personal and collegial relationship with him. In my previous dioceses I had enjoyed frequent interaction with the bishops and I suspected that he would find a vast reduction in tension if he could make himself more available to his clergy. I was surprised when he told me that he couldn't be a colleague because he had to be a disciplinarian. I tried to assure him that the priests would respect him more if he adopted a different position, but he disagreed. I left the meeting saddened, but determined to have a good working relationship with my new bishop.

Other than this odd event, I quickly adapted to my new role as an assisting clergyman for the first time since 1977.

The memory of Andrews and Kerrville seemed very distant in this environment. At St. Barnabas, Dan led a team that seemed very focused on accomplishing its mission and ministry, and there was little friction or competition for time or resources, and a great deal of respect for each other's abilities.

In the fall, Dan started advertising for a youth minister to join the staff. Robbie suggested a young man from Texas that she remembered from camps and youth events there. After a series of interviews, Dan invited him to join the staff.

Robbie went to work with the City of Phoenix in their Head Start program, returning to her first love of education of the underprivileged children of the city. Though the daily commute was sometimes a trial, she loved her work and made a mark for herself in her career. Both of us felt the hand of God guiding our ministries and lives in Arizona.

In October, Dan was called out of his office to make an emergency visit to a man he had been counseling. When he hadn't returned in time for staff meeting, John got us together for our weekly coordination session. As we were finishing, we received a call from Dan saying he wanted to see us in his office right away. When we walked in we were stunned. He was covered in blood. When he had walked into the young man's home, the young man had shot himself, and Dan had held him as he died.

Father Miner was visibly shaken by this horrendous experience, and John and I urged him to take some time off and to seek some counseling for himself as he tried to make sense of the suicide. As John cleaned his glasses and gently washed the blood from his face and arms, we assured him that we would support and uphold him through this crisis. In the next few days, he seemed to have recovered his confidence and vision. I wondered how anyone could adjust to the horror of that experience without the help of someone skilled in traumatic stress management.

Chapter 16

In the fall of 1995 St. Barnabas was working with a consultant to engage in a capital funds campaign to build another classroom building for the parish and to donate an adult lodge for Chapel Rock, the diocesan camp and conference center in Prescott. When I heard the consultant's presentation, I took Dan aside and told him I didn't think this company was going to work out. The Vestry had insisted that the consultant also conduct the annual budget canvass; but he had insisted that he would not do it. Neither side seemed to have heard the other.

I urged the rector and senior warden to fire this company and to talk with the people who had worked with St. Alban's on that campaign a few years earlier. I was told it was too late, and that I was wrong about my assessment. At that point, I backed away from further discussions. I did not want to take on the pressures of another capital campaign, especially after the way my friendship with the campaign chair in Harlingen had turned out in its aftermath, and I did not want to encroach on the prerogatives of the Rector and Vestry.

In early June 1996, our son Stephen was married on South Padre Island. He had met his fiancée on the job and seemed thrilled and deeply in love. The wedding was attended by many members of the family and by old friends from Harlingen, and I was assisted as the officiant by Stephen's Godfather and by the rector in Brownsville. When I got choked up with joy, I was glad to have back-up. A rainstorm that had hovered over the chapel before the service gave way to bright sunny skies by the time they embraced as husband and wife. My prayer for them was that their life together would be clear of all storms and that our family would grow stronger with this new addition.

In July, I returned to the Air Force Academy for my annual tour of duty, working the first half of Basic Cadet Training. Several times through the year, a team of us had been brought to Colorado Springs to develop the pastoral care and character development curricula for the cadets.

The senior staff chaplain also had hopes of gaining space for a chaplain supervised cadet center. All facets of my duties were enjoyable and fulfilling.

Because of the high cost to the Air Force of placing temporary duty reserve chaplains at the Academy, the ARPC Command Chaplain called me to discuss reducing our strength. I told him I didn't think that would serve the ministry in that place very well, since the active duty chaplains were understaffed and over scheduled all summer. Rather than reduce the reserve strength, I suggested that we billet the chaplains assigned to the second half of basic training in tents in Jack's Valley with the cadets. That way, we could eliminate the cost of housing, meals, and rental cars to practically nothing. He accepted the suggestion for implementation the following summer.

As I drove home through northern Arizona, I stopped into Prescott to visit Mary, who was working along with her fiancé at Chapel Rock as a counselor. Mary was studying religion and philosophy at Texas Christian University, and we talked about her growing sense of vocation to the priesthood. I felt pride in her faith and a sense of fearful joy in her sense of calling. We talked of the difficult parts of ministry that she had seen growing up but she believed she could find fulfillment only by pursuing the calling. Ministry is difficult, but not nearly as difficult as avoiding it. She was additionally blessed by having a fiancé who also had a deep faith and believed in her sense of call.

As we walked across the camp, a young man came up to me, greeted me with a salute, and called me "Colonel." I returned the salute and exchanged brief pleasantries. I asked Mary who he was, and she told me it was a deacon named Sean Cox, who wanted to be a Marine chaplain.

Chapter 16

In November, Bishop Shahan called to ask me to consider acting as a mentor to Deacon Cox. Several things Sean had done had irritated the bishop, and he had decided to postpone Sean's ordination to the priesthood and wanted me to try to "turn him around." I explained to the bishop that my experience in Harlingen with my associate and youth minister had left me with deep reluctance to try to work with any young minister again.

He pressed me, and I agreed to meet with the deacon. As we gathered in the bishop's office on the appointed day, I was shown the files and listened to the concerns of various people who had been working with Sean. When Sean was brought in, he was polite and controlled, but his emotional strain showed in his posture and in his face.

The next hour reminded me of several interrogation sessions I had experienced in Hanoi, including a statement from the bishop's psychologist assistant that my job was to "break" Sean. I was so aggravated by that comment that I decided to do everything I could to be a good guy, to help Deacon Cox find his way, and to prove the bishop and his staff wrong. First, though, I had to struggle through my own reluctance to form a friendship with the 27-year-old and to begin to trust him.

The arrangement for supervision was that Sean would work at St. Barnabas two days a week and one Sunday a month, while continuing his other duties at Trinity Cathedral in Phoenix under the supervision of the Rev. Rebekah McClain, who served both as cathedral dean and as Canon to the Ordinary (Bishop's assistant). While we would begin in early December, most of our work would have to wait until 1997 because he was getting married in Texas between Christmas and the new year.

When we first met in my office at St. Barnabas, I was not yet convinced that this young man was anything other than a repeat of my youth minister from Harlingen. However, as he told his story, I came to trust his honesty and to believe in his call to vocation.

Every task I assigned was accomplished with grace and ease, and the people who received his ministrations were laudatory in their reports.

In mid-January 1997, Dan Miner called to say he would be late because of a flat tire. I teased him about not being able to change it himself, but his voice sounded despairing. I decided to drive over to his house to see what was wrong, and found him very upset. His car had obviously hit a curb; the front right tire was missing and the right rear wheel was severely bent. Dan couldn't tell me what had happened and asked me to take him to see a doctor. He seemed terribly disoriented, and I wondered if he was finally reacting to the trauma of the suicide of the young man over a year earlier.

Although John Hall had been on the staff longer, the Bishop and Senior Warden asked me to take charge of the parish during Dan's absence because of my experience as a rector. As I became more involved in administration, Deacon Cox eagerly picked up some of my pastoral duties.

Dan stayed away from the office for a couple of months, working at home building a bed for his son. Having been through a similar experience in Memphis, I wanted to give him as much time as he needed without worrying about the state of the parish. While he was recuperating he did the woodworking, using it as a spiritual mantra much as I did. As he began to return to work in March and April, I was happy to return his responsibilities to him a little at the time.

Fr. Certain, Bp. Shahan, Fr. Cox

By Easter, Sean had shown himself to be a man of character and devotion, a hard worker and a team player. My relationship with him had also healed the wounds of betrayal, and I was blessed when he asked me to preach at his service of ordination to the priesthood in June. Once more I was able to see the hand of God at work in the world around me.

When I went to my annual tour at the Air Force Academy, Sean rode as far as Albuquerque to assist with the driving. I completed the trip alone, arriving for the second half of basic cadet training. Since I had suggested living in the tents, I decided I needed to lead by example. The reserve team of chaplains, chaplain candidates, and NCOs who lived and worked among the new basic cadets that summer did a superb job of counseling and leadership. Several young men and women, who might have otherwise withdrawn from training, decided to stay the course after talking to one of us. The experiment was very successful.

On September 16, I made an appointment with Bishop Shahan to show him the growth plan John Hall and I had developed for St. Barnabas to start a new parish in the rapidly growing section of north Scottsdale. We were very excited about it and expected to be able to build a substantial congregation for that future parish within ten years. He liked the plan and commended us to start work.

That evening Bishop Shahan suffered a heart attack. The notice we received did not include the name of the hospital and the request was that all notes be sent to the diocesan office. I thought that odd, but Canon McClain called to tell me where he was. She said I was the only priest the bishop wanted to have visit. I was both surprised and pleased to be trusted with that responsibility and went by to visit and pray with him in his hospital room following his bypass surgery.

The next day, Dan came to my office to tell me he was giving me a raise. I was grateful and told him I was committed to staying there for another five years. Robbie and I really loved the community and the parish, and I was thrilled with my ministry and with my friendship with him. We went on to discuss some problems we were having with our youth program.

Tension was running high on the staff as the rector considered discharging the youth minister for poor work and lack of coordination. He seemed to be at the center of a growing friction that involved the other program leaders, and his own ministry was stagnant. The three priests had discussed the situation and agreed that he would be released the following week. After the staff meeting on Tuesday, Dan called me aside and asked me to fire him by the end of the week.

That same day, the Canon told me she was going to Tucson to meet with the clergy there, and was afraid they would verbally attack her for not revealing the bishop's whereabouts. I offered to drive down with her. The clergy meeting turned out to be civil. On the way back to Phoenix we talked more of the plan John Hall and I had developed for starting a new parish in northern Scottsdale. I was very energized by the proposal, but it soon faded into the background of my concerns.

For the next several days, Father Miner did not come into the office and none of us were able to locate him. Once again, he seemed to be having a stress reaction that led him to withdraw alone. This time, the problem was much worse and would affect all of us on the staff, as well as the entire parish. When he returned, John Hall and I encouraged him to seek medical evaluation. Within a few days, he was diagnosed with rapidly progressing Parkinson's Disease. This severe blow to the rector ended his tenure at St. Barnabas, forcing him to accept a medical retirement within the month.

Once again I was asked to take full charge of the parish, and called Canon McClain for guidance. She informed me that the bishop would want John and me to stay in place as an interim team for three years while the parish worked through this development. That surprised me, because every diocese I had served had a policy preventing associates from becoming the rector of the parish. I invited her to attend our October vestry meeting to lay out the plan.

In the meantime, I gave the youth minister the option of resigning his job in lieu of dismissal. He accepted the offer and left to work in another parish. In early October one of our part-time priests reached his mandatory retirement age and could no longer continue on the payroll. In January, the other part-time priest would arrive at his retirement date and leave the payroll.

As John and I faced leading the parish with a much-reduced staff, Canon McClain told the vestry that it was the bishop's desire that they begin their search for a new rector in January 1998. She assured them that both John and I would be able to find other positions fairly easily, since the church law required us to resign when the rector retired. Neither of us could be considered for the position of rector.

Title III, Canon 14 of the canon law of the Episcopal Church specifies that all assisting clergy serve at the discretion of the Rector and "may not serve beyond the period of service of the Rector except that, pending the call of a new Rector, the assistant may continue in the service of the Parish if requested to do so by the Vestry of the Parish and under such conditions as the Bishop and Vestry shall determine." While a new rector could offer John and me a continuing position on his staff, I was not sure I wanted to trust my longevity to another priest again.

An interim contract would give me the opportunity for a leisurely search for another place and the possible chance to participate as a candidate for Suffragan Bishop for the Armed Forces, which should open up in 1999 or 2000. I had long thought of that position as one in which I could best serve both the Church and the military chaplaincy. If I had to move before 2000, I would not be in a position to consider becoming a candidate. Robbie and I both were beginning to desire positional stability more than career progression.

We prayed that whatever change we had to face in the next few months would be the final one before my retirement.

Canon McClain's statement to the vestry made it clear that a change would definitely happen.

After the vestry meeting I called the Canon and demanded an explanation. The last she had told us was that it was the "bishop's desire" that we serve as an interim team, and now she had reversed that position. While she apologized for not calling ahead of time, I felt badly manipulated. The events of the last month appeared to be converging toward disaster very much as had the night of December 18, 1972. My stress level was through the roof, and I found myself becoming extremely focused on getting my job done, just as I had done on that fateful combat mission.

John busied himself with a search for another call; and within a month he had been elected rector of a parish in the Phoenix metropolitan area. When he accepted the call, Canon McClain telephoned to tell me that it was now the "bishop's desire" that I be given a three-year interim contract to lead the parish and continue its ministries and growth. I couldn't believe this new reversal, and told her the vestry needed to hear that from the bishop himself. Since we were now into Advent and Christmas and he had to attend a House of Bishop's meeting the first of the year, she suggested the January vestry meeting as the first opportunity.

In the meantime, I needed clergy help to lead the parish. I told her I wanted Sean Cox to come back to St. Barnabas full time. He was already known to the parish, and would be able to pick up behind the youth minister as well as to assist with pastoral care and liturgies. Since I would not be able to call anyone else to move to the parish, he was my best and only choice.

When I met with the vestry in December I told them I was looking for another place to be; but if they wanted me to stay, they needed to agree ahead of time and go into the January meeting with a firm plan. I was not interested in a fight between them and the bishop and would have nothing to do with it. I understood and agreed with the policy. Whatever they and the bishop agreed upon would be the course I would take.

Chapter 16

When the Bishop and Canon arrived for the January meeting, I was allowed to introduce them and was then dismissed. As I left the building, he called the meeting to order and told them that the policy prohibiting associates from staying on as rectors in the parish was firm. The vestry was stunned, but managed to discuss the idea of an interim contract, a fairly common practice in other parishes in the diocese. As they broke up, they understood the bishop to say he would consider the idea and they agreed to meet again in two weeks to discuss it.

When the wardens described the meeting with the Bishop, I wrote a letter to say that I would not accept an interim contract and that they should get on with their search. They asked me to wait until after their next meeting, confident that the bishop would accede to their wishes.

The day before the vestry planned to meet to decide their course of action, I was talking with Bishop Shahan about another matter. When we were done, I told him the vestry was meeting the next evening and would have a proposal for him the day following. "What will you do if they ask to give me a three-year contract?"

His response was quick, "I'll tell them it's inappropriate. We only give those to conflicted parishes. St. Barnabas is strong."

When I put the phone down, I called the senior warden. "My letter stands. Read it to the vestry and end the meeting. I'm not going to have you start a fight with the bishop. If I'm still here when you find a rector, maybe I will be able to work with him."

As all of this was going on, I had received correspondence from St. Margaret's Parish in Palm Desert, California to consider their search for a new rector. I agreed to meet with them, and a group from their search committee was scheduled to drive over to Scottsdale the first weekend of March to interview me and to hear me preach.

On Tuesday, February 24, 1998, Robbie had given final approval to the genetics research department of St. Joseph's Hospital in Phoenix to test her blood for Huntington's disease. With the passage of time, the cost and accuracy of the test had been improved and her sister's DNA had been tested the previous fall. Mary O'Connor's diagnosis was now confirmed just as our children were beginning to marry and plan their own families. If Robbie did not have the offending gene, the children were home free.

On Ash Wednesday, February 25, Sean and I led a group of parishioners on a hike to the top of Camelback Mountain for a Eucharist and Imposition of Ashes. As we came down in the early afternoon, Sean went to the church to shower and change while I drove home. As I neared my street, he called on my car phone. Robbie had been in an accident in north Phoenix and was trapped inside her car. It would take another half hour before she would be free and then would be transported to a hospital. I reached her on her cell phone and was relieved to hear her voice. The conversation was ended quickly because her rescuers were ready to cut her free with the "jaws of life." Since it would take nearly an hour for me to drive to the location, and since the hospital hadn't been decided upon, all I could do was go home, clean up and wait for more news.

By the time I was dressed, the call came in and I headed to the hospital. She had suffered ten fractures in the wreck and was undergoing evaluation for internal injuries. When I arrived at the hospital, the senior warden and her husband, as well as the bishop, were already there. Robbie was strapped to a board waiting results of X-rays and a CT scan. The bishop had been in to see her, but he seemed awkward in the midst of this scene of worry. Given my disappointment at the monthly reversals in guidance from his office, I was in no mood to accept any ministry from him or anyone else from the diocese.

Chapter 16

That night, I called the search committee chairman in Palm Desert to tell him of Robbie's accident. Since none of her injuries were life-threatening they were free to come on over, but they shouldn't expect me to be at the top of my game. Since I would not be able to spend more than an hour a day in the hospital, their visit would not take me away from her.

As we met and conversed that weekend, I was unconcerned about what they thought of me. I was incapable of putting on airs, or even of putting my best foot forward. That did not seem to matter, and on Sunday afternoon, barely six hours after they had left Scottsdale to return to California, I received a call to invite me to fly there to meet the entire committee. I agreed to fly over on Tuesday, spend the night, and fly back Wednesday in time to see Robbie. The visit went well, and another portion of the committee asked to come to Scottsdale the following weekend.

As I was driving home from the airport, Sean called on the car phone. One of our parishioners, a gentleman I deeply admired, had committed suicide. The burden of the previous year was beginning to feel like a crushing weight. This tenure was definitely not turning out the way I had envisioned even six months earlier, and this Advent-Easter season was the worst since Memphis. The difference this time was that I was severely focused on maintaining some semblance of order in the parish, a credible interview process, and reasonably calm care of Robbie.

Robbie, for her part, was determined to recover from the fractures and to recover her ability to walk. Though she was in tremendous pain, she forced herself to participate in every facet of physical and occupational therapy assigned. Drugs helped, but she was eager to put them aside, too. The Huntington's test was relegated to the back of her mind as she labored to finish her therapy and return home. Stephen and Rachel had moved to Phoenix and were able to visit as her schedule allowed. Mary and her fiancé, Stephen Vano, flew out from Texas during their spring break from college, but found they could do little to calm the turmoil that had captured our lives.

I placed a call to the bishop to ask for reconsideration. I told him of the DNA test for Huntington's and pointed out that Robbie's support community were all in Scottsdale and Phoenix. Her recuperation would be long and we would need a good bit of help while she regained her ability to walk. If the DNA test was positive we would both need a tremendous amount of support. I asked what it would hurt for me to have a three-year contract with St. Barnabas. His response left me cold, "You know we don't make decisions about that based on the pastoral needs of clergy." I was feeling the old rage boil to the surface again. I hated feeling forced along a path I did not want to travel. But by now I knew both intellectually and in my soul that God was working to bring good out of this colossal mess. Whatever else was going on with Bishop Shahan, he was being used as an instrument of God's grace for my life.

The following week, I received a bill for Robbie's DNA test. When I called the genetics center, the counselor said she had not seen the results yet. I told her I knew she had the report and my request was simple. I explained about Robbie's accident and asked her to consider the best place to give her the results – the hospital or home.

After a month of hospitalization Robbie was released from the rehabilitation center on March 27 in time for her to have dinner with the third and final calling group from Palm Desert. She was brave and cheerful as I wheeled her into the restaurant to meet the people I had gotten to know during the time of her hospitalization.

On Sunday, March 29, twenty-five years after my release from prison in Hanoi, the chairman of the search committee at St. Margaret's called to tell me they were going to recommend me to the Vestry for election as their next rector. Since it was so close to Holy Week, he suggested we wait until after Easter before I came out to meet the Vestry. I thanked him, but felt a deep foreboding. The next day the genetics counselor was planning to come to our home to tell us the results of the test.

Chapter 16

When she told us that Robbie had tested negative for Huntington's we were overjoyed. The dark shadow of fear that had threatened her and our children for all those years was now gone in a moment. The final block to my willingness to take responsibility for leading a parish also vanished.

With that, I called the chairman and suggested we get on with the visit that weekend. I reminded him that one member of their search committee lived next door to another Vietnam War POW and that it would be very difficult to keep the secret for two more weeks. Since many of the people in St. Barnabas knew members over there, it would likely be all over both parishes by the time the vestry could act.

The search committee and vestry conferred and decided to invite us over to Palm Desert that weekend. In the meantime, I drove out to the Mayo Clinic in Scottsdale for a thorough physical examination. Because the last rector of St. Margaret's had died the previous summer with prostate cancer, I believed it was important to present the search committee and vestry with my own clean bill of health.

We drove so Robbie would be more comfortable and we could stop as necessary. The meeting went well over dinner on Friday night, and we returned to Scottsdale the next day in time for Palm Sunday.

The Vestry met Palm Sunday afternoon and elected me as their fifth rector. On Monday, Bishop Hughes of San Diego called to congratulate me and to arrange a meeting so he could give his approval. He decided to fly over to Scottsdale on Wednesday so the election could be announced in Palm Desert on Easter Day.

After our meeting, I invited Sean Cox to join us for lunch, since the Vestry of St. Margaret's had asked me to offer him a position on the staff as my associate for evangelism and young adult ministries. Bishop Hughes was surprised, but gracious and welcoming.

I had a letter prepared and mailed on Saturday so our people would get the announcement in the mail on Monday. But by the time I left the last service of Easter Day, some of them had already received calls from their friends in Palm Desert to find out about me.

Within a few weeks, Robbie was feeling well enough that we were able to fly to Dallas for the twenty-fifth anniversary reunion of the Vietnam POWs. Though she wasn't able to do everything on the schedule, we really enjoyed seeing our old friends again. It was the first time that Dick Johnson, Tom Simpson and I had been together since Operation Homecoming.

In one session, one of our Navy members encouraged all of us to get involved with the Center for Repatriated Prisoners of War at Pensacola Naval Air Station in Florida. The program was originally set up to follow the Navy and Marine Corps POWs in a longitudinal study of the long-term health outcomes and medical effects of torture and deprivation in the prisons of Vietnam. Beginning in 1974 the Air Force ex-POWs had been included, with the Army joining in 1997. Neither of those two services had continued their medical evaluations in a formalized study after five years.

Over time, the Center began to focus on increased incidence of carotid artery disease, diabetes, traumatic arthritis, calcium loss from starvation diets and its affect on bone density, and psychological epidemiology. The stated goal of the program is to evaluate the former prisoners and their experience both in captivity and through repatriation and reintegration into society so that the lessons learned from their experiences may be used to help others from future conflicts.

Chapter 16

Over time, many of these physical and psychological ailments were identified as rooted in our experience in Vietnam, making them "service-connected" in the lingo of the Department of Veterans Affairs. As such, each malady became part of the formula for awarding a disability pension to the former POW and for determining the responsibility of the VA to treat us in our retirements.

Congress appropriated permanent funding to enable the military services to place the former POWs on travel orders, pay for transportation, lodging and per diem, and to provide the annual physicals at no cost to the participant. Spouses were also welcomed to participate in the physicals without cost except for travel, lodging, and meals. Robbie and I decided to begin our participation in 1999.

Once again we were blessed with the quick sale of our house and easy location of a new home in Palm Desert. When we returned from the reunion, we made the move west. On Pentecost Sunday, I preached my first sermon as the rector of St. Margaret's Parish, Palm Desert, California. The previous three years had been tumultuous in every way, but a tumult firmly in God's hands.

Chapter 17

New Challenges and Old Ghosts

Ecclesiasticus 34:9-12
A man with training gains wide knowledge;
  a man of experience speaks sense.
One never put to the proof knows little,
  whereas with travel a man adds to his resourcefulness
I have seen much in my travels,
  learned more than ever I could say.
Often I was in danger of death,
    but by these attainments I was saved.

On May 31, 1998, I approached the pulpit of St. Margaret's for the first time. Many of the seasonal residents of the parish had stayed late in the spring to greet me, and I was eager to set the tone for our life together. Not only was it Memorial Day weekend, it was also the Christian Feast of Pentecost, celebrating the gift of the Holy Spirit to the Church.

I opened the sermon by saying, "The whole thing started back around the beginning of Lent. As we read the story of the final journey to Jerusalem, interesting things happened on Palm Sunday, something new was announced on Easter Day and now something new again. The story of Jesus Christ has come to its fullest expression with the Feast of Pentecost and the gift of the Holy Spirit.

It also parallels our story which began between you and me early in Lent, finished on Palm Sunday, was announced on Easter Day and now culminated on the Feast of Pentecost. It is tempting to talk about this parallel, but I just wanted to point it out to you because I believe the Holy Spirit is alive and well and moving in St. Margaret's parish, in our lives as individuals and family and as the people of God.

"Sometimes the best we can say to another person who does not know the grace of Christ in their lives is, 'I do not know what it is that is changing my life, but someway and somehow it has to do with my participation in this crazy organization known as the church. With all of its warts, with all of its problems, with all its frustrations, it's still there. And how exactly it is there in the church community, I do not know. I do know it includes the liturgy; I do know that it includes music; I do know it includes education and fellowship; I do know it includes attractive buildings and cared for grounds — because those things show others how much we love the Lord. It also includes social ministries, caring for the poor and the dispossessed and the hungry. And it includes, most importantly, changed lives.'

"It all begins with expectant waiting, like the disciples during the ten days from Ascension Day to Pentecost. We don't know exactly what to do, but we do know the Lord is going to lead us and we are going to follow the Holy Spirit to lead us into all truth. We do know that expectant waiting will be, and is, empowered by joyful infusion of the Holy Spirit and then is led in complete trust of God in all circumstances of life, especially those circumstances where we do not understand what it is that is going on. As individuals we are simply a collection of promises. We're a hodgepodge of people with different talents and different abilities, and no single one of us will accomplish the mission of the kingdom of God. Not even will we accomplish it if we gather together as a totality.

It takes more than that. In order to usher in the kingdom of God, it is done as community of the people of God — the glue that holds us together." The words were directed as much to myself as they were to the people.

By the time Robbie and I had the house settled, it was time for me to return to the Air Force Academy for what I thought would be my final tour of duty before retirement the next year. I picked up Sean Cox in Phoenix to assist with the drive and this year he went all the way to Colorado Springs. He was able to get in a few days for his own reserve service with the Navy by participating in the Academy chapel program before flying back to Phoenix.

When I called the Air Reserve Personnel Center to arrange for my retirement papers to be processed, I was surprised that my final date was in July rather than June, which meant that I could return one more time to greet the next class of aspiring Air Force officers. I was ending my Air Force career on a high note. After twenty-two years in the reserves I felt I had finally repaid the educational obligation I had acquired in seminary. I also believed I had made a contribution to the spiritual well being of the men and women in uniform to whom I had ministered since I first became active again in 1983. Perhaps in the process I had even made a small contribution to the institutional chaplaincy.

Back in Palm Desert, I busied myself getting to know as many people as possible, and with working with the Vestry and School Board to plan for a capital campaign to retire the church debt and to grow our ministries into the future. In that process I became profoundly impressed with the health and strength of the parish, as it had grown under the leadership of my predecessor. The challenges in front of us were those of a rapidly growing parish already united in vision. In almost every respect, it proved to be the easiest transition Robbie and I had ever had, alleviating the stresses of the previous months and lighting new hope for our future.

Chapter 17

As we prepared to celebrate the festival of our patron saint, Margaret of Scotland, in November, I felt it important to acknowledge what we were all feeling as we learned to work together as priest and people. On Saturday, November 14, Bishop Hughes came to officially install me as the rector and to stay over the next day for the big festival.

My words in the sermon were heart-felt: "We have come to this Celebration of New Ministry one year too soon. You, the people of St. Margaret's Parish, had hoped and expected that your rector of thirteen years, Brad Hall, would be the one to present the organ and this new chancel to Bishop Hughes tomorrow; that you would celebrate Brad's 65th birthday and retirement together next spring; and that the fifth rector of this wonderful parish would arrive next fall. Robbie and I had planned to be in Scottsdale another five years. But circumstances of life both here and in Arizona transpired to change all of our hopes about the timing of the changes that have rolled over us in the past eighteen months.

"So tonight we have come one year too soon to this Celebration of New Ministry. The big question before us is 'what will be different?' I am quite confident that the answer to that question is 'nothing of substance.' The vision for the mission and ministry of St. Margaret's Parish does not change with a change of clergy leadership – not if that vision was God's to begin with. God's vision for this parish was articulated with great eloquence by his servant Brad Hall; that vision has been reviewed and validated throughout the interim year and as recently as one month ago by the Vestry and School Board. God's vision for this parish will continue to give us work to do in the Kingdom for the next fourteen years of my tenure as your rector; and I am confident that the sixth rector will discover in 2013 that St. Margaret's continues to be a beacon on the hill, drawing people to a saving relationship with Jesus Christ as Lord and Savior.

"I believe that the differences we shall experience are the differences of growth and maturity. Personality and style will certainly be different; but that is a matter of God's creative variety. As we grow together over the next decade and more, I think we might liken our movement as one from youth to adulthood. St. Margaret's is already a strong, healthy, dynamic parish. In order to remain so, we will exercise, broaden our horizons, increase our depth and continue to strive to discern God's will for us as a community of faith. Because we stand on the tall and broad shoulders of those who have gone before, we will see farther and wider into the Kingdom of God.

"God's vision of St. Margaret's beyond 2000 is for us to build on the foundation that has been so well laid, to build our heart as a caring, compassionate incarnation of Christ on earth."

After the sermon, the people of the parish presented me with the tokens of the office of rector. I knelt in their midst and prayed, "O Lord my God, I am not worthy to have you come under my roof; yet you have called your servant to stand in your house, and to serve at your altar. To you and to your service I devote myself, body, soul, and spirit. Fill my memory with the record of your mighty works; enlighten my understanding with the light of your Holy Spirit; and may all the desires of my heart and will center in what you would have me do. Make me an instrument of your salvation for the people entrusted to my care, and grant that I may faithfully administer your holy Sacraments, and by my life and teaching set forth your true and living Word. Be always with me in carrying out the duties of my ministry. In prayer, quicken my devotion; in praises, heighten my love and gratitude; in preaching, give me readiness of thought and expression; and grant that, by the clearness and brightness of your holy Word, all the world may be drawn into your blessed kingdom. All this I ask for the sake of your Son our Savior Jesus Christ."[1]

---

[1] 1979 Book of Common Prayer, p. 562-563.

Chapter 17

The months ahead would be a difficult trial, with a major capital campaign looming. I still had a lot of ghosts, old and new, locked in my anxiety closet. The Christmas to Easter cycle of fear and rage would make the door bulge against the locks until the hinges finally failed at the staff meeting on April 3, 2000. On that day, a scheduling and proofreading error was enough to send me into the events of the previous three decades to seek the hand of God at work in the world.

Chapter 18

A New Direction?

"Fill my memory with the record of your mighty works; enlighten my understanding with the light of your Holy Spirit."

My life didn't begin in Vietnam, but it didn't end there either. Through the grace of God I was repatriated, at least in part. Though the cell doors had opened and the Starlifter had flown me out of that terrible place, the chains of the past continued to have a very long reach, snapping me back into the dungeons of a dark night of the soul, often when my life events were at their most expectant. I frequently felt like the eagle depicted in the shield of the "4th Allied P.O.W. Wing," with wings spread for flight, but with the shackle and chain holding me down. Only after decades of struggling with the continued meaning of the events of the winter of 1972-73, were my eyes finally open to

recognize that the chain was not connected to a post, that while its weight might continue to effect my perspective, it no longer had the power to imprison me. As I worked to commit this story to print, another more ancient story kept coming to mind.

In the Gospel according to Luke (24:13-35) there is an intriguing story that speaks of the filling of memory and the enlightenment of understanding. Two of Jesus' disciples, Cleopas and a companion, are returning to Emmaus on Easter Day. They've been walking with Jesus for several miles, talking with him and not knowing who he was until he broke the bread at dinner. Suddenly, their eyes are opened and they recognize Jesus.

Earlier in the day, Mary Magdalene had been in the garden by the tomb weeping and carrying on a conversation with a man she thought was the gardener. When that gardener spoke her name, "Mary," she finally recognized that it was Jesus. Again, in a simple thing that had happened before, the speaking of her name, Jesus was known to her.

In Emmaus, he was known to the two men in a simple thing that he had done with them, day in and day out, for months on end – the saying of the blessing and the breaking of the bread. When they finally recognized him, they realized that on the entire journey from Jerusalem to Emmaus, their hearts had burned within them, not out of grief as they must have thought, but out of Christ's presence in their lives, out of something larger going on in their lives than they ever imagined or dreamed possible. The stories contained in this book raise the same question that first Mary and then Cleopas and his companion faced in Luke: "How is it that Jesus is known to us?" Those two men were so wrapped up in the tragedy of Good Friday, and the depression and the fear of Saturday and Sunday morning, that they could not see how God's hand could have been at work in that weekend. The women amazed them, but that didn't change their minds because the men didn't see anything when they got to the empty tomb. In their sadness and confusion, they said to Jesus as he walked with them, "We *had* hoped that he would be the Messiah."

The trip from Jerusalem to Emmaus was a trip of despair and hopelessness, in so far as they knew when they started out. It was only when they recognized the Lord in Emmaus, at the close of the day, that they finally realized the trip was rather a walk with the Lord.

I have been very much like those two men in my own tragedies, and sometimes even in my inconveniences, in failing to ask where Jesus can possibly be. Many of my plans have not turned out the way I envisioned them, and out of the depths I have cried that the Lord would open the eyes of my faith that I might behold him in all his redeeming work.

I was trained in seminary in theological reflection, but it has been a daily chore to apply that training. Writing this story set me on the road to Emmaus, walking with the Lord as he explained the passages of my life that showed his hand at work. I had always seen many parts of my life as a diversion from the ministry, and so much of it as painful and outside of the realm of redemption.

Through the ministry of a young Christian psychologist at the San Bernardino Vet Center, I was sent back in time to reevaluate events that I had understood to be "coincidence." She said, "Go back and read your story again, and instead of seeing only coincidence, ask yourself was God working in that story, in every part of it, not just the parts you want him to be working in?" Through the subsequent ministry of a Christian family counselor in Riverside, California, I finally glimpsed the light of Christ shining before me on the path in my darkest nights of the soul.

In committing this story to the written word, I realized that throughout my life my heart had burned within me in places where

I did not want to return. When I went there, I found that Christ was walking beside me all the way, carrying the keys that would eventually free me from my chains of fear, doubt, and grief. I do not believe that I am any different from other pilgrims along the way, and no different from Cleopas and his companion.

In Psalm 116.10, the question is asked, "How shall I repay the Lord for all the good things he has done for me?" Anyone can read all the answers of the Scriptures, but only the individual can read his or her own life. Only the pilgrim can go back into his own journey from Jerusalem to Emmaus to discover where Jesus has walked with him, and in ways he did not then understand.

Looking again at the tapestry of life and seeking the hand of God working in every thread, my eyes have been opened to his redeeming work in surprising places. Tragedies have become times of God's immanent presence, and coincidences and the routine events of daily life form the intricate design of God's hand at work in the world. Perhaps now I can understand and experience that the fullness of joy is found not just in the people and events that I have called blessings, but even more in realizing God's hand at work in those moments, relationships, and events that I had locked so securely in my closet of unredeemable things.

While the road I have taken may be unique in its details and in the footsteps I have left behind, the themes of dark nights and glorious days are common to us all. By looking back at the stories in the wake of life, perhaps we can all see more clearly where we are heading in whatever future God has granted us.

Glossary
People, Places, Acronyms and Things

340th Bombardment (Heavy) Squadron: B-52 Squadron at Blytheville AFB, Arkansas

72nd Strategic Wing: B-52G Wing (Provisional) based at Andersen AFB, Guam

97th Bombardment Wing: B-52/KC-135 Wing at Blytheville AFB, Arkansas

AAA: Anti-Aircraft Artillery

AC: Aircraft Commander (Pilot)

AFB: Air Force Base

AFIT: Air Force Institute of Technology

Alexander, Fernando (Alex): Major, USAF. RN on Rose 1. Shot down early on 19 December 1972. Capt. Certain's cellmate throughout incarceration.

Andersen: Air Force Base on Guam, Mariana Isalands

APN 69: Rendezvous beacon

Arclight: B-52D deployment to Southeast Asia

B-52: "Stratofortress": Heavy 8-engine jet bomber

Barn: Cellblock in the Zoo

BCP: Book of Common Prayer

Blytheville AFB: Air Force Base in northeast Arkansas

BUFF: Big Ugly Fat Fella (B-52)

Buff, Charcoal, Olive: Colors refer to B-52 cell call signs

Bullet Shot: B-52G deployment to Southeast Asia

BYH: Aeronautical designator for Blytheville (later Eaker) AFB

Capt.: Captain

Cell: A flight of 3 B-52s in formation

Certain, Robbie: Robert's wife

Certain, Robert: Navigator, Charcoal 1. POW

Charcoal 1: Lead B-52, Charcoal cell

Col.: Colonel

Contrail: "Vapor trail"; ice crystal "cloud" formed behind jet engines

Cu Loc: Prison in Hanoi, North Vietnam; The Zoo

Dash-1: Flight Manual (1B-52G-1)

Defense Team: Electronic Warfare Officer and Gunner

Eaker AFB: Later name of Blytheville AFB

ECM: Electronic Countermeasures

EW (E-dub, E-Dubya): Electronic Warfare Officer

EWO: Electronic Warfare Officer

Fairchild AFB: Air Force Base near Spokane, Washington. Home of USAF Survival School

Ferguson, Walter (Fergie): Gunner, Charcoal 1. KIA

FNG: Freaking New Guy

FOG: Freaking Old Guy

GMT: Greenwich Mean Time

Guns: Gunner

Haiphong: Major coastal port city of North Vietnam

Hanoi: Capitol city of North Vietnam

Hanoi Hilton: Hoa Lo Prison, Hanoi, NVN

Heartbreak Hotel: Cellblock in Hanoi Hilton

Johnson, Richard (Dick): RN, Charcoal 1; POW

KC-135: "Stratotanker"; provides aerial refueling; doubles as cargo and troop carrier

KIA: Killed in Action

Linebacker I: Overall interdiction bombing effort; spring – autumn 1972

Linebacker II: Bombing campaign against Hanoi and Haiphong, December 1972

Lt.: Lieutenant

Lt. Col.: Lieutenant Colonel

Maj.: Major

MIA: Missing In Action

MiG: Mikoyan/Gurevich series of Soviet-built fighter aircraft

MSgt: Master Sergeant

Nav: Navigator

Nordick, Casper (Cap): Former copilot, BYH S-18

NVN: North Vietnam

Offense Team: Radar Navigator (Bombardier) and Navigator

Pig Sty: Cellblock in the Zoo

Plantation: Prison in Hanoi, North Vietnam

Polek, Mel: Former Aircraft Commander, BYH S-18

POW: Prisoner of War

Quail: Decoy missile

Radar: Radar Navigator (Bombardier)

Rissi, Donald: Lt. Col., USAF; Pilot, Charcoal 1; KIA

Rissi, Joan: Wife of Don Rissi

RN: Radar Navigator (Bombardier)

S-18: Crew designator for crew of Charcoal 1

SA-2: Soviet-built surface-to-air missile; NATO designator "Guideline"

SAC: Strategic Air Command

SAM: Surface-to-Air Missile

SEA: Southeast Asia

Simpson, Richard Thomas (Tom): Capt., USAF; EWO on Charcoal 1; POW

Sortie: A combat mission

Stable: Cellblock in the Zoo

Takhli: A Royal Thai Air Force Base

TDY: Temporary Duty

Thomas, Earline: Wife of Bobby Thomas

Thomas, Robert (Bobby): 1st Lt., USAF; copilot, Charcoal 1; KIA

TSgt: Technical Sergeant

U-Tapao (UT): Royal Thai Navy Air Base near Sattahip, Thailand

USAF: United States Air Force

Wave: A flight of three B-52 cells (9 aircraft)

Zoo: Cu Loc prison in Hanoi, North Vietnam

Bibliography

Books

Baker, Mark. **NAM: The Vietnam War in the Words of the Soldiers Who Fought There.** New York: Berkley Books, 1983.

Boyne, Walter J. **Beyond the Wild Blue: A History of the U.S. Air Force 1947-1997.** New York: St. Martin's Press, 1997.

Butler, David. **The Fall of Saigon.** New York: Dell Publishing Co., 1985.

Eschmann, Karl J. **Linebacker: The Untold Story of the Air Raids Over North Vietnam.** New York: Ivy Books, 1989.

Groh, John E. **Air Force Chaplains: 1971-1980.** Washington: Office, Chief of Air Force Chaplains, 1986.

Lipsman, Samuel and Stephen Weiss. **The Vietnam Experience: The False Peace.** Boston MA: Boston Publishing Company, 1985.

Legacies of Vietnam: Comparative Adjustment of Veterans and their Peers. Washington: U.S. Government Printing Office, 1981.

McCarthy, James R. and George B. Allison. **Linebacker II: A View From the Rock.** Maxwell AFB AL: Airpower Research Institute, Air War College, 1979.

McNamara, Robert S. **In Retrospect: The Tragedy and Lessons of Vietnam.** New York: Times Books, 1995.

Michel, Marshall. **Clashes: Air Combat over North Vietnam 1965-1972.** Annapolis MD: Naval Institute Press, 1997.

Michael, Marshall. **The 11 Days of Christmas: America's Last Vietnam Battle.** San Francisco: Encounter Books, 2002

Rochester, Stuart and Frederick Kiley. **Honor Bound: The History of American Prisoners of War in Southeast Asia, 1961-1973.** Washington DC: Historical Office, Office of the Secretary of Defense, 1998.

Risner, Robinson. **The Passing of the Night: My Seven Years as a Prisoner of the North Vietnamese.** New York: Random House, 1973.

Rowe, James N. **Five Years to Freedom.** Boston MA: Little, Brown and Company, 1971.

Rutledge, Howard. **In the Presence of Mine Enemies.** Carmel NY: Guideposts Associates, 1973.

Smith, Philip E. and Peggy Herz. **Journey Into Darkness.** New York: Pocket Books, 1992.

Stockdale, James B. **A Vietnam Experience: Ten Years of Reflection.** Stanford CA: Hoover Institute, 1984.

Stockdale, Jim and Sybil. **In Love and War.** New York: Harper & Row, 1984.

Wheeler, John. **Touched With Fire: The Future of the Vietnam Generation.** New York: Franklin Watts, Inc., 1984.

Magazines

Boyne, Walter J. *Linebacker II.* **Air Force Magazine.** November 1997, 50.

Cooper, Dale B. *Lost Linebackers.* **Soldier of Fortune Magazine.** February 1993, 40.

Davis, Shelley. *The Journey Home.* **Retired Officer Magazine.** February 1998, 32.

Hemingway, Al. *Into the Teeth of the Tiger.* **VFW Magazine.** December 1997, 26.

Jalenak, Natalie. *Soldiers' Story.* **Memphis Magazine.** April 1989, 96.

Stricklin, Charles R. *The End and the Beginning.* **Airman Magazine.** June 1973, 10.

At Last the Story Can Be Told. **Time Magazine.** 9 April 1973, 19.

More Bombs Than Ever. **Time Magazine.** 1 January 1973, 8.

Nixon's Blitz Leads Back to the Table. **Time Magazine.** 8 January 1973, 5.

Operation Homecoming: 15 Years Later. **Airman Magazine.** March 1988, 13.

What Went Wrong? **Newsweek Magazine.** 1 January 1973, 8.

When the POWs Came Home. **Air Force Magazine.** February 1998, 18.

Newspapers

The Air Force Times. 20 February 1974.

The Capital Times (Madison WI). 19, 20 December 1972.

The Chattanooga Times (Chattanooga TN) 23 March 1975, D14.

Chinh, Anh. *Capture of B-52 Pirate Crew.* **Nhan Dan**. Hanoi, NVN. 20 December 1972, 4. English version in *Translations on North Vietnam No. 1327.* Maxwell AFB AL, Air University Press, 20 March 1973, 42.

The Collinsville Herald (Collinsville IL) 12 April 1973.

The Commercial Appeal (Memphis TN), 19 December 1972 – 25 May 1973.

The Courier News (Blytheville AR) 19 December 1972 – 1 June 1973.

The Evening Star (Washington DC) 19 December 1972 – 1 April 1973.

The Washington Post (Washington DC), 19 December 1972 – 1 April 1973.

Original documents

Certain, Robert. *What, In Hell, is a Chaplain Good For?* Montgomery: Air War College, 1995.

Intelligence Debriefing Document of interview with Robert Certain on 29 March – 5 April 1973.

Personal correspondence between Robert and Robbie Certain, 10 July 1972 – 15 December 1972.

Tallman, K. L., Maj. Gen., USAF: Notification letters to Wife and Parents. 19 December 1972.

Various letters from government officials and family friends. 19 December 1972 – 23 June 1973.

Wade, Margaret. Letter to friends and family concerning Robert's capture. 10 January 1973.

Interviews

FAMILY

Certain, Alan
Certain, Eugenia
Certain, Glenn
Certain, Neal
Certain, Phillip
Certain, Robbie
Forinash, Glennell

OTHERS

Alexander, Fernando (cellmate in Hanoi)
Buckley, William (co-pilot)
Johnson, Richard (Radar Navigator and POW)
    Rissi, Joan (Widow of Aircraft Commander)
Rose, Howard (Scheduling officer on Guam)
Simpson, Tom (Electronic Warfare Officer and POW)
Whitmire, Teresa (Friend of the Rissi family)